SPORTING SENSATIONS

Great Moments in World Sport

Evening Standard
Sports Writers

WARD LOCK

First published in 1993 by Ward Lock

Villiers House, 41–47 Strand,
London WC2N 5JE, England

A Cassell imprint

ISBN 0–7063–7127–5

Typeset by Litho Link Limited, Welshpool, Powys.
Printed and bound in Great Britain by
Hartnolls Limited, Bodmin

The photographs in this book were
provided by Associated Newspapers and reproduced
with their kind permission.

Front cover illustrations: Creators of sporting
sensation throughout their illustrious
careers, both Ian Botham – with his ability to
snatch victories from the jaws of defeat, and
Carl Lewis – record-breaking all-rounder in
track and field athletics, have demonstrated
the ability to draw participants and spectators
to their sports by dint of their outstanding
performances and high-profile charisma.

CONTENTS

CONTRIBUTORS

Michael Herd is Assistant Editor and Head of Sport at the Evening Standard. An award-winning writer, he has covered Olympic and Commonwealth Games and a string of World Championship boxing matches including the 'Rumble in the Jungle' between Muhammad Ali and George Foreman. He has been the Standard's Sports Editor, News Editor and Assistant Editor (news), and acted as Editor of the Evening News when it returned briefly in the 1980's. During a five-year spell away from Fleet Street, he was Editor-in-Chief of a provincial group with 23 titles.

Neil Allen writes on Athletics and Boxing for the Evening Standard. In a career of over 30 years as a sports writer with the Standard and The Times, he has won a British Press Award and has been President of the International Athletic Writers Group. His occasional full-length interviews with sporting celebrities are a feature of the Standard's sports page.

Peter Blackman has been tennis correspondent of the Evening Standard since 1983 and has covered all the major tournaments around the world in that time. He has strong views on the overpayment of players and the power they exert, and on the lack of depth on the women's tour. Before switching to tennis he worked for 18 years as a soccer reporter, travelling extensively in Europe with the successful English clubs.

Mick Dennis is the Evening Standard's Deputy Sports Editor. Born in West London he began his career with the Easter Daily Press in Norwich before returning to the capital to work for The Sun and The Daily Telegraph.

Michael Hart the Standard's chief soccer correspondent, began his Fleet Street career with the Reg Hayter Agency and joined the Standard in 1969. He has been chief football writer since 1976, covered the last three World Cups and has been present at all but one of England's last 200 matches. His most difficult assignment: being re-routed from an England match in Israel to cover a civil uprising in Egypt.

Chris Jones has been the rugby correspondent of the Evening Standard since 1986. He had previously covered the sport for the Western Mail in Cardiff and for Extel, a national sports agency. He has reported tours in South Africa, Australia, New Zealand and Argentina.

Renton Laidlaw is the most travelled golf writer in the world. Each year, as the Evening Standard's golf correspondent – a post he has held since 1973, he covers over 40 events in America, Australia, South Africa and Europe. He spends a total of three weeks a year at 35,000 feet commuting between tournaments, making an average 100 flights every 12 months. He also works for televison and radio.

Christopher Poole has been racing correspondent of the Evening Standard for over 20 years, has made over 2000 broadcasts for BBC World Service Radio and written or edited fourteen books devoted to the Turf. He is former holder of the coveted Derby Award as racing journalist of the year.

David Smith joined the Evening Standard in 1980 after spells with local papers in Hertfordshire and the specialist publication, Motoring News. As a member of the Standard's sports writing team he covers motor racing, football, boxing, golf and tennis; he has raced in several types of racing car and partnered leading driver, Roger Clark in the Autoglass Tour of Britain.

INTRODUCTION

Michael Herd

The greatest gathering of British sporting champions in the history of these islands took place at Buckingham Palace on 9 July, 1992. The country has never seen anything like it, not even when our archers won themselves a gold medal or two in 1415 and our yachtsmen outsailed the Spaniards 173 years later!

To mark the 40th anniversary of the Queen as patron of the Central Council of Physical Recreation and of the Duke of Edinburgh as president, a unique garden party was held in the Palace grounds. Invitations were sent to those men and women, either as individuals or as members of a team, who had achieved world-class status in sport during the Queen's reign. In other words, they were the Queen's Champions.

It delighted many and surprised more than a few that it was a long, long list of men and women we had watched with awe, pleasure and respect. When the list was finally closed, mainly because searching officials had run out of time, it consisted of more than 1500 names from more than 30 sports. Coe, Cram, Ovett, Wade, Cooper, Conteh, Davies, Whitbread, Charlton, Hurst and Moore, McColgan, Carling, Compton, May, Bedser, Peters, Bannister, Brasher, Hunt, Hunt and Hunt.

Many of them appear in this book. *Sporting Sensations* records the derring-do of the world's greatest sporting personalities and the events that have led to their place in history, not always for the right reasons. They are the men and women who, in our lifetime, have taken sport from the back pages of our newspapers to the front, moved into our living rooms via television and radio and lived out the dreams of the rest of us.

They have been different nationalities, varying shapes and sizes, some introvert, some extrovert. Some have been merry and others morose. Some have even died in the pursuit of excellence, while others have suffered unbearably. Others have thrived and survived but each and everyone has deserved a place in this little piece of literary history. Americans like Muhammad Ali and Joe Louis.

Once upon a time, as he prepared to challenge George Foreman for the heavyweight championship of the world, Ali received a letter. The date was October, 1974, the place Kinshasa, Zaire, the writer former light-heavyweight titleholder Archie Moore. Moore was working with Foreman.

'Ali, you remind me of the fable of the dog that had everything – the top dog,' Moore wrote. 'You had skill, the swiftest feet in your sport and a thinking man's brain. The dog in the fable had everything, too. Then he looked down in the water and saw a bigger dog with a bigger bone. He dropped his own bone and leapt into the water.

'For you, Ali, the bigger dog isn't just a reflection . . . it's George Foreman. The leap isn't going to just cripple your future, it's going to cripple your ego. I think the big thing that is going to beat you is Foreman's total concentration . . . Even if Foreman misses with a punch, the whoosh of the air will lower the ninety degree temperature of Zaire very considerably.

'My logic is that the quiet cunning and deadly patience of the Spider Family, in this case the Tarantula Family, whose game is really the big bananas, will settle this time for a mouthy, noisy bee. Foreman is the most improved heavyweight since Joe Louis. In contrast, you have performed outlandishly, boring and bombarding the champion with threats.

'Much of your prose is timeworn, an act now as thin as a Baltimore pimp's patent leather shoes. This time, you are in real trouble. I publicly and privately warn you. After the fight, you can even hide out a few years in the jungle, then slide into Louisville about midnight and nobody will ever know. The reason I'm writing this to you is that I don't want the blood of one of my talented ex-students on my otherwise clean and saintly hands.

Yours in prayer for your life.

Archie Moore.

Of all the letters Ali ever received, none got to him more than Moore's. After Ali had closed the living room door of his bungalow on the banks of the River Zaire (formerly the Congo) and gone back to his bedroom, he found himself looking up at the ceiling. Was it time to retire? Was he too old? How does a fighter know when it is time to quit? When the end came, would he know it before other people? How would he know? Would it come to him down on the canvas, bleeding, unconscious, his face pulverised by some new hope?

Not long afterwards we all knew that Moore was wrong. In the eighth round of a fight set in the middle of an African night, Ali shot out a straight right to the jaw with all the snap and power that was in him. The blow struck Foreman almost flush on the chin and the champion stood still. Ali was ready to follow through with combinations but, as he explained later, he could see Foreman was slowly falling, a dazed look in his eyes.

Ali said, 'I knew he was entering the room of the half-dream for the first time in his life. George was down, his eyes glazed. He was listening to the tuning forks humming in his head, bats blowing saxaphones, alligators whistling, neon signs blinking. The referee began to count, and later George was to protest that he was a victim of a short count. I could understand that. In the half-dream room, time seems to stretch out slow, like rubber, and unless you've been there before, you'll never know how fast it goes by.'

Alas, as we all know, too many years and too many fights later, Muhammad Ali also entered the room of the half-dream. There are those today who say that, as a result of Parkinson's syndrome or of what is generally described as punch-drunkenness, Ali has never left the room. Nevertheless, he and other boxers, men like Louis, the Brown Bomber, will for ever have a place among the men and women who have made this book possible.

The last time I saw Joe Louis he was in Las Vegas. He was just a shell of the man described as the greatest heavyweight of all time. It was his job to greet gamblers entering Caesar's Palace Hotel. Louis, crippled by a series of strokes, was in a wheel chair. His head tilted to the left then to the right as the man pushing the chair changed direction. Men and women touched his hand for luck as they rushed past him to the casino tables and slot machines. 'That's Joe Louis' they said and kept moving. Some posed for photographs but no-one stopped to talk to him.

Louis died nearly a decade ago. He was buried in Arlington National Cemetery close to John F Kennedy. The former boxer received full military honours during a service at which the mourners included Frank Sinatra. Louis defended the world heavyweight championship a record 17 times. He lost three fights in 17 years and he died broke. Thank God, the Alis and Brown Bombers are in a minority in this book. All the same, without them, there would be no book.

There would be no book, either, without men like Denis Compton and Bill Edrich, the batsmen who put a smile back onto the face of English cricket and English sport not long after the end of the Second World War. The Middlesex pair scored more than 7,000 runs between them in the glorious summer of '47. Edrich had a rare talent, Compton was a genius. Both men played excellent cricket and were a joy to watch.

R.C. Robertson-Glasgow, one of the finest writers of the time, portrayed Compton thus:

'He has the habit of batting, as the sun has the habit of journeying from east to west, and the fielders are his satellites. They say Compton's feet are wrong. So, once, were Whistler's hands. They turn up the diagrams and manuals and grumble about the direction of his left leg. But why legs and feet only? I saw him playing strokes to Kent's Doug Wright when his body went one way, his arms the other way and the ball the same way, past the fielders. It was genius.'

Sport has become big business, a division of the entertainments industry where agents and advertisers and athletes live and thrive side by side. Multinational companies clamour to be associated with it. Today fame more often than not goes with fortune. The people in this book, covering a half-century or more, have helped make sport what it is today.

Robertson-Glasgow described Compton and Edrich as fitting adornments and exponents of a game that was meant not as an imitation of, but as a refreshment from, the worldly struggle. He could and would have said much the same thing about many of the other people who appear in this book.

ATHLETICS

Neil Allen

August 23, 1886, Lillie Bridge, West London, England.

Walter Goodall George, long of leg and of moustache, a former cyclist and footballer from Calne in Wiltshire, was the great amateur runner of the time, a hard-training prodigy who had won AAA titles or set world records for a whole range of distances from 880 yards up to the testing one hour event in which he had managed to cover no less than 11 miles 392 yards.

Looking at photos of him now, or the Spy cartoon on the wall of my dining room, people find the long, almost drooping, shorts, and the somewhat lugubrious Victorian face, an unlikely subject for athletics immortality.

If they knew his favourite training exercise was called "The 100 Up" and consisted of running on the spot with knees high they would simply smirk. In fact this 5 ft 11 in, 9 st 10 lb all-round runner was a sporting giant.

In the mid 1880s George, an apprentice chemist looking for further fields to conquer, and no doubt hoping that somehow the exercise would eventually prove profitable, applied to the Amateur Athletic Association for permission to race against William Cummings of Paisley, the leading professional who, in 1881, had run the mile in 4min 16.2sec compared with George's amateur record in the following year of 4min 18.4 sec.

Permission was denied, even though George, in some financial difficulties, swore that none of the gate money would come to him. W.G.G. promptly turned 'pro' and the clash was on.

In the first meeting in August 1885 between George and Cummings, George – who had done an incredible mile time-trial of 4min 10.2sec at Mitcham just before, ran right away from his Scottish rival. Passing the half-mile mark in 2min 2sec, George, who had found his pursuer tapping his heels with his finger tips in the early stages, eventually won by over 50 yards, easing up, in 4min 20.2sec.

For the return race in 1886 at the Lillie Bridge ground a crowd of 11000 watched George set a fierce pace again. But the tall Englishman and the diminutive Scot were still level when the third lap was finished in 3min 7.75 sec.

It was Cummings who charged ahead first, pulling into a six yard lead. But then George fought back and passed Cummings so confidently that the Scot collapsed about 70 yards from the finish. George strode on to finish the race out on his own in the astonishing time of 4min 12.75 sec.

Because of the professional aspect of the race this could be given no record status. But no athlete, amateur or pro, was to run faster until the American Norman Taber recorded 4min 12.6sec in 1915.

No wonder that the crowd that day stormed the track, banging and buffeting George on the shoulders, finally causing him to seek refuse in a hut while they cheered the hero of one of the most sensational sporting feats of the 19th century.

George, who had been the very first champion of the Amateur Athletic Association on 3 July 1880, had helped draw crowds of 130000 to the New York Polo Grounds in 1882 when he raced against the American Lon Myers in a series of amateur races which the Briton won 2-1.

By 1886 both men were professionals and a new series of 'test' matches were held first in the States for prize money of $4500, and then in Australia. Walter George, a sportsman in advance of his time who would have earned a fortune today, was to die in June 1943 at the ripe old age of 84.

23 July, 1908, White City Stadium, West London, England.

Everything was looking rosy for Lt. Wyndham Halswelle of the Highland Light Infantry as he went to his marks for the start of the Olympic 400 metres.

Starting with victory in the 1905 AAA 440 yards, he had taken a second and a third in the 400 and 800 metres interim Olympics at Athens the following year, won four Scottish titles in a single afternoon and then lowered his personal best for the quarter-mile to 48.8sec in winning the AAA title of 1906.

Concentrating on the short sprints during 1907, Halswelle was in his sharpest-ever form when it came to the Olympic season and the celebrations of the 1908 Games at the marvellously appointed stadium at Shepherds Bush.

In just a fortnight the young Army officer had established a world's best 330 yards time and a British 440 yards record of 48.4sec which was to last for 26 years. No wonder that, when it came to the Olympic semi-finals, Halswelle set a Games 400 metres record of 48.4sec with the American William Robbins, the next fastest at 49.0sec.

Still, on paper, the Scot looked up against it when it came to the four man Olympic final in which he was to race not only against Robbins but also his US team-mates, John Carpenter and John Taylor.

In those days no lanes were drawn to protect the runner from being impeded, and even in the opening 50 metres of the final Halswelle was briefly blocked out by Robbins. It got much worse, however, according to Halswelle's own post-race testimony.

'Reserving my efforts for the finishing straight, I attempted to pass Carpenter on the outside. Carpenter's elbow undoubtedly touched by chest for as I moved outwards he did likewise, keeping his right arm in front of me.

'In this manner he bored me across quite two-thirds of the track and entirely stopped my running. When about 30 or 40 yards from the tape I saw the officials holding up their hands so I slowed up, not attempting to finish all out.'

The Olympic judges, all chosen by the AAA, declared the final 'no race' and subsequently disqualified Carpenter following evidence from an umpire stationed on the last bend. Then a re-run was ordered for two days later and US – British relationships at the Games soured rapidly.

Both Robbins and Taylor announced they would boycott the re-run in sympathy with Carpenter. American reporter John Keiran claimed that there had been such strong pre-race hints in the English press of Halswelle being 'ganged-up on' by the US athletes that their coach Mike Murphy had warned his three finalists to keep clear of trouble.

Kieran then declared: 'In loud language, the US officials said they were being rooked, bilked, cheated, swindled and robbed – to put it mildly. If there had been a boat leaving Shepherd's Bush that night for New York the US party would probably have torn down what they could of the stadium and rushed up the gang-plank for home.'

But the storm abated and Halswelle, perhaps wishing the ground would swallow him up, ran alone in the White City to win, in 50sec flat, one of the most unsatisfying of all Olympic gold medals in athletics.

Seven years later Halswelle serving in the First World War, and still only 32, was killed by a sniper's bullet in France.

July 11, 1924, Paris, France

Eric Liddell had already made his mark on the international rugby field as a seven-times capped winger for Scotland. But here, on the 500 metres, single turn track at Colombes stadium he was to revolutionise the way men ran the 400 metres.

Just two days earlier, the 22-year-old Liddell had won a bronze medal in the Olympic 200 metres final. In 1923 he had won the AAA 100 yards title in 9.7sec, just one-tenth of a second slower than the then world record. Obviously the Scot had speed but did he also have the strength to cope with American 400 metres specialists, capable of returning times close to 48sec.?

Many years later, the romantic film, *Chariots of Fire*, was to create the myth that Liddell decided to concentrate on the 400 only when he arrived in Paris and found that the 100 metres heats, scheduled for a Sunday, would clash with the religious views of this child of missionary parents.

In fact Liddell, admittedly a man of strong faith, had virtually decided the previous April, when returning by boat from America after competing in the Penn Relays, that he would concentrate on the 200 and 400 rather than the shortest sprint.

He was still very much the outsider in Paris until he won one of the two semi-finals in 48.2sec, just 0.4sec slower than the new Olympic record set a few minutes earlier by the American, Horatio Fitch.

For the six men final, Fitch and Coard Taylor for the USA, plus Switzerland's Joseph Imbach, the Canadian David Johnson, and Britain's Guy Butler, the draw had the inexperienced Liddell in the unfavoured outside lane from where he would have problems in judging the pace.

The atmosphere was very tense in the final minutes before the start. Then there came a ripple of amusement when the starter had to point out to the nerve-wracked Butler, silver medal winner for Britain in the 1920 Olympic 400 final, that he had left the laces of his running shoes untied.

When the gun did sound, it was Liddell who was best away, bounding forward in his ungainly but effective way, eventually to reach the half-way mark in 22.2sec; an astonishing feat considering that the 200 metres gold medal in Paris had been won in 21.6sec.

Experts in the crowd, watching Liddell's head begin to go back, swore that he would 'blow up' by the time the finishing straight was entered. But then they had not had the benefit of a comment in the British press from Olympic 100 metres champion to be, Harold Abrahams.

He had written: 'People may shout their heads off about Liddell's appalling style. Well, let them. He gets there.' Even so, Abrahams himself admitted years later that, sitting in the Olympic stadium that day, he cried out in disbelief 'Eric'll never keep it up to the end'.

But now Liddell, head right back, arms pumping, was 'keeping it up and getting there', somehow even slightly increasing his advantage over a shell-shocked field in the final few metres.

On the line Liddell, with an extraordinary Olympic record of 47.6sec, was no less than 0.8sec ahead of Fitch with the gallant Butler third.

Behind them, the track looked like the end of a Wild West shoot-out, with Imbach tripping so heavily over a marking line that he had to be taken to hospital and the second American, Taylor, suffering so badly from ankle pain that he fell a few metres from the finish, then crawled across only to collapse.

Liddell, who had raced about 1.7sec faster than ever before, was said to have been inspired by a note, with a text from the Bible, pushed into his hand before the day's competition. It read: 'In the old book it says: 'He that honours me I will honour.'

The new champion was to have just one more season, winning the sprint treble in the 1925 Scottish championships, before he joined his father as a missionary in China. It was there, in 1945, that the Rev. Eric Liddell died while in a Japanese internment camp where, so the story does, he once came to terms sufficiently with his Sabbath observance principles to serve as an umpire for a Sunday hockey game for the imprisoned children.

May 25, 1936, Ann Arbor, Michigan, USA
The great Jesse Owens didn't feel like top class track and field athletics today even if the Western Conference Big Ten meet was an important inter-

collegiate fixture for his Buckeye team from Ohio State University.

To tell the truth, James Cleveland Owens could hardly move about at all because of the back pain he had suffered after an impromptu, cheery wrestling set-to with a fellow student.

Years later, while visiting Australia for the 1956 Melbourne Olympics, Owens confirmed to me: 'I was really scared that when I went to my holes (we weren't using starting blocks) for the start of the first event, the 100 yards, I was afraid I just wouldn't be able to raise my body into the 'set' position. The cramped-up pain was that bad that day.'

But Ohio coach Larry Snyder, the canny motivator they nicknamed the Grey Fox, insisted to Owens that once his personal timetable of four events – 100 yards, long jump, 220 yards and 220 yards low hurdles – in 75 minutes got under way he would be fine.

As Owens was to recall: 'I wasn't at all convinced but before the afternoon's track meeting got underway my team-mates helped me to take a very hot bath for my back and then I started to go about my warm-up very, very cautiously. When the gun went off, at 2.45 pm for the start of the 100 yards, my only thought was to do nothing but try to run as relaxed as possible.'

That relaxation and superb upright technique, demonstrated from a photo of that opening sprint, was what certainly allowed the relieved and briefly astonished Owens to equal the official world 100 yards record of 9.4sec, with some stop-watches actually registering 9.3sec.

The 21-year-old student had little time to reflect on his achievement. In just 10 minutes from the end of the 100 yards he had to join the queue of 20 competitors for the first round of the long jump.

"Because there were so many long jumpers, and I had the 220 yards coming up in about another quarter of an hour, I decided I only had time for one leap.'

What the young man did next, as a cool as a cucumber, was to have a piece of paper placed in the long jump pit at 26 ft 3in (7.98 metres) from the take-off board, dramatically indicating the four-year-old existing world record by Chuhei Nambu of Japan.

'I can't hide the fact' admitted Owens 'that I really felt the world record was in my grasp having been only a fraction behind it in the Drake Relays. And, immediately I'd jumped, the shouts of my team-mates told me I'd done something special.'

He had indeed. Owen's single leap, measured as 26 ft 8 and a quarter inches, or 8.13 metres, was to last as the world record for quarter of a century.

But the star of the Buckeye squad was not finished yet in his search for team points. From the long jump celebrations and remeasurements he went over to the start of the straight 220 yards which he was to win in 20.3sec. Last but hardly least came the 220 yards hurdles with Jesse first again in 22.6sec.

Under the rules of the International Amateur Athletic Federation world record status in the last two events could also embrace the 200 metres flat and

200 metres hurdles events. So Owens, on what is surely still the greatest afternoon's achievement by any single athlete in the history of the sport, had equalled one and broken five world records.

If what Owens did at Ann Arbor was sensational then his feat of winning four Olympic gold medals in Berlin was nearly as remarkable and certainly far more publicised.

From August 2 to 9, Owens, the outstanding member of what Adolf Hitler's Nazi press smeared as 'America's black auxiliaries' won the 100 metres in 10.3sec by a metre from team-mate Ralph Metcalfe and then the long jump, after a tremendous duel with Germany's Luz Long, with a final effort of 8.06 metres.

Then Owens went on to gain perhaps his most impressive Olympic victory – the 200 metres – in which he was to beat his compatriot Mack Robinson by four metres, the biggest margin yet seen in this event in any previous Games, the respective times being 20.7sec to 21.1sec.

All that was left, in the swastika-draped stadium was the 4x100 metres relay in which Owens led off for Uncle Sam, gaining an advantage of some five metres for the team-mates who went on to set a new world's record of 39.8sec.

Pressurised by the amateur officials of his country, a young man from a poor family whose great track talent was earning him nothing, Owens competed only a couple of more times in Europe in post-Olympic meetings, plus a sprint relay stage at London's White City, before he turned professional, still not quite 23 years of age.

French writer Robert Pariente sums Jesse up perfectly: 'He remains an absolute reference point when we need to compare the giants of today with those of yesterday. He remains a kind of Beethoven in his field.'

May 6, 1954, Oxford, England.

Travelling down in the train from London that morning, Roger Bannister told his coach Franz Stampfl that the weather looked far too windy for the record attempt. His concern was heightened when they got to Oxford University's Iffley Road ground and the flag of St. George on an adjacent church tower was straining at the halyards.

But eventually the mile record attack, in which Bannister and his pacers, Chris Brasher and Chris Chataway, were out to achieve the years-old dream of four laps in less than four minutes, was declared still on.

For this annual match between the Amateur Athletic Association and Oxford University, the 25-year-old Bannister, a medical student at Queen Mary's hospital, Paddington, had trained with high quality interval work during the Spring following the 1953 season in which he had run the mile in 4min 2sec.

That performance, though never ratified as a British record because it was

16

not regarded as having been done in a bona-fide event, compared very favourably with the existing world mile record of 4min 1.4sec by Sweden's Gunder Haegg in 1945.

The planned pacing on the afternoon at Oxford may also have lacked true competitive flavour for some athletics purists. But the 1200 of us fortunate enough to be there could not fail to be stirred in the way that Brasher, destined to become Olympic steeplechase champion in two years time, set just the right tempo with 57.4sec for the opening 440 yards and 1min 58sec for the half-mile.

Standing on the back straight I can remember Brasher wisely refusing to respond when Bannister shouted 'faster, Chris.' The pace was right and sporting history was in the making.

As Brasher began to fade it was Chataway, possessing the strength of a 5,000 metres world record breaker, who took over and moved into the lead for the third and most of the first half of the lap. With about 230 yards left Bannister, like a racing yacht with all sails stretched, surged ahead and clapping at last broke out from a most restrained, if fascinated, crowd.

Bannister was to write later in his autobiography, First Four Minutes 'I felt at that moment it was my chance to do one thing supremely well. I drove on, impelled by a combination of fear and pride. My body had long since exhausted all its energy but it went on running just the same. The physical overdraft came only from greater will-power.

'Those last few seconds seemed never ending. The faint line of the finishing tape stood ahead as a haven of peace after the struggle. I leapt like a man taking his last spring to save himself from the chasm that threatens to engulf him. I knew that I had done it before I even heard the time.'

Dramatically prolonging the suspense, announcer Norris McWhirter, later to earn fame as the founding editor of the Guinness Book of Records, at last unleashed the cheers with the words: 'The time is THREE . . .' with the announcement drowned by the crowd it took some considerable time before we knew what the new world record was.

At last it was established that Roger Gilbert Bannister, formerly of Exeter College, had run the classic English distance of one mile in 3min 59.4sec to beat the most celebrated barrier in athletics history.

Just how much of the challenge had been mental as much as physical might be judged from the fact that it was less than two months after the nine-year-old record had been beaten that Australia's John Landy had the next word. Running in Turku, Finland and chased hard to the bell by Chataway, Landy set a new record of 3min 58sec.

In a classic Commonwealth Games mile final later that summer, though, it was Bannister the victor over Landy as he fought back against the Australian's powerful front running and won in 3min 58.8sec. For miling it had been a sensational summer.

October 13, 1954, White City, London

Chris Chataway had had two months to think about the way he had underestimated the strength and confidence of the blond-haired Ukranian, Vladimir Kuts, who was lined up against him for the London v. Moscow 5000 metres event.

At the European championships in Berne, the 23-year-old Chataway had focused all the attention on the reigning Olympic champion, Emil Zatopek of Czechoslovakia, only to find that Kuts, who had shot off at a fast early pace, held on to win with a world record breaking 13min 56.6sec. Later, old Zatopek had said dryly: 'Chataway said he had backed the wrong horse but we were there to race against men, not horses.'

On this evening, 45 days after the failure in Berne, Chataway, the former Oxford Blue nicknamed 'The Red Fox', had a crowd of 45000 to urge him on as well as an estimated TV audience of 15 million. But Kuts, a one-time Soviet marine and boxer, was ready to crush any challenge.

From the start the European champion tried to impose his will by his front running tactics. When he threw in a sixth lap of 62.4 sec, with an extraordinary mid-race surge, it seemed only by a miracle that Chataway was able to remain in contact.

When the bell sounded for the final 400 metres lap it was still the burly, aggressive Kuts in front with Chataway just a stride behind. And they stayed like that all the way down the back straight and into the home stretch without any sign of Chataway's customary finishing burst.

Commentor Norris NcWhirter later suggested the final seconds were symbolic. 'Could a spare time amateur businessman, who trains 35 miles a week live with a full-time State athlete who trains 135 a week, in this waging of "total" sport?'

The answer came in the final 10 metres when Chataway, his finishing sting almost drained, pulled himself past his powerful rival and broke the tape first for one of the most unforgettable victories ever seen in Europe, let alone this country. When the cheering finally died away it was no surprise to learn that Chataway had lowered Kut's world record by five seconds, to 13min 51.6 sec.

Just 10 days later, in Prague, Kuts clipped the new record by 0.4sec, but it was Chataway who would be remembered by British sports fans, long after the White City stadium was levelled to the ground.

October 20, 1964, Tokyo, Japan.

Ann Packer, a fresh-faced physical education student from Dartford College, had come to the Olympic Games hoping to win the 400 metres. But three days earlier, worried about her pace distribution, she had stayed back too much in the first 200 metres, forgot to duck into the strong wind and then found herself with too much to do in the home straight.

Ahead of her she found Australia's Betty Cuthbert, an Olympic triple medallist in the 1956 Melbourne Olympics who had at last successfully moved up from the shortest sprints after being dismissed as a has-been for four years. And it was Cuthbert who, thanks to Packer's misjudgement in the third 100 metres section, held on to win the Tokyo 400 gold.

Now Packer was facing an entirely new experience – an Olympic final in an event which she had run only six times previously, including her heat and semi-final in these Games of the XVIII Olympiad.

Nervous and fatigued from her 400 metres races, Ann had looked tense in her first round 800 heat. But now, in the final, competing without any inhibitions, she was to be so relaxed that, on the second and last backstraight, she was able to look up the electric scoreboard and think: 'First lap in 58.6sec. It doesn't seem that fast.'

She was still not well placed as the runners came off the final bend. Later she explained: 'I thought the New Zealand girl, Marise Chamberlain, would be one of the strong ones at the finish so I got behind her and waited for her to sprint.'

It never happened and in the end Packer, inexperienced at 800 but with excellent basic speed, went wide, accelerated and finally passed the leader, Maryvonne Dupureur of France, to take the gold medal looking as fresh as a buttercup.

'When I went by', Ann later confessed a little shyly 'it just all seemed so easy.'

In this seventh two-lap race of her life, Ann Packer had clipped the official world record of 2min 1.2sec by just 0.1sec and proved that she was capable of running well below 2 minutes.

But apart from one anti-climatic post Olympic meeting in Osaka, athletics was ended for Ann Elizabeth Packer, later to marry the British athletics captain, Robbie Brightwell.

For this writer at least, her victory was to remain the outstanding memory of a summer Olympics in which Great Britain's athletes did better than ever since – winning other gold medals through Mary Rand and Lynn Davies in the long jumps and Ken Matthews in the 20000 metres walk.

October 18, 1968, Mexico City, Mexico.

Directly opposite us, in the great Estadio Olimpico, no less than 2248 metres above sea level, we could see the men long jumpers warming up for their Olympic final.

European sportwriters were wondering what place in the final order would be taken by the defending champion from 1964, Britain's Lynn Davies, or the experienced Igor Ter-Ovanesyan from the Soviet Union who, in October 1967, in the helpfully thin air of Mexico City, had equalled American Ralph Boston's world record of 8.35 metres.

19

The number one American that summer was not Boston but New York born, Bob Beamon, who had been undefeated during the season, beating Boston six times and having best pre-Mexico jumps of 8.33 metres and 8.39 metres, the latter wind-assisted.

Boston had warned: 'Bob has terrific abdominal strength and amazingly strong hamstrings. When he's jumping it seems that he can hold his legs in the air forever. I know that one day he may put all his great talent together in one great jump.'

There did not seem too much chance of that in the Olympic qualifying competition on October 17. After two no-jumps, the obviously nervous Beamon jumped for safety and, taking off around 30 centimetres before the board, cut the sand at around 8.19 metres while Boston set a new Olympic record of 8.27.

Following a shower of rain, after lunchtime on the day of the final, the weather was cool plus the obvious advantages at high altitude of 27 per cent less atmospheric pressure and 23 per cent less air density. Three of the finalists registered fouls in their opening efforts and then it was the first jump of the 22-year-old Beamon.

Running down the approach, using a new stride pattern taught to him by Boston, Beamon seemed to some observers to float right off the board from the fulcrum of his six-spiked right foot. Others likened his rise to the leap upwards from a trampoline.

There was no doubt in any case that the American leaped high and long enough to soar beyond the limits of the special Cantabrian measuring device. While a steel tape was introduced, a huddle of incredulous athletes and officials began to gather round that long jump pit which was the cynosure of all eyes on the backstraight of the stadium.

Then, with news that the wind assistance had been just 2 metres (4.47 mph) per second, the maximum allowed for world record ratification, the unbelievable distance was displayed. Beamon had cleared 8.90 metres or 29 ft 2 and a half inches, surpassing the previous best by no less than 55 centimetres.

The sensational news brought Beamon to his knees, half laughing, half crying as he kept asking team-mate Boston, who was embracing him,'Tell me I'm not dreaming.'

Though Boston was to have an outstanding foul of close to 8.50 metres, the rain which followed Beamon's mind-blowing record helped to dampen the spirits of the already deflated opposition. Finally the Olympic silver medal went to East Germany's Klaus Beer with only 8.19 metres.

The Beamon record, described as 'one for the 21st century' survived right through the Seventies and Eighties, until, as the result of an unforgettable duel in the 1991 world athletics championships in Tokyo, American Mike Powell, clearing 8.95 metres, deprived even the great Carl Lewis of victory.

October 15, 1968, Mexico City, Mexico.

'Mid Atlantic' was what they called David Hemery sometimes when he returned to London from his lengthy periods in the United States.

A classic English gentleman in profile, accent and character, the British athlete had first made his mark in winning the Commonwealth Games 110 metres high hurdles in 1966 in Jamaica.

But by the time of the Mexico Olympics two years later he was enrolled at Boston University and competing for them when he won the American national collegiate title in the 400 metres hurdles in the personal best time of 49.8sec.

Hemery relied equally on advice from his Boston coach Billy Smith and his English mentor Fred Housden. The two men were determined to bring him to his peak in the challenging conditions of the Mexico Olympics where the thin air would help competitors in events up to one lap of the track but after that could cost them dear in oxygen debt.

By the time of the Games the leading American was Geoff Vanderstock who won the US trials in a world record time of 48.8sec. Hemery remained cool as the Olympic pressure built up, even maintaining his politeness when he was offered money to change the brand of spikes he was wearing between semi-final and final.

Drawn in lane 2, Hemery was away confidently, using 13 strides between the hurdles for the first six flights and then fifteen strides to the remaining fences. Timed at 23.3sec for the first half of the amazing race, Hemery took the field apart.

Possessing the strength to hold on and keep his form Hemery had said before: 'The secret of the 400 hurdles is keeping your rhythm in spite of the heaviness growing in your legs as the race progresses.'

Now Hemery showed true character by the way he covered the last half of the event known as 'the man killer of track and field' in 24.8sec.

He admitted later: 'The biggest problem was when we reached the sixth hurdle and the time had come to switch from 13 to 15 strides. I began to wonder if I would be able to hold on. But then the thought flashed through my mind – 'This is the Olympic final – you have to hold on. I got a real shot of adrenalin and I concentrated on attacking the last flight as if it was the end of 110 high hurdles race . . . '

Lungs burning, desperately reaching out for oxygen, head pounding, almost blacking-out, Hemery for a moment looked without understanding at a piece of paper which a first aid man handed to him.

Then, when the man repeated: 'It's your time', the gold medal winner appreciated that he had smashed the world record by 0.7sec, winning his Olympic title in 48.1sec, so far out on his own that the silver medallist, Gerhard Hennige of West Germany, had a time of only 49sec.

The impact of Hemery's run on the opposition was best underlined by the incident in the tunnel leaving where the stadium where this reporter accidentally trod on the hand of the prostrate Geoff Vanderstock. 'Don't apologise' gasped the ex-world record holder 'I'm in a world beyond pain right now.'

September 3, 1972, Munich, Germany.

The Olympic 10000 metres field had covered just 4500 metres of the 25 laps event when the crowd gasped. Two figures, soon identified as Lasse Viren of Finland and Mohammad Gamoudi from Tunisia had collided and fallen, Viren on the track and Gammoudi in the infield.

Somehow both not only regained their feet but then, after being completely out of the race for at least three seconds, set off in pursuit of the field. For Gammoudi, the Olympic 5000 metres gold medallist at the previous Games in Mexico City, the fall and then the effort of catching up was to prove too much. He was forced to retire.

But Lasse Artturi Viren from Mryskyla (population 2400), who had set a world two-miles record in Stockholm just before these Games, was to prove himself in the true gritty tradition of the Flying Finns of the 1920s, spearheaded by the immortal Paavo Nurmi.

While Britain's David Bedford was leading the field coming up to the half-way mark, Viren steadily worked his way back though the pack. Then when Bedford, the courageous front runner, fell back it was Viren who was to prove by far the strongest of the leading group of five.

Ruthlessly, the man who had run more than 7000 kilometres in training in the past 10 months applied the pressure. With complete confidence in his finishing speed after some 200 metres repetitions under the eye of coach Rolf Haikkola, Viren took off from the other medal hopefuls with a last 800 metres in 1min 56.2sec a final lap in close to 56sec.

Astonishingly, the man who had survived a trackside tumble to become Olympic champion had the extra bonus of becoming the new world record holder at 10000 metres with a time of 27min 38.4sec, just a second faster than the previous best by Australia's Ron Clarke.

Only one week later Viren was in unanswerable form for the 5000 metres, letting the field amble through at a pace which, at 3000 metres, was no less than 14 seconds slower than it has been for the 10000.

The tall, goatee-bearded Finn could afford to smile at the nervous way the 5000 field was watching each other. When the pace did at last increase it was only he, vainly followed by Gammoudi, who was able to release another strong last 800 metres and a final 400 in 56sec.

The final time was a forgettable 13min 26sec, nearly six seconds slower than the world record Viren was to achieve at Helsinki after the Games.

For Viren and his countrymen what mattered was that his 5000 and 10000 Olympic victories in Munich made him only the fourth man in history to achieve the distance running double.

Four years later, in Montreal for the 1976 Games, it was Lasse, the ultimate competitor for getting it 'right on the day', who took hold of the history books even more firmly.

By retaining both the 5000 and 10000 metres titles in Montreal, content to impose his unyielding personality in the final stages of slowly run races, it could be argued that Viren had surpassed, in the Olympic arena at least, even the feats of both Nurmi and Emil Zatopeak of Czechoslovakia.

Rumours were rife in Montreal that Viren owed his success to having been 'blood doped' in the final months before the Games to the benefit of his red blood cells. Viren, when questioned, kept his temper, pointed out that running up to 8000 kilometres a year was pretty good preparation and then smiled. 'My real secret' he confided with an almost straight face 'is that I drink reindeer milk every day . . . Trouble is . . . it makes you go bald.'

February 2, 1974, Christchurch, New Zealand.

About 10 days earlier, after a long search through the training fields used by competitors for the British Commonwealth Games, we had found the 'mystery man' of the track – 21-year-old Filbert Bayi from Tanzania, 'unknown' winner of the 1973 African Games 1500 metres, ahead of the great Kenyan Kipchoge Kieno.

Shyly, the slightly-built but long-legged Bayi explained that apart from one valuable season racing in Europe in 1973 he was also almost an Olympic veteran – having competed in Munich in 1972. There, he had proudly, he had achieved personal records in both the 1500 and 3000 metres steeplechase.

'But I do not like steeplechase so much' he added 'when I get hurt jumping over the hurdles. So here in Christchurch I shall be doing my very best in the 1500 metres.'

And now, on such a sultry day that the temperature was measured at 30 degrees centigrade in the shade, Bayi lined up with a field which included Olympic steeplechase champion Ben Jipcho from Kenya and his countryman Mike Boit, plus the talented New Zealanders John Walker and Rod Dixon.

The starting gun cracked and, right from the line, Bayi shot straight to the front, covering the opening 400 metres in 54.4 sec. After a moment of disbelief the crowd began to roar their appreciation of the Tanzanian's blaze-away tactics. Behind him, runners like Jipcho, who had twice overhauled a fast-starting Bayi in races in Europe, bided their time.

But after 800 metres, reached by Bayi in 1min 51.8sec, Jipcho and the others were lagging 20 metres behind. And with 1200 metres of the race run the gap was still the same if not more.

Only in the last back straight, with Bayi needing 300 metres in just 42.7sec to erase the world 1500 record of American Jim Ryan, did his pursuers wake up to their task. Both Jipcho and Walker took off at last, and it was Walker, in the black vest and silver fern kit of the hosts, who seemed the most likely to catch the extraordinary pacemaker.

Walker seemed inspired by his home crowd. But in the last few strides, as his shaggy head arched back in frustration, it was Bayai who regained his poise and crossed the line with a new world record of 3min 32.2sec.

Never before, not even in Rome 1960 when Australia's Herb Elliott had attacked from the front, had a major international 1500 been won by a man leading from gun to tape. No wonder, with this unique kind of 'hare,' that – in Bayi's wake – the next six men behind him all ran faster than ever.

Bayi's success, which was to be followed by a world mile record of 3mins 51sec in Jamaica the next year, can be regarded as one of the peaks of the mass African takeover in middle distance racing.

The modest man from Tanzania, who was later to be seriously handicapped by bouts of malaria, deserves to be remembered on equal terms with such great African athletes as Kipchoge Keino, Henry Rono, John Aki-Bua, John Ngugi and Said Aouita even though his career at the top was to be so short.

July 26, 1980, Moscow, Soviet Union.

Seb Coe came to his marks for the Olympic 800 metres final as the reigning world record holder for the event. Statisticlly, the nearest man in the field to his fastest ever time of 1min 42.4sec, in Oslo the previous year, was Jose Marajo of France with 1min 43.9sec. And no-one fancied Marajo was going to have any say in the hunt for medals today.

The form sheet for this race had been summed up only a few weeks earlier by athletics specialist Mel Watman writing: 'Coe brings to the event such a dazzling combination of speed, stamina and style that it is difficult to conceive of anyone being able to stay with him for the entire two laps. Who else could aspire to run the first lap 50 sec and the second in 52? Or be capable of the reverse in pace?'

When the gun went, in the Moscow stadium, however, it could be seen that this was going to be more about push, bunch and shove than fast flowing movement. No-one was more able to look after himself, as the field came together like a log-jam on the first backstraight, than Coe's arch rival, Steve Ovett from Brighton.

Ovett brought to the cut and thrust of battle not only a wealth of experience even before the 1976 Montreal Olympics, when he was a finalist in both the 800 and 1500 metres, but also height and weight and a readiness to use both if necessary. With a shove the 6ft 4in East East German, Detlef Wagenknecht, was sent sideways into Marajo and everyone knew that Ovett was ready to race uncompromisingly.

Meanwhile, what of Coe? Drawn in the outside lane, the slightly built world-record holder reached the bell for the beginning of the last lap in eighth position with a time of around 55.3sec. Keeping out of trouble was one thing but this amount of hanging back looked far too risky.

At 600 metres the Russian Nikolay Kirov was in the lead but it was Ovett who was now waiting on his shoulder. For those British observers who remembered that Ovett was on a streak of 43 successive victories at 1500 metres, Steve's position had to be highly encouraging.

Just 70 metres before the end Ovett opened up and a final surge took him closer and closer to a now inevitable gold medal in the event he was not 'supposed' to win. 'Here comes Seb' shouted someone in the press box and here indeed came Coe, moving from fourth at the beginning of the home straight to third and then second. But it was too late, Coe's time being 0.5sec slower than the 1min 45.4sec by the triumphant Ovett.

Afterwards Ovett, who had raced with almost bursting confidence throughout, confessed in a TV interview: 'If anyone was guilty of doing more than their fair share of pushing in this race it was probably me. People were wearing half-inch spikes and if anyone gets close to you, you fend them off because they're dangerous. . . . it's really a matter of safety precautions.'

Coe, grey-faced with shock, said: 'I know I threw it away on the second lap. When they broke (for the inside) I didn't have the speed of thought or movement necessary. Don't ask me why. Some days you perform well, others you don't . . . '

August 1, 1980 Moscow, Soviet Union.
The strain of waiting had been part agony, part eagerness. Sebastian Newbold Coe had taken an unexpected drubbing from Steven Michael Ovett in the Olympic 800 metres, the event for which he held the world record. Now here was the 1500 and a chance for revenge, a clutch at Olympic gold which must not be missed.

As Coe said emotionally in one pre-race interview: 'I've got to come back and climb the mountain again. The 1500 was going to be a hard event anyway, but now it's going to be the big race of my life. I MUST win it.'

Eight men qualified for this final and three of them were British for, apart from 'COVETT' as the star duo were nicknamed, the line-up included a tall fair-haired teenager named Steve Cram. Two East Germans, too, in Andreas Busse and the rugged ex-steeplechaser Jurgen Straub.

After a dawdling pace for two laps, the 800 metres was reached in an almost risible 2min 4.9sec with Straub in front and Ovett and Coe right on his back. It was almost time to start yawning when Straub, realising he had nothing to lose against two such big 'kickers', took off like a rocket.

Coe happily went with him, followed by Ovett, and the three reached 1200 metres having covered a mid-race lap in astonishing 54.2sec. Now the race was on, now there was a chance for Ovett to become the supreme track champion of the Moscow Games.

But Seb, though placed in front of master strategist Ovett on the final bend and therefore theoretically at an unsighted disadvantage, had his own secret weapon, honed to sharpness by father and coach Peter Coe.

That was the double 'kick' which Coe applied just as Ovett was gathering himself and so caught the admittedly leg weary 800 metres gold medal winner totally unable to respond.

Indeed it was not Ovett ('there was no power there, I didn't realise how tired I was') but the determined Straub who took the silver medal as Coe, Olympic champion at last in 3min 38.4sec, crossed the line with arms wide and his face contorted in a grimace of relief. Years later Coe admitted: 'I never, ever want to look like that again.'

August 1984, Los Angeles, USA

The sprinters were coming out for the final of the Olympic 4x100 metres and Frederick Carleton Lewis, an elegant 6 ft 2in 12 st 7 lb could be easily forgiven if his mind flashed back to a childhood meeting – when he was only about 10 as a matter of fact – with a gracious gentleman named James Cleveland Owens.

Young Carl Lewis had been attending a track and field meeting in Philadelphia when his father had taken him over to be introduced to a hero from the 1936 Olympic named Jesse Owens. The kid in his shorts and shirt and the balding man with a pencil line moustache had even posed for a photo together which Owens had later signed.

Now Carl had become the three times world champion, at 100 metres, long jump and 4x100 metres relay, in Helsinki in 1983. And it seemed as if the whole of America, and maybe even the shade of the late Jesse Owens, was waiting to see if he could equal the all time Olympic feat of his boyhood hero.

Years later, when he came to write his self-analytical, controversial life story, *Inside Track*, Lewis was to take a very matter of fact line to this relay in which he would have the chance to follow Owens by winning four gold medals for himself and Uncle Sam.

'The 4x100 relay was supposed to be a lock for the United States, the easiest win of my four events. And it was. The team was made up from the four top finishers in the 100 final at the US trials and the baton went from Sam Graddy to Ron Brown to Calvin Smith to me.

'It was as simple as that sounds and we won by seven metres. Our time of 37.83sec was a world record, the only track world record of the Los Angeles Games. That was one way to look at the relay – a record. And I was thrilled to be part of an American team that accomplished that.

'But there was another way to look at the victory. My four events were done and I had survived. I had been challenged from every direction, criticised for reasons I still failed to understand, but I had survived. I felt relief. It was over – finally.'

The often almost agonised memories of Lewis the author from those Games, his suspicion of the press and failure to be accepted then as warmly as he might have liked, as an Olympic hero, must not be allowed to obscure what Carl the athlete did in that stadium.

Beginning with the 100 metres in which he was to erase any true challenge, winning his first gold medal in 9.99sec compared with 10.19sec by silver medal winner Graddy.

After Lewis had won, and celebrated by running a half lap waving a huge Stars and Stripes which a man had thrown to him, he met his coach Tim Tellez outside the stadium. The coach's first, brisk words were not of congratulation. 'Technically, you were bad out of the blocks' said Tellez. 'You should have broken the world record.'

With that kind of kick up the bottom, Lewis was most positively on his way to his next Olympic medal test – the long jump final in the evening of August 6 and it showed with his opening leap of 8.5 metres which no-one, including Lewis's regular American rival Larry Myricks, could even approach.

Misunderstood Lewis got booed by a section of the Olympic crowd of 92000 in the Coliseum that evening because they could not understand why a swirling wind, and a fear of injury from a very sore hamstring, made him decide to take no more than four out of the possible six jumps. Lewis was upset but not so much as to lose any of his admirable concentration when it came to the 200 metres final.

'My leg was still sore for the 200 metres heats' Lewis recalls 'and all I wanted to do was finish the race. But I felt good out of the blocks and ended up with one of the best 200s ever, just by staying relaxed. My time was 19.80sec, an Olympic record.'

Lewis himself had run only one faster 200 metres, a 19.75sec a year before in Indianapolis. The only man ever to have gone round the track curve faster was Italy's Pietro Mennea with 19.72sec in the helpfully thin air of high altitude Mexico City in 1979.

At last, of course, the relay which Lewis was to say brought to a perfect end 'the time of my life.' Yet his life inside track and field was far from over.

Ahead lay the world championships of 1987 in Rome with another triple gold because Canadian 'winner' Ben Johnson was to be subsequently disqualified following his positive drugs test at the 1988 Seoul Olympics where Lewis turned his four Games golds into six.

Ahead, too, was the final proof that Carl Lewis should really be unarguably regarded as the greatest athlete this or any other century has seen – victory in the 1991 Tokyo world championships 100 metres final in 9.86sec plus silver in the long jump and yet another gold in the sprint relay. 'Have fun'? Carl Lewis certainly kept trying to do so.

September 29, 1988, Seoul, Korea.

The amazingly long finger nails, the sleek fitting body suit, the thighs seemingly constructed of tungsten steel, had already amazed the Olympic audience when glitzy Florence Griffith-Joyner had won the women's 100 metres for the United States four days earlier.

'Flo-Jo's' time had been a wind assisted 10.54sec which, though outstanding, hardly compared with the almost unbelievable electronic recording of 10.49sec two months earlier when she had won a quarter-final of the US Olympic trials with, officially, no wind assistance.

That record had, it must be said, been much queried on the basis that one briefly shown wind measurement on the official score-board had suggested a powerful following gust of 4.3 metres per second, double the allowed maximum.

Still, Griffith-Joyner's supporters could point out that the 28-year-old from Los Angeles had also run the 100 metres in 10.61sec and 10.62 sec without any wind assistance, both inside the previous world record of 10.76 by 1980 Olympic champion Evelyn Ashford.

An improvement over 100 metres of 0.47sec seemed almost phenomenal at Flo-Jo's age. But the dazzling lady, who had won an Olympic silver medal in the 200 metres at the Los Angeles Olympics and silver again at the 1987 Helsinki world championships before marrying Olympic triple jump champion Al Joyner, put it all down to hard work.

It still almost seemed as though we were watching an athletics visitor from Mars when Flo-Jo took off in the Olympic 200 metres final in Seoul. Veteran press observers were left simply shaking their heads in disbelief as Griffith-Joyner moved further and further away from any possible challenger.

Never had any woman sprinter, and very few men for that matter, shown such powerful leg drive. What made it seem all the more like a clip from a science-fiction film was that as Flo-Jo approached the final 30 metres she could be seen to be smiling widely like a film star attending a photo call in Cannes.

Having already set an impressive world record of 21.56sec in her Olympic semi-final earlier the same day, the American now stopped the timers in 21.34sec with a following wind of only 1.3 metres per second. Gallant runner-up Grace Jackson of Jamaica finished all of 0.38sec behind.

For all the crescendo of applause which greeted her triumphs in Seoul, Flo-Jo was later to suffer from continuing innuendo and factually unsupported hints that her feats were the results of taking banned drugs. Her retirement from sprinting after the Games in Korea helped to fuel the rumours even though she subsequently started to talk about taking up the marathon as a totally new venture.

All we can say is that the American gold medallist and record-breaker passed all the anti-doping tests she was asked to take. And no-one can disagree, whatever the debatable background, that the sight of Flo-Jo in full flight during those memorable days in Seoul was truly . . . sensational.

BOXING

Neil Allen

March 17, 1897, Carson City, Nevada.

As the crowd surged into the arena under a blazing sun they were dispossessed of their revolvers by sheriff Bat Masterson. No spontaneous acts of violence were going to be allowed to distract the public's attention from the feud between the ropes, featuring world heavyweight champion James J Corbett and Bob Fitzsimmons, an unlikely-looking challenger from England via many years of living and fighting in Australasia.

Fitzsimmons, born in Helston, Cornwall on 26 May 1863, was nicknamed 'Ruby Robert' and 'Freckled Bob' because, apart from the remnants of his reddish hair, his balding pate was covered in freckles. Though 6ft tall, with powerful shoulders, he had a waist measured at only 28 inches and long skinny legs.

Yet this odd figure had the power to thrash heavyweights outweighing him by more than 50 pounds as well as the speed to become the middleweight world champion in 1881 with a 13th round knockout of Jack 'Nonpareil' Dempsey.

Gentleman Jim Corbett was a former bank clerk from San Francisco who had introduced an unexpectedly polished kind of personality to the rough world of the old prize ring when he whipped John L Sullivan in the 21st round in New Orleans in 1882.

Corbett had stayed idle for years after toppling the Boston Strong Boy who used to boast in saloons 'I can lick any son of a bitch in the house.' But now, after a long campaign of needling by Fitzsimmons, Corbett was ready to teach the brash Bob a lesson.

After a cautious start at mid-day, with Corbett working his left jab steadily, reddening Fitzsimmon's face, the champion was well ahead on points after the first five rounds. In the sixth a prolonged attack by Corbett, ending with a right to the chin, sent Fitz down for a count of nine.

But the Englishman, famed for his powers of recovery, came back surprisingly well in the seventh. From then on he kept pressing, trying with feints as well as actual punches to get Corbett to raise his guard. 'I'll win with a left and a dig in the body' he had told his camp 'it ain't so easy to hit his chin.'

The freckled battering-ram became so confident that, by the end of the 13th, he called out to his manager and his wife Rose to bet everything they had on him winning in the next round.

Even though the fight was jerkily filmed, descriptions of the final 14th knockout differ. But Fitzsimmons himself declared 'Corbett was fighting a little wild and made a swing which I sidestepped. In a flash I saw a clean opening on his stomach, came in with a left hand shift to his wind and then, without changing the position of my feet, shot the same hand against his jaw.'

What made the result a sensation, apart from the world title changing hands, was the description of the body shot which left Corbett wheezing helplessly on his haunches. Reporter Robert Davis heard two doctors discussing the final blow and promptly labelled it 'the solar plexus punch.' The fight ended as it had begun, with the two men loathing each other. While Corbett was being counted out, sneering Fitz is supposed to have called out, 'How do you like the view from there, you son of a bitch?'

When Corbett recovered he screamed at Fitzsimmons, 'If you don't fight me again I'll lick you every time I meet you in the streets.' Bleakly, Ruby Robert replied, 'If you ever lay a hand on me outside the ring I'll kill you.'

July 4, 1919, Toledo, Ohio, USA

'The Massacre at Toledo' was how it came to be known in fight lore – nine minutes of bludgeoning of an almost helpless quarry called Jess Willard by William Harrison (Jack) Dempsey, the Manassa Mauler from Colorado who travelled the roughest possible way up from the hobo camps to make a fighting fortune through his fast talking manager Jack 'Doc' Kearns.

The crowd surging into the 80000 seater stadium which had been built by promoter Tex Rickard from more than one and three quarter million feet of timber believed almost to a man that reigning champion Jess Willard from Kansas, was the favourite. After all didn't big Jess outweigh this fellow Dempsey by nearly 70 pounds as well as being about five inches taller?

Even worldly-wise Rickard was concerned enough about what seemed a one-sided match to visit Dempsey's dressing room before the fight and suggest, 'If he hurts you, go down and stay down before he kills you.'

Manager Kearns, on the other hand, had bet $10,000 to $100,000 that his young, black haired, steely-eyed tiger would win in the very first round. And that money looked completely in the bag when Dempsey walked out, bobbed and weaved round his huge prey for half a minute, and then attached ferociously, knocking down Willard by the ropes.

The champion, hopelessly overweight and out of real ring action for more than three years, could offer nothing to the shirt-sleeved, straw-hatted crowd except courage. In that very first round Willard was smashed to the canvas no less than seven times.

Referee Ollie Pecord actually counted Willard out on the seventh knockdown and raised Dempsey's right hand as the winner and new champion. But as the hysterically delighted Kearns was about to collect his wager, and Dempsey was in the act of leaving the ring, it was discovered that the bell had saved Willard, his jaw already broken in two places, for more punishment.

Desperately retreating, Willard somehow held the now arm-weary Dempsey off for most of the second. He even managed to score with one right hand early in the third. But then Dempsey was on him again, cutting and slashing until the round ended.

Back in his corner, 'a bleeding, trembling, helpless hulk' in the words of ringside reporter Damon Runyon, Willard muttered through his ruined mouth, 'I guess I'm beaten, I can't go on any longer.' Second Walter Monahan sent the towel whirling into the ring and Jack Dempsey's victory had begun the first Golden Age of Boxing.

September 14, 1923, New York, N.Y., USA

A crowd of 125000, paying the then extraordinary total gate money of $1,188603, had come to the New York Polo Grounds to see America's own world champion Jack Dempsey defend the title against Luis 'Angel' Firpo from Argentina, nicknamed The Wild Bull of the Pampas, though it was said he had begun his fighting career as a clerk in a Buenos Aires chemist shop. Most 'experts' agreed that the crude Argentinian did not stand much of a chance against Dempsey.

Still, Firpo stood 6 ft 3in, scaled around 15 st 6 lb and had a big enough punch in his right hand to have stopped nine successive opponents since he had arrived in the States.

At the bell it was Dempsey who went straight into the attack, nailing Firpo with a stunning right hand but only after he, the champion of the whole world, had been briefly down, half slip, half punch, from a right hand. Those who hoped then that this might prove a thrillingly even fight, soon began to shake their heads as Firpo was floored by the merciless title-holder not once or twice but no less than seven times in this opening round.

A round that was to be unforgettable in the history of boxing caught flamingly alight when Firpo, hitting out with utter desperation at this beetle browed assassin of a man, connected with a right hand of his own.

Unbelieving, yet screaming with excitement at the slug-fest they were witnessing, the crowd saw Dempsey propelled back so fast that he fell right over the ring ropes, landing in the lap and onto the typewriter of a reporter named Jack Lawrence.

Ironically, Lawrence had remarked to columnist Grantland Rice, just before the fight, 'They're both big guys but if somebody goes through the ropes I hope it's Dempsey. At least he's lighter than that truck Firpo.'

Luckily for Lawrence he did not have to use all his strength to push the 14 st Dempsey back into the ring. The world champion, crying out 'Allez-oop' like a circus acrobat, heaved himself straight back, claiming later, 'The people at ringside just put up their hands to break my fall. No-one tried to help me – it was all instinctive. I was fighting to keep from being killed.'

Dempsey survived the last few seconds of that last round, the over-excited and still bewildered Firpo unable to capitalize on his sudden advantage. When the second round opened, both men were understandably a little cautious until Dempey opened up again, sending Firpo down for counts of 'two' and 'four' before an explosive left-right combination saw Firpo counted out in 57sec. After a total of 3min 57sec what is still rightly regarded as the most action-packed, short-fused world heavyweight title fight of all time was finally over.

September 22, 1927, Chicago, Illinois, USA

No less than 104,943 people, paying $2,658,660 had come to Soldier's Field, an American football stadium by the edge of Lake Michigan, to see whether Jack Dempsey, the former Colorado mine worker, could retain the world heavyweight title by beating Gene Tunney, an ex-US Marine who came close to besmirching the trade of professional pugilist by admitting that he liked reading books.

Clearly out-pointed by Tunney when they had met for the first time on the night of September 12, 1925, Dempsey, accused in the past of being a First World War shirker, had gained popularity with the way he had accepted defeat. Highly circulated was his immediate post fight reaction when his film star wife, Estelle Taylor, had asked him what had happened. 'Honey' replied the battered but unbowed Dempsey with a grin, 'I just forgot to duck.'

For six rounds in Chicago it looked as though Tunney would win the return match even more easily than the first. The ex-Marine jabbed crisply with his left, moved fast and landed some solid, strength-sapping right hands to the head.

Everything changed about half-way through the seventh round when Dempsey, who had never stopped trying to connect with his famed left hook, caught Tunney by the ropes and struck home with the best weapon in his armoury.

Dempsey himself confirmed to me in 1973 when I met him in London. 'Got him first with a pretty good right and then with a real solid left hook. I hit him about seven times while he was going down, hit him with all the punches I'd been trying to land on him even in my sleep. He went down all right and then I forgot about the rule that the Illinois Boxing Commission had insisted must be observed for this fight – it says that a man scoring a knockdown should immediately retire to a neutral corner.'

While champion Tunney lay on the floor, Dempsey stood glaring over him, right by the corner where Tunney, on his back, was clutching the ropes. While referee Dave Barry shouted at Dempsey and then eventually grabbed him round the waist and pointed towards the corner where he must go, the seconds ticked away.

Most of the gathered evidence at the time, and generally accepted since, is that at the high point of what became known as 'The Battle of the Long Count' Tunney was down for about 14sec. Certainly the champion was given time to recover. But equally certain, Tunney was up on one knee, seemingly clear headed, when the delayed but official count reached 'nine'. And in the ninth round it was Tunney, later to win unarguably on points, who floored Dempsey – though this time the referee acted much more quickly in pushing Tunney to a neutral corner.

Dempsey took the ultimate sporting standpoint in his later, mellow years. 'Gene's a great guy' he used to say 'He's often told me he could have got up anyway and I have no reason to disbelieve him. Everything happens for the best.'

June 22, 1938, New York, N.Y. USA

Outside the Yankee Stadium, before the most awaited return match of the decade, the 80000 crowd were passing pickets carrying signs reading, 'Down with Hitler and Mussolini.' Inside the dressing-rooms a black share-cropper's son from Alabama originally named Joe Louis Barrow was waiting to trade blows with a German heavyweight Max Schmeling who, whether he liked it or not, had been adopted by the Nazi regime of Adolf Hitler as a symbol of the Ubermensch or Superrace.

For two long years Joe Louis had waited to avenge the unexpected 12th round defeat he had suffered at the hands of Schmeling. Not even winning the world heavyweight title from James J. Braddock in June 1937 had made up, in Louis's mind, for that protracted beating when Schmeling exploited Joe's frequent opening to a right cross counter whenever he dropped his left glove after jabbing. Louis had been floored in the fourth and then, in 2min 29sec of the 12th, counted out for the first time in his career.

The night before the return match Louis was talking with his friend, sportswriter Jimmy Cannon. 'You make a pick?', the Brown Bomber asked the columnist. 'Six rounds' replied Cannon. Louis shook his head and raised one of his fingers. 'No, just one' he said. 'It go one.'

Joe Louis was so right. In just two minutes and four seconds, less time than it would take a chain-smoker to finish a fag, he had wiped out Max Schmeling in such summary fashion that, between the first and third knockdown of the outclassed challenger, the radio broadcast back to the land of Dr Josef Goebbels somehow, most mysteriously, got cut off.

At the sound of the bell Louis had come half way across the ring to meet Schmeling. The first of what was later calculated to be a total of 50 blows landed by the ruthless champion was a thudding left jab which snapped back the German's head. Schmeling tried his trusty right hand but Louis promptly countered with his own right, sending his opponent careering onto the ropes with his body half-turned.

It was then that Louis showed his superb fighting instinct by leaping in with a sequence of head blows as the German stood half-collapsed, supported only by the top rope under his right armpit and his chin. As the referee hovered half-protectively by, Louis aimed and then drove a huge right-hand, deep into the unprotected left side of his opponent's body. No wonder that Schmeling screamed – that body punch had displaced a vertebrae in his backbone.

Soon the grievously handicapped fighter was down three times, never in with a chance of defending himself while the towel came into the ring, thrown by Schmeling's trainer Max Machon as a complete act of surrender. The referee kicked the towel aside but only continued his count for a couple of seconds more before he spread his arms wide. It was one of the most complete victories and utter defeats in the saga of modern championship fighting.

September 23, 1952, Philadelphia.

'One of the stubbornest matches ever fought by heavyweights' was the way the New Yorker magazine's outstanding boxing writer Joe Liebling summed up the 13 rounds battle for the world heavyweight title between veteran champion Jersey Joe Walcott and rough, tough, youthful challenger Rocky Marciano.

Walcott, who first made his name when he took the legendary Joe Louis all the way to a much-disputed 15 rounds points verdict for the world title in December 1947, losing a return with Louis in the 11th round the following year, had had his first pro fight when Marciano was still only seven years old.

But this evening in Philadelphia's Municipal Stadium the two were to provide the perfect match, boxing and slugging at such a pace that even years later any rare glimpse of the film of the fight would leave young fight followers amazed by the conflict.

Walcott from the start defied his years by taking the fight to Marciano, moving him back and then landing a powerful left hook to the side of the jaw which put Rocky down in the very first round of the bout. Marciano, so strong, still got up after a count of only 'three'.

But Walcott kept taking the brawl to the younger man until, in the third, fourth and fifth it was Marciano who started handing out heavy punishment. Between rounds six and eight Walcott was on top once more. Then the control kept switching between the two men right through to the 12th when Walcott, ahead on points on the cards of all three fight officials, looked the stronger.

It looked all over except, perhaps through the years creeping up on him, Walcott suddenly suffered a moment of fatal loss of concentration during the what proved to be the unlucky 13th round. Parrying a couple of blows with his left arm, Walcott fatally lowered his left glove. At that very moment Marciano threw a short, straight right which crunched onto Walcott's chin, distorting his features with its power.

As Liebling wrote, 'Walcott flowed down like flour out of a chute. He didn't seem to have a bone in his body. After old Jersey Joe had piled up a lead by fighting the way he wasn't supposed to, Rocky knocked him out with the kind of punch he wasn't supposed to know how to to use.' The richest prize in sport had suddenly become the personal oyster of the young son of an Italian-American shoemaker from Brockton, Mass. who was to retire as undefeated champion of the world four years later.

July 10, 1951, London, England.
Statistically, there seemed little chance that Britain's Randolph Turpin was going to last very long in his challenge for the world middleweight title held with such style and swagger by America's Sugar Ray Robinson. Turpin, an outstanding, hard-hitting amateur champion, had lost two out of his 43 professional fights whereas the 31-year-old Sugar Ray had been beaten just once, by Detroit's Jake La Motta eight years earlier, in a total of 133 matches.

The vast body of informed opinion suggested that Robinson, already being hailed as 'pound for pound, the greatest fighter in the world' would win before the end of the scheduled 15 rounds at Earls Court arena. The only possibility of a more even contest was if King Sugar, who was accompanied by a pink Cadillac and a retinue including a chauffeur, masseur, barber, three trainers and a dwarf jester, was not taking former Royal Navy cook Turpin seriously enough.

So far as the public was concerned, this was an 'event' as much as a boxing bout and they flocked to buy tickets from Britain's most show business-minded promoter, 'Jolly Jack' Solomons. Apart from cheering on the brave challenger from Leamington they also licked their lips at the chance to see in action a man who had already won nine world fights at welterweight and middleweight, including a comprehensive 13 rounds thrashing of his former conqueror, La Motta.

Certainly Turpin did not seem overwhelmed by his task. 'I shall feel a little bit jumpy' he conceded 'but once I've had a look at him at the weigh-in I'll be OK.' At least he was entitled to have confidence in the body he brought to the fight with the world champion. Randy Turpin had become an enthusiast for physical fitness after surviving double pneumonia and pleurisy as a young boy. By now his stomach was teak hard with, it was said, abdominal muscles about two inches thick after regularly withstanding assaults from a 150 lb medicine ball.

From the start it was Turpin who did the leading, using his long reach to advantage and, awkwardly but effectively, bending back from the waist when Robinson tried to counter. As early as the second round Turpin landed a left hook and Robinson, eyes screwed up, was forced to clinch. But in the third it was Robinson's turn to get home with a solid left after feinting. Turpin was clearly wobbled.

Yet coming towards half-way, in the seventh round in fact, there was a collision of heads which was to prove of vital importance to the future passage of the championship. Though Turpin at first seemed the more dazed, it was Robinson who eventually stepped back with blood pouring from cut over his left eye, an injury with which Robinson's corner seemed unable to cope. Between rounds, the frustrated Sugar Ray himself grabbed at a towel and dabbed ineffectually at the cut.

Gradually, Turpin with his rather stiff, wide-legged stance, broke down Robinson's strength and his confidence, forcing the illustrious title-holder to retreat. Later Turpin was to explain that he had learned a great deal about Robinson's style from Mel Brown, an American middleweight. 'He took the Robinson machine to pieces for me' said Randy. 'He explained how to deal with the bolo punch so that every time Robinson let it go, my elbows were tucked in to deflect the punch on to arm or elbow. Mel sparred every round with me the way Robinson would fight.'

Sugar Ray, well aware that the six fights in six weeks on the continent and all the soft living had been hardly the best preparation, tried desperately towards the end of the 13th to hurt Turpin. But the British champion, even though the ringside radio commentators seemed hesitant about the points margin, was now ahead and staying there, right through to the final bell. At 10.35 pm the new world champion was announced as the winner on points, the capacity crowd celebrating in true English style by singing, 'For He's a Jolly Good Fellow.'

On 12 September, 1951 in agreement with the fight contract, they met again, in New York City's Polo Grounds where 61370 people turned out to see this unknown Limey in action against the King of Harlem.

Robinson, boxing in front of his own people, looked nervous. But during the first half a dozen quietish rounds it was the American doing the leading. After nine rounds the referee had scored four rounds each and one even.

But then, in the 10th, Robinson's left eyebrow was split and he knew he was in danger of being stopped. As his mother screamed, 'Go get him, Ray', Robinson landed a right which knocked Turpin down. When the defending champion climbed back to his feet he was forced back against the ropes where Robinson pounded him with both hands until referee Ruby Goldstein stopped the fight with just eight seconds of the round to go.

June 18, 1963, London, England.

Anyone in Britain who, by this evening, had not heard of Cassius Marcellis Clay must surely have been tucked away in a Trappist monastery. Never since the prewar arrival of Italy's Primo Carnera had a heavyweight boxer so

36

easily captured the headlines and photo lens. And unlike Carnera, celebrated only for his size, this man Clay never stopped talking.

In the days leading up to his fight with British champion Henry Cooper, the 'Lip from Louisville', later to be even more famous as Muhammad Ali, assured everyone that he was 'The Greatest'.

We had seen him first in the 1960 Rome Olympics, winning the light-heavyweight gold medal before turning professional with the backing of a group of wealthy businessmen from his hometown of Louisville, Kentucky. The backers showed they knew something about boxing by hiring the much respected Angelo Dundee from Florida to train their investment.

Clay turned pro in October 1960 and then ran up a string of 18 victories, including a fourth round stoppage of veteran Archie Moore, before deciding to widen his reputation by boxing Cooper in London. Clay promptly announced, on arrival, that he could pick the round in which he would beat Cooper. 'If he wants to jive' he shouted 'he'll fall in five.'

Cooper and his manager Jim Wicks reckoned they had prepared particularly well for the flashy style of Clay by importing an American sparring partner named Alonzo Johnson who had lost a close enough points decision to Clay and could imitate him beautifully. Even so Cooper was to admit later 'We knew Clay was going to be fast but it's not until you are in there with him that you realise just how fast he is. As far as I'm concerned he is the fastest heavyweight of all time.'

After two reasonably even rounds Cooper once again suffered his old bug bear of cuts, a chopping right hand slitting his left eyebrow with a cut of about two and a half inches long. The British champion knew now that he had to go all out at the start of the fourth round before the fight was stopped.

'I jabbed once, twice, three times. Each time he went back. But now he was right back on the ropes and he couldn't go any further. The fourth punch hit him, a genuine left hook with all my power behind it. The ropes helped make the situation but they also saved Clay. If he had fallen more heavily I don't think he would have got up. As it was he slid gently down the ropes, there was a count of five, Clay started to get up and then the bell went.'

My memory, with Clay landing only a foot in front of my ringside seat, is the American landed on his bottom, bouncing from the impact even while his back brushed the ring ropes. But what neither I nor Cooper realised was that in Clay's corner, after the bell to end the dramatic fourth round, the ever opportunistic Dundee noticed a minute tear in one of his fighter's gloves. Dundee inserted a finger, worsened the tear and then was able to call the referee over. By the time one of the ringside stewards had found a replacement pair of gloves, the normal interval between rounds of only a minute had doubled. Cassius Clay was fully recovered from that left hook by now.

The bell rang for the fifth and Clay went straight for the obvious target – Cooper's damaged eye. Long powerful left jabs snapped time and again into

Cooper's face and eventually the blood was pouring down his chest. Manager Jim Wicks was soon up on the ring apron, calling for a merciful end and the referee needed no second bidding.

Nearly three years later, Clay who had now adopted the Black Muslim faith and taken the name of Muhammad Ali, returned to London to defend against Cooper the world heavyweight title he had won from Sonny Liston. This time the fight, promoted at Highbury football ground, had no knockdown or between the rounds controversy. Cooper was gallant in his aggression but in the sixth round he suffered the worst cut of his career when he was caught by the heel of Ali's right hand glove. Once against Henry Cooper had lost to the Greatest without ever being off his feet or even outpointed.

March 8, 1971, New York, N.Y. USA

It was billed simply as 'The Fight' and for those of us who were there in a capacity crowd at Madison Square Garden there will simply never be another one like it. The first of three mega-matches between Smokin' Joe Frazier and Muhammad Ali saw them both undefeated with Frazier the dignified total pro from the deep South and Ali the so called 'uppity nigger' who had refused to serve in the Forces during the Vietnam War and now was back in the ring after an enforced lay-off of more than three years.

In the pre-fight ticket selling Ali was as outrageous as usual, claiming that he was going to retire Frazier for good. But to many of us it seemed that Smokin' Joe, a superb in-fighter, might be able to stay close enough to Ali to nullify his disadvantages in height (almost four inches), reach and speed. Frazier, who as a youngster in Beaufort, South Carolina had suffered from white racism, also had a personal score to settle with the garrulous 'Greatest'.

'I'll be talking to him in there' he promised. 'I like to hit guys and see their knees tremble. He says that I won't reach him but that's a broad statement. He'll find the ring will get smaller and I will get bigger. I always talk in my fights and I've got something special to say to him after all the crap he's been saying about me being an Uncle Tom.'

Hard words which a hard, proud man did his best to carry out during the unforgettable 15 rounds of high skill, blatant gamesmanship and full-blooded slugging for which Ali, ending with a swollen jaw and no title, was to earn around $2,500,000 and the renewed affection of his millions of supporters.

To start with Ali was able to dominate with his speed of hand and foot. But as the rounds went by he was forced to rest for longer and longer on the ropes. And that was where Frazier, worrying away like a wild boar to the ribs and kidneys, could do his ferocious, painfully weakening work. Frazier's face was swelling from all the jabs he had taken, especially in a particularly damaging ninth round. But in the 11th he was all over Ali with

38

his left hooks and even had his man briefly down though the referee wrongly regarded it as a slip.

Frazier would not give up, quarrying away at the body of the taller man even through a testing 14th when Ali somehow reached down into his fading reserves of stamina. And the war of attrition reached fulfilment in the 15th and last when a huge left look smashed against the right side of Ali's face and sent him smack on his back, the tassels on his boxing shorts bobbing up towards the arc lights.

Ali, whose heart has never been questioned all through his unique career, got up at the count of only 'two' and then took the mandatory 'eight', standing, before doing his best to retaliate until the final bell. But all three officials rightly voted for Frazier as the points winner after that crunchingly convincing knockdown. Next time, promised Ali, would be different. And he was to be proved right.

January 24, 1973, Kingston, Jamaica.

They called it 'The Sunshine Showdown' but it was a beautiful tropical evening when we made our way down to the ringside seats, escorted by black policemen wearing white pith helmets, to see Joe Frazier, a 7 to 2 betting favourite, defend the heavyweight championship of the world against 1968 Olympic gold medal winner George Foreman.

Underdog Foreman may have been, with the only British writer tipping him to win being the late Walter Bartleman of the Evening Standard. But Big George, though often dismissed as too crude in the ring, had beaten 37 successive opponents, all but three of them failing even to last the distance. Before the fight Foreman commented, 'All of Joe's punches are left hooks. He only knows one way to fight and he comes at you straight ahead and wide open.' That was not strictly true but it was certainly the way Frazier fought this night, being knocked down by a left hand early in the opening round.

After taking an 'eight' count, Frazier came charging back in, head down, and paid the price for his lack of caution. Before this explosive round was over, Frazier had been floored twice more by the giant from Marshall, Texas.

Just a few seconds after the second round had begun Foreman put Frazier down with a short right. Then came one of the most sensational of all moments in the history of the heavyweight. A punch by Foreman actually lifted the shorter Frazier right off his feet, in the air, before he collapsed. When Frazier somehow rose again even Foreman now seemed sickened by the slaughter, calling for the fight to be stopped. A few punches more and referee Arthur Mercante obliged.

October 30, 1974, Kinshasa, Zaire.

'The Rumble in the Jungle' was the way it was sold and no heavyweight championship fight had a more exotic setting – the African land of Zaire, formerly known as the Belgian Congo, now ruled by ex-Army sergeant President Mobutu Sese Seko. A new, imaginative American promoter named Don King had come up with the idea of selling former champion Muhammad Ali against title holder George Foreman in what he called 'the land of their forefathers.'

With a soccer stadium in Kinshasa ready for the fight, all the promotional plans for worldwide television coverage were upset when Foremen suffered a cut eye in training and the fight had to be postponed by a month. Keeping the hype going, Ali announced blithely to Foreman 'My African brothers is going to boil you in a pot.' His trainer Angelo Dundee insisted, 'Foreman's only human – my guy ain't.'

The odds still seemed in favour of the 25-year-old, hard punching Foreman against a man who had won his first world title fight against Sonny Liston no less than 10 years ago. Before the fight began, mischievous psychologist Muhammad led the crowd in chanting 'Boom Aye Yea' again and again. Even the African lady busily breast-feeding her child at ringside gave him, the ex-champion, an encouraging wave.

When the first round opened Ali went into his old dancing routine but then found he was a little winded. Any lesser fighter might have felt discouraged.

Instead Ali 'decided I'd go to the ropes where I could handle him without getting hurt. Let him burn himself out, let him blast his ass off and pray he keeps throwing punches. I kept asking him if he couldn't hit any harder. Then I'd jab him until his head was turning away. Those punches took the heart away from George, they sickened him.'

Ali certainly had the master plan to beat the big puncher. But on the night it looked so lacking in pattern, with Ali seemingly content to take body punches as he lay against the ropes that writer George Plimpton was heard to wonder aloud whether the fight was a 'fix.' By the fifth round, however, you could sense Foreman was tiring and in the sixth he was almost pawing with some of his attempts at punching.

The 'rope-a-dope' tactics as Ali called them, were working. But, even so, very few must have been prepared for the way Muhammad took back his title in the eighth round. One moment Ali was back against the ropes, arms at his side in a mimicry of helplessness. The next he had launched himself forward and crashed home a long right hand to Foreman's head. Big George went down like a tree from an axe, laying on his back and then scrambling about in vain on the floor as the count was completed for the end of his reign.

It has been an extraordinary finish and, as if even the gods had been impressed, a tremendous storm broke over the scene as the crowd were leaving the ground. Much later, the 32-year-old, born-again title holder was to explain at length his awesome confidence.

'An experienced pilot flies a plane through a storm without panicking. If things happen he's cool. I have been boxing 20 years and I'm a pretty good fighter. I can walk into the firing line with a man like Foreman and I got no fear. Nothing can happen that I don't understand. I been to school and I was a pro nine years before he was. I knew what I was doing. You know I wouldn't go in there to let no street fighter mess me around.'

15 April, 1985, Las Vegas, Nevada, USA

Thomas 'The Hit Man' Hearns against Marvelous Marvin Hagler was a match appetising enough in anticipation to make any true fight fan think about selling his house in order to be there.

After all, Hearns from Detroit had been an outstanding welterweight champion and then such a hard hitting light-middleweight king that he had stopped, in just two rounds, the great Panamanian, Roberto 'Hands of Stone' Duran. On the other hand, Hagler, the shaven-headed warrior from New Jersey, was unbeaten in nine years and making the 11th defence of the middleweight title he had won from Britain's Alan Minter back in 1980.

At Caesars Palace, the glittering casino capital of the modern boxing world set in the middle of a desert, the pre-fight line this evening was that Hearns was the betting favourite. After all, the wise guys argued, hadn't Hagler been forced to travel the full 15 rounds with Duran when they had met back in 1983? Surely Hearns, the Cobra Man from Motor City, would hit too hard and too fast. Already Tommie had told his fans that tonight he would become the world champion at yet another weight within 10 minutes.

Yet significantly, perhaps, Hagler could be observed, standing in his corner before the first bell, pummelling his chest and shaven head as if he was drumming up the fires within him. And it was Hagler, normally a slowish starter, who came out with all guns firing at the start of a first round which most of us there believe to be the most memorable three minutes of non-stop fighting we have even seen.

First it was Hearns driven back on those long legs right across the ring by a middleweight champion who seemed possessed by demons. Then the Hit Man, fighting for his life, came punching back and unarguably shook Hagler to the soles of his boxing boots with a couple of jolting counters. The first two exchanges provided the fuse wire for the action to explode like a giant firework display under the night sky. Punch for punch, grunt for grunt, biting down on their gum-shields, neither Hagler nor Hearns would yield until the bell to end the fiercest round brought them to their senses.

Staring across at the press during the moment's interval, British TV commentator Reg Gutteridge mouthed 'I can't believe this'. Boxing News editor Harry Mullan was to say later, 'I thought I was going to have a heart attack.' But there was more heart-stopping action for ringsiders to marvel at during the second as Hagler kept pressing and Hearns kept pounding.

By the third round, mere human flesh, or at least Hagler's, was showing signs of weakening. The middleweight champion, who had been cut as early as the opening round, now had gashes above and below his right eye. Twice the referee, Richard Steele, stopped the fight to examine the wounds. There were groans from the crowd at the possibility of this battle of the ages coming to an unscheduled, totally unsatisfactory ending.

Only one thing could avert the likely anti-climax. And that was the fierce fighting pride of Hagler. Right after the second examination by Steele, Marvelous Marvin charged across the ring, slammed home a left and a right to Hearn's head from his southpaw stance and then, with his opponent reeling, chased him and struck home with two more looping rights. Hearns, whose heron like legs had been buckling ominously from time to time in the second round, could take no more. He crashed down on his back, his goatee beard sticking up almost like a grave marker.

Animal courage somehow got Hearns staggering up unsteadily as the referee reached the count of 'nine'. But there was no way he could continue. Hagler's hand-grenades, and sheer bloody-minded refusal to take his foot off the accelerator, had won the war.

April 6, 1987, Las Vegas, Nevada, USA

This was the one that was not supposed to happen, on sheer humanitarian grounds. If you cared about the handsome, stylish fighter named Sugar Ray Leonard there was surely no way to justify the return to the ring of a man who had had just one fight in four years, a May 1983 win over Kevin Howard during which Ray had been floored. What on earth was Leonard, who had had surgery for a detached retina, doing in the same ring with middleweight champion Marvin Hagler?

It was not a need for money, stressed multi-millionaire Leonard. The fact of the matter was that he just couldn't keep away from the buzz of big time boxing. Plus, 'I've always wanted Hagler. I need this man.' Big, bad Marvin, told that people were concerned about Leonard's sight being endangered, chillingly replied, 'If he's foolish enough to step in the ring with me, I'm foolish enough to rip his eye out.'

In spite of this bloodcurdling comment what we saw was not an exhibition of Grand Guignol savagery but a classic boxing match with a result which, to this day, can cause argument. Not a single knockdown in 12 rounds marked as much by fainting and blocking as battering but always full of tension as Ray Leonard produced every trick from his box of gamesmanship ploys to fool and frustrate Hagler.

Even when Leonard's legs were weakening, towards the end of the ninth, he had the coolness under fire to half turn and listen to Angelo Dundee telling him the round was nearly over.

'OK' said Leonard and turned to catch the advancing Hagler with a crisp one-two. Three rounds later, with Hagler successfully 'conned', the sensation was not only that Leonard turned back the clock but the breakdown of the different official scores with which he won the title that I made Ray sneak by a round.

Lou Filippo scored it 115-113 (seven rounds to five) to Hagler while Dave Moretti scored it by exactly the same margin, the other way round, to Leonard. The roar of incredulity came when it was announced that Judge Jo Jo Guerra from Monterrey, Mexico had Leonard ahead by 118-110 having given Hagler only two rounds out of the 12. Not even debatable computer 'evidence' that Leonard connected with 306 punches to 291 by Hagler could sway the claim of Marvin's supporters that he had been robbed in the city where the one aim is to take your money.

February 11, 1990, Tokyo, Japan

So easy was Iron Mike Tyson's latest task as heavyweight champion supposed to be that most leading newspapers in the United States had not bothered to send their boxing specialist on the long flight to the Japanese capital. After all, Tyson had had little trouble in beating up Tony Tubbs in a couple of rounds there, back in 1988, and no-one could argue that this latest 'challenger', James Buster Douglas from Columbus, Ohio, was any better.

Douglas, born in April 1960, had been boxing as a professional since 1981 with a fair measure of success, motivated by his tough, ex-middleweight father. But he had been out-pointed by Jesse Ferguson in 1985 and when he got his first big chance, meeting Tony Tucker for the International Boxing Federation's version of the heavyweight title, he ran out of gas and got stopped in the 10th. Even a handful of wins since then had not altogether removed the suspicion, in the minds of some fight followers, that Buster might just lack heart when the going was tough.

It did not seem it could be much tougher than he would find, at this lunch-time duel in the Tokyo Dome stadium, when he came out against the undisputed champion of the world. After beating Tubbs, Iron Mike Tyson, the brutal fighter from Brooklyn, had stopped Michael Spinks in the first round, Britain's brave Frank Bruno in the fifth and then Carl 'The Truth' Williams in another first round job, the 17th of his career so far.

Tyson was supposed to have eschewed the beer drinking which had made his weight balloon up before he fought Bruno. He was also supposed to have settled down with a new, inexperienced training group after splitting with long time adviser Kevin Rooney.

There was still a good possibility, felt some of us who had travelled on to Tokyo from the British Commonwealth Games for this fight, that Douglas could extend Tyson if he could use his best weapon, a powerful left hand, as well as his inches in height and reach. But no-one, except the young, inexperienced reporter from Douglas's home town of Columbus, actually predicted the shock result which was to lead to a shamefully manipulated 'controversy'.

For this was surely the upset fight of the decade, possibly of the century. Mike Tyson, previously unbeaten, actually knocked out for the first time in his career after taking a steady beating for most of the nine full rounds before he went down for good in the 10th.

What made this fight all the more eerie was that the 90 per cent Japanese audience remained almost unmoved, certainly not cheering, as ring history unfolded itself. So hushed was the crowd that in the early rounds, as Douglas slowly began to gain in confidence, sometimes the only voice you could hear was the wild mixture of advice shouted at ringside by one of Buster's sparring partners.

After a tentative start, Douglas began to appreciate that if he used his 16 st and 6 ft 4in fully behind the left hand Tyson was a far more open target than usual. The world champion seemed to forget that he must shift and roll his head for protection as he tried to get to close quarters for short arm slugging.

At the end of the nine completed rounds American judge Larry Rozadilla had Douglas ahead 88 points to 82. I made the margin a couple of points closer than that but certainly could not agree with the Japanese official Masakuzu Uchida's levelling of the scores or Ken Morita who incredibly scored the battered Tyson one point ahead before the knockout made all scorecards irrelevant.

The unexpected knockdown of Douglas in the eight round, from a smashing uppercut by a suddenly never-say-die Tyson, led to a controversy later fuelled by Tyson's promoter Don King. The fact that the referee fumbled in picking up the count certainly gave Douglas needed respite. But there was never any doubt, amongst the unbiased observers, that Douglas would have been able to get up in time without the break.

The proof is that within another couple of rounds he had Tyson staggering backward, bullied about the ring, caught by a series of savage blows to the head. Tyson could not respond at all, now, his head jerking back again and again until he was sent crashing to the floor. There he crawled about, trying, in his half-conscious state, to thrust his gum-shield back in his mouth, while the count above him continued to the end.

The man of iron had turned to putty. While 'unknown' James Buster Douglas, the boxer no-one believed in, was left so amazed, and also so perturbed by Don King's subsequent machinations, that it was many days before he could bring himself to sign for autograph hunters, under his name, the proud words 'World Heavyweight Champion.'

44

CRICKET

Michael Herd

The D'Oliveira Affair

Basil D'Oliveira said he wanted to be a cricketer who had been chosen as a cricketer and not as a symbol. The South African prime minister, John Vorster, said guests who have ulterior motives usually find they are not invited. They were both correct. The D'Oliveira Affair was and still is one of the greatest sensations in sporting history. It exiled a nation from the playing fields of the world.

In the summer of 1968 England was preparing for a Test tour of South Africa. Basil D'Oliveira, a Cape Coloured who played for Worcestershire, was first excluded from the touring side and then included. Neither decision seemed to make cricketing sense. There was a huge row within MCC, South Africa refused to accept a side with 'Dolly' in it and the tour was called off. As a result, the Sprinboks were banished from the world of cricket. Years later, some like Allan Lamb and Robin Smith joined English counties and after qualifying periods became England players. Some English-born players joined rebel tours to the Republic and were banned from playing Test cricket for their own country. Thus a situation existed in which South Africans could play for England and Englishmen couldn't. By any standards, it was bizarre.

Other South African cricketers started and ended their careers without ever knowing international competition. For 25 years the South Africans were in exile. That ended in 1992 when apartheid was blown away, the Springboks were welcomed back to the World Cup and lovely, likeable Basil D'Oliveira walked through Customs at Johannesburg airport and handed his luggage to a white porter. 'Time for you to carry my bag,' he said with a light laugh. 'Things are different now.'

Basil Lewis D'Oliveira was brought up playing non-white cricket in Cape Town. He was an outstanding player and one day he sat down and wrote a letter to a voice. John Arlott, the BBC commentator, was known throughout the world. Two years later D'Oliveira was playing Lancashire league cricket and five years after that he joined Worcestershire.

In his first season he made six centuries, Worcestershire retained the county championship and 'Dolly' was an established star. Twelve months on he was in the England team. He went on to play 44 Tests, scoring 2,484 runs for an average of just over 40.

In 1967-68 D'Oliveria performed only moderately during a tour to the West Indies, held his place for the first Test against Australia that summer then was dropped. He was back before the end of the series and after scoring 158 in the Final Test was asked by Doug Insole, the chairman of selectors, whether he was available for the tour to South Africa. 'Dolly' said yes, he was.

Surprisingly, he was not chosen. Was it because the selectors wanted to remain outside politics? Was it an act of political expediency? At the time, Ted Dexter, now chairman of selectors, said he believed it was a good honest piece of bungling by good honest men. Whatever, Tom Cartwright of Warwickshire was chosen. But the fates were not finished. Cartwright had to withdraw because of injury and 'Dolly' took over. But why replace a bowler with a batsman?

South African representatives flew to London to try to save the tour. But as the South African government led by John Vorster, refused to accept D'Oliveira, so the MCC had no option but to call off the visit. The whole affair had been conducted in a blaze of publicity. Sir Alec Douglas-Home met Vorster, a meeting which came to nothing. D'Oliveira was offered £40,000 in a 10-year contract, a car and a house to coach in South Africa, provided he was unavailable for the tour. The MCC Committee faced three votes of censure, their accusers led by the Rev David Sheppard, the former Test player and then Bishop of Woolwich.

Years later, when D'Oliveira was talking about The Tour That Never Was, he explained that he had wanted to go to South Africa with the England side, to mix in the white community with the England side and to come away from the Republic leaving doubts in the minds of people he'd met. His behaviour, he stressed, would have been impeccable. 'I think if I had gone there as a personal example for people to look at, they might have said 'Somewhere, something is wrong. It is us or them?' Quarter of a century on, with 'Dolly' fatter and grey, he knows they know it was them.

The Hutton 364

To quote a former cricket correspondent of the Yorkshire Post, Len Hutton made no romantic gestures, lit no fires of inspiration. He invited admiration rather than affection and would have exchanged both for obedience. He could not countenance a light-hearted approach to any cricket match when the result of that match had a meaning. He wanted team-mates to be untiringly purposeful.

Len Hutton, years later to be knighted for his services to cricket in general and as England captain in particular, was never more purposeful than in the Third Test against Don Bradman's Australians at The Oval in the third week of August, 1938. He was established on a pinnacle of lasting fame when he hit 364, the highest score ever made by any man in a Test Match (until it was passed by Gary Sobers of the West Indies 20 years later). Hutton's score

46

included 35 fours and lasted 13 hours and 20 minutes.

It was the best score ever made by a Yorkshireman in first class cricket and was one of several records broken by England in that memorable Test. Hutton's total was the highest individual Test innings, passing Don Bradman's 334 against England eight years earlier and Walter Hammond's 336 against New Zealand in 1933. Other records set were the England total of 903 for seven declared. It was the highest Test total in history, compared with the old 729 and the highest total in first class cricket, the previous record having been 887. Hutton also took part in two record stands; 382 for the second wicket with Maurice Leyland (who scored 187 before he was run out) and 215 for the sixth wicket with Joe Hardstaff (who was 169 not out at the declaration).

But back to Hutton and that remarkable innings. The previous day the dour Yorkshireman, the archetypal Northern batsman, had set about the Australians as no-one had done for years. Residents of his home town of Pudsey had sat glued to the radio as young Len had passed his first century and then his second. At the end of the day he was 300 not out and the whole country knew that the gritty Tyke had his eyes set on one target: Bradman's record. Hutton had ben a boy wonder in the Yorkshire town. A schoolboy cap at the age of 13; a place as opening batsman in the town team at the age of 13. His dad explained that Len had been handling a cricket bat almost as soon as he could walk and, yes, Pudsey had expected him to break records. 'He were that sort o' lad' just as Herbert Sutcliffe had been before him.

The following morning, with the whole country joining the good citizens of Pudsey round radio sets, nothing seemed to matter except the record. Hardstaff made some delightful strokes but all eyes were glued on Hutton. He scored 10 in the first half-hour, exactly the same number in the second. Young Len ticked on as remorselessly as Big Ben. At 12.45 with his score at 332 and the whole of England barely daring to breathe, Hutton late cut Fleetwood-Smith savagely to the boundary and the trick was done to a perfect pandemonium of noise.

Immediately Don Bradman – who as to be injured later in the day and take no further part in the match – followed by the whole of the Australian team (except O'Reilly who was lying on his back at third man) walked up and shook hands with England's hero. The crowd of 31,000 stood as a man and sang 'For he's a Jolly Good Fellow' and on the side of the ground opposite the gasometer, successive 'hurrahs' were bellowed by the crowd. During the interlude, as drinks were taken out, O'Reilly got to his feet and joined the throng of Australians congratulating Hutton.

It was a great moment for Hutton and justification, if it were necessary, of the faith placed in the young batsman by Sutcliffe, his discoverer, friend, tutor and impresario. At 2.30 the great innings ended when Hutton, tired after more than 13 hours at the crease, his mind reeling after such total concentration and commitment, was caught by Hassett at cover point off O'Reilly. Sutcliffe had been a Pudsey lad, too. He was called 'Our Herbert' and was Hutton's great hero. Three years before Hutton's record-breaking innings, Sutcliffe had said, 'I cannot teach Hutton anything about the finer points of batting. He knows them all instinctively. He is going to accomplish feats for Yorkshire and England of which we shall be proud. In fact, I think he will be one of our greatest batsmen for the next 25 years.' Hutton made his first Test appearance in 1937 and his last in 1954. In all, he scored 6971 runs, including 19 centuries, for a Test average of 56.67.

The Summer of '47

The late R.C. Robertson-Glasgow, one of cricket's most gifted writers, described Denis Compton and Bill Edrich as being of the happy philosophy which keeps failure in its place by laughter, like boys who fall on an ice slide and rush back. In the golden summer of 1947, the England and Middlesex 'twins', Compton, the role model for the sporting young men of the country, and Edrich, a former bomber pilot who had been awarded the DFC, revelled in a run spree the like of which has never been seen since.

Something sensational happened to cricket that summer. Crowds of 30,000 attended midweek country matches, festivals and weeks were hugely successful and, while glorious weather had something to do with it, the greatest contribution came from two men. A 29-year-old unspoilt genius called Denis Compton was responsible for more converts to cricket then anyone or anything in the sport. Aided and abetted by his county and Test colleague, Bill Edrich, Compton set record after record. In one scintillating summer Compton scored 3816 runs to smash Tom Hayward's 41-year-old record aggregate of 3518 runs in a season. He also hit 18 centuries to pass Jack Hobb's 1925 record of 16 centuries in a season. In the final game of the season, between champions Middlesex and The Rest, Edrich also beat Hayward's record, finishing with 3526 runs. The Middlesex pair finished first and second in the record books, first and second in the season, with no-one within sniffing distance.

Compton's playing attitude was carefree to the point of cockiness but the crowds loved him. He batted right-handed, bowled and fielded left-handed. He played golf to a handicap of 10, good club tennis and squash. He was an England international soccer player – he played for Arsenal on the left wing – and there was a story about how he had scored most of the tries and kicked all the goals in his very first rugby game. But it was at cricket that he was in a class of his own. In that summer of 1947, he finished with an astonishing record. In 50 innings, he was not out eight times, hit his record 3816, had a highest innings of 246 and averaged 90.85.

In 13 innings against the South Africans, he made 1157 runs for an average of 89. A Springbok later explained, 'We just kept on bowling and pegging away in the hope that he would make a mistake. We had no idea about bowling him or tempting him into making a wrong stroke. We studied the question for hours and came to the conclusion that he had no flaw in the whole of his cricket make-up.'

Compton was not content with his batting achievements, either. His bubbling enthusiasm earned him 73 wickets at a cost of 28.12 runs apiece. He was destructive against batsmen who were reluctant to use their feet to get to the pitch of the ball. Against Surrey he took 12 wickets in the match.

Compton had been born at Woodford, Essex, learned his cricket in the backyard with a bat or, perhaps, a piece of wood or against a lamp-post in Hendon, to which his family had moved. In his early teens had scored a century for London Elementary Schools and had won a England schools soccer cup.

His great partner, Bill Edrich, had quite a different background. Born in Norfolk, his family could have produced several cricket teams in which every member was called Edrich. Compton's 'twin' also had a remarkable war record, rising from pilot officer to squadron leader in three months as a daylight bomber pilot. On one occasion, he appeared at Lord's to play for the Lord's XI against The Army wearing a DFC ribbon. He refused to say how he had won the award. Subsequently, it was learned, it had been awarded for bravery in a massed raid over Cologne.

Stories were legion about Compton and Edrich. It was said that Compton was the only player who used to call Edrich for a run and wish him good luck at the same time. In the summer of '47, the pair of them didn't need any luck.

Laker at Old Trafford

Jim Laker once said the older he got, the better a cricketer he seemed to become. When the former Surrey and England off-spinner died in 1986 at the age of 64, he took with him the most extraordinary analysis ever recorded in Test cricket – 19 wickets for 90 runs against Australia in the Fourth Test at Old Trafford in 1956. Incredibly, it was the second time in the season he had taken 10 Australian wickets in an innings. He had already done so for Surrey at The Oval. And six years earlier, he had ruined a Test trial at Bradford by taking eight wickets for two runs bowling for The Rest against England.

As an obituary explained, Bradford-born Jim Laker had considerable powers of spin, unwavering accuracy, a haughtiness which reduced hesitant batsmen to trembling wrecks and a fine temperament. He also had an unusual spinning finger. It was a lot larger than the first finger of the left hand and it had a slightly mysterious curve on it. On the top joint was a sort of carbuncle. It ached in cold weather, it split with the spin but it could produce magic.

Laker also had the Yorkshire canniness, the dour confidence, to discover how best to make the most of his natural talent. He made the best of his ability on the evening of Saturday, 28 July, 1956. In reply to an England first innings total of 459 (with centuries from Peter Richardson and the Rev David Sheppard), Australia had been skittled out for 84 with Jim Laker taking nine for 37. His Surrey partner, Tony Lock, had taken the tenth. Nobody in modern times had taken as many wickets in an innings as Laker and there were doubts that anybody ever would.

The Australians followed on and at close of play that evening they were 53 for one. Only one wicket had fallen. Neil Harvey caught Cowdrey bowled Laker 0. There was no play on the Sunday and by Monday there was rain and gusting wind howling across Old Trafford. No play before lunch. No action, no hint of what was to come.

After the meal there was time for a brief snatch of play before the rain returned, washing out any hopes for the rest of the day. In that interlude, another wicket went. Burke caught Lock bowled Laker 33. On Tuesday morning, with Australia hoping to save the game, play was delayed for 10 minutes. It finally resumed under leaden skies. Was it too late for Laker to weave a magic spell? McDonald and Craig carried the score to lunch and England hearts were sinking. A draw seemed to be the best bet after so many hopes the previous Saturday.

During the lunch interval, as Laker ate his food and wondered whether his luck would change, the sun came out and the wicket began to dry. Cricket, lovely cricket! Perfect for spin. Craig played back when he should have played forward, Ken Mackay edged a ball to Alan Oakman in the slips, Keith Miller was out for a duck, bowled by Laker. Score: 130 for five and all five wickets had gone to Laker. Would he, could he?

Ron Archer probed at his second ball and Oakman snapped up another at short leg. McDonald and Richie Benaud (who was to become Laker's commentary partner with BBC television) survived until tea. By then, though, Laker knew he had them.

The Surrey bowler's second ball after day stood up and McDonald edged, again to Oakman. The tough Australian had made a valiant 89 but the writing was on the wall. And it was Laker's writing. Benaud had made 18 when he was deceived, played back and was bowled. Laker said afterwards that it was only at that moment, as Benaud ambled back to the pavilion, that he realised he could achieve cricket history. He knew there would be no conniving from Tony Lock. They might have been chums for Surrey and England but they were friendly rivals, too. It's wickets that count and both men knew it.

The Australian captain, Ian Johnson, joined Ray Lindwall at the wicket. They poked and prodded at Laker, played and missed at Lock and for 20 minutes defied the wiles of the England pair. Not long after five o'clock Lindwall was caught by Lock round the corner. Jim Laker was poised to make history. He already had 18 wickets. Could he get the 19th and the 10th of that second innings?

Len Maddocks was last man in. He hit Laker for two, which meant that Lock had to bowl at Johnson. The Aussie captain had a weakness; he didn't like any ball that was aimed straight at his wicket! Nevertheless, the Aussie showed commendable restraint, refusing to be tempted to do anything rash. He withstood Lock's six-ball assault and so Laker had his chance.

Maddocks, his cap pulled down over his eyes, survived the first delivery from Laker. It was a few minutes before 5.30 and there was an outside chance, no more, than the Australians would beat the odds and pull off a draw. Oh, no, they wouldn't, thought Laker. The Yorkshireman had bowled a mammoth 51 overs. He was tired but determined. His arm swung over and Maddocks shuffled across his wicket. The ball smacked against his pad and Laker turned, his arms by his side. Wicketkeeper Godfrey Evans let out a bellow. Laker appealed in a more sedate way. The umpire seemed to wait a lifetime then his arm rose slowly, his finger pointing upwards. Maddocks lbw Laker 2. Australia out for 205. England's Test by an innings and 170 runs. Laker's figures. 51.2 overs, 23 maidens, 53 runs, 10 wickets. The following morning's headline in The Daily Express said it all. 'Ten little Aussie Boys Lakered in a Row.'

Sober's Six Sixes

Gary Sobers (Sir Garfield Sobers as he was to become) once told one of his West Indian team-mates, 'You can't consider yourself a county cricketer until you've eaten a ton and a half of lettuce.' Sobers played for the West Indies no less than 93 times, captained his country and the Rest of the World (against England) and in his heyday was the greatest cricketer on earth. But the single feat for which he will be remembered until the millenium, occurred during his salad days as a member of Nottinghamshire.

During a county match against Glamorgan at Swansea at the end of August, 1968, Sobers put himself into the record books by hitting the maximum six sixes in a single over. The luckless bowler on the receiving end of the savage onslaught was 23-year-old spinner Malcolm Nash. The record has never been equalled in first-class cricket and probably never will. One man has told the story better and more often than anyone else. Bowler Nash says, wruly, that at least he got himself into the records books. Even if it was the hard way.

'I'd already bowled three overs at Gary and it was pretty obvious he was looking for quick runs. I wasn't all surprised to see the first ball go for six. It was a half-volley, anyway, and if you bowl like that to a man like Sobers you expect to get hit. Though not out of the ground.

'I thought about it a bit while I went back to bowl the second ball and decided not to worry but just to keep the ball up to him. This time I flighted it up on a good length and that one went into the crowd over long-on. I thought about pitching the third ball wide but decided it was my job to get him out and the best way to do that was to keep bowling straight. I tossed that one up, too, and watched it sail into the crowd over long off. After that I didn't know quite what to do.

'I looked hopefully at the skipper, Tony Lewis, but he just smiled and told me to keep bowling. I looked down the wicket at Gary and told him, 'I bet you can't hit the floodlights with the next one.' He just smiled back and said they were too high for him. So he hit the fourth ball out of the ground instead. Gary hooked it like a bullet and I swear he had both feet off the ground when he hit it.

'By now the crowd was going mad but I was still only thinking about getting him out rather than avoiding more punishment. I kept telling myself how wonderful it would be to get the greatest batsman in the world. I nearly did it with the fifth ball. I pitched it on a good length just outside the off sump. Gary made his only mistake. He mistimed it slightly and it dropped straight towards Roger Davis who was standing on the long-off boundary. Roger caught it low down and I thought I've got him. Then Roger overbalanced and part of his body went over the boundary so the umpires decided it had to be another six.

'It wasn't until then that I began thinking about a world record. Even then I just wanted to get him out. My only thought was to get him out. But how? I thought I'd try him with a yorker. It was a miserable failure. When it got there it was more of a long hop and when Gary swung at it I didn't have to follow the ball to know that one was out of the ground, too.'

The ball landed in a street outside the Swansea ground and was taken home by a passing schoolboy. The following day, the boy's father rang the club and explained that he had the ball. Nash wanted to keep it as a memento of how he got into the record books the hard way. Instead, the ball was mounted and placed in the Trent Bridge cricket museum.

There was a chance of more history, too, because later in the same match, the clobbered and the clobberer came face to face. This time Nash was the batsman and Sobers the bowler. Could the Glamorgan player despatch the ball out of sight. Alas, no. He was clean-bowled by Sobers for eight. 'It wasn't my match, was it?' he lamented later.

Gary Sobers is older and greyer now. The bones creak, too, and he doesn't care to recall all his records. Oh yes, he will tell you, he remembers the day he hit six sixes. It was also the day he backed three winners. A 10-1 shot, a 20-1 outsider and a horse, which won at 4-1, called Jubilation!

Botham's Test

Tim Hudson, who acted as Ian Botham's agent for a time, always claimed the cricketer represented everything that is best in Britain. He was Biggles, the VC, El Alamein, and the tank commander, the agent explained. How could a schoolboy not want to be like Ian Botham?

Peter Roebuck, Botham's captain when they played for Somerset, used different words to say the same thing. Roebuck said that Botham wanted to roar around the land, waking up the sleepers, showing them things could be done. As it was, he had to play cricket all the time and worry about newspapermen; a Gulliver tied down by the little people.

For two days in July, 1981, Botham was everyone and everything listed above. He threw off the ropes and in one giant leap became the country's hero in the greatest comeback in Test history. England defeated Australia in the Third Test at Headingley and brought Britain to a standstill. Botham himself acknowledged it as The Incredible Test.

Two weeks earlier Botham had quit as England skipper, only for the selectors to announce they had been going to sack him in any case. The Test careers of lesser men would have been over at that point. Instead Botham bounded back. He made 50 in England's first innings, took six for 95 in 39.2 overs in Australia's first, scored an unbeaten 149 as England rushed to 356 in their second and watched as Bob Willis tore out Australia's heart with eight for 43 in 15.1 overs to give England victory by 18 runs.

Briefly, England had been bowled out for 174, then watched as Australian made 401 for nine declared in their first innings. In the second innings England had slumped to 135 for seven and, with 92 still required to make Australia bat again, even the most cockeyed optimist thought everything was lost. They had reckoned without Botham, sidekick Graham Dilley, Chris Old and fast bowler Bob Willis.

This is Botham's own description. 'You don't fancy hanging around on this wicket for a day and a half, do you?' I said to Graham Dilley when he walked to the wicket to join me at Headingly. 'No way,' he replied. 'Right,' I said. 'Come on, let's give it some humpty.' At that stage in mid-afternoon on Monday, 20 July, Botham and Dilley set about the Australian attack with a ferocity unequalled all summer. Botham had been at the wicket for threequarters of an hour when Dilley, a left-handed batsman, arrived. They matched each other stroke for stroke during an 80-minute partnership that put on 117 runs for eighth wicket. When Dilley was finally bowled by Alderman for a fighting 56, Botham had contributed 57 towards the stand and, as the great man himself said, England's innings was starting to live again.

Indeed it was. Botham, bearded like a brigand, was joined by Chris Old, another left-handed batsman. The pair put on 67 for the ninth wicket before Old was beaten by a Lawson yorker. While they were together, Botham reached his seventh Test century. It brought all the England players onto the balcony, where the new captain, Mike Brearley, made a signal telling the batsman to stay out there. Botham gave him a signal back, the type showjumper Harvey Smith had been known to give. Of Botham's 103, he had scored 82 in boundaries with 19 fours and one six.

Big Bob Willis went in to join Botham with 45 minutes' play remaining. They were still together when stumps were drawn. In the last two hours after tea, England had put 175 runs in 27 overs! The following morning Willis did not last long. Botham was still there on 149 – including 27 fours – and England, totalling 356, had a lead of 129.

It couldn't be enough, could it? Certainly, it didn't look that way. Botham dismissed Wood in his second over but the Australians moved smoothly to 56 without further loss. It meant they needed only 74 to win. Then Willis switched to the other end. Instead of bowling into the wind and uphill, the old man (as he described himself) glowered at the Australians as he powered in to find some extra bounce. Trevor Chappell was caught behind off a shortish ball, Hughes was beaten by pace and edged a catch to Botham and Yallop lasted three balls before he was caught by Mike Gatting at short-leg.

Willis had taken three wickets in eleven deliveries without conceding a run. After lunch the extraordinary rout continued. Old bowled Boder with a delivery that cut back and Willis simply swept up the rest of the Aussie batsmen. Dyson, Marsh and Lawson went in quick succession, followed by Lillee and Bright. Australia were all out for 111 and England, victors by 18 runs, had squared the series. As Botham put it, the whole country went beserk, the England players were besieged in their dressing room and, two weeks after quitting as England's Test captain, he was back in business.

The Sound of Leather on Metal!

Dennis Lillee was a great fast bowler, the best I have ever seen and one of the finest of all time. He had everything: courage, variety, high morale, arrogance, supreme fitness and aggression. So said Bob Willis, former England captain and another world-class bowler. Once upon a time, Lillee had all of these things and something extra. He had an aluminium bat which threatened to tear cricket apart.

In December, 1979, Lillee, the great Australian Test player, then 30 and by his own admission on the wane, had plans to front an international drive to launch and mass-market a 'tin bat' and put the traditional King Willow out of business. He and another Australian, Graeme Monaghan, ploughed £50,000 of their money into producing a bat that would have sent a square cut clanging to the boundary or made a thick edge sound like a dinner gong. It was a gamble that did not pay off.

Lillee made no friends in cricket's governing bodies by the manner in which he drew attention to his baby. He used the aluminium bat for the first time in the Test match against England at Perth. He played two shots before being ordered to change the bat. And he indicated his displeasure by hurling it the length of the pitch. Afterwards, wearing a T-shirt that carried the words 'Think Aluminium', he explained that his gesture, angry or not, futile or not, was a protest at the way in which the game was run.

Others tried and tested the bat. Brian Close, formerly of England and Yorkshire, one of the most powerful hitters in the game, put the bat under exhaustive tests at Alf Gover's Cricket School in Wandsworth, London. Against some formidable bowling in the nets, Close's trial was with two new top-grade cricket ball as used in the county championship. He smashed 150 shots against each, the first with a traditional willow bat and then with Lillee's invention.

Close was a careful, shrewd Yorkshireman. If he thought Lillee's bat could have helped kids who couldn't afford any other kind of bat he would have been all for it. After all, Lillee's would have retailed at £37.50 compared to the £50 of many willow bats. There was a stark difference, not so much in the feel of the bat but in the damage Lillee's inflicted. After 28 shots against one ball, the ball was distinctly out of shape and when Close mistimed a shot and got bottom edge, there was a deep V-like incision across the seam which would have rendered it useless for top-class action.

The bat as an instrument of destruction did not impress Close, either. 'From the batsman's point of view, the metal just feels alien. There is no difference when you are glancing or late-cutting but you feel it almost every time on the drive. What cricketers call the sweet spot, where the drive comes off the blade perfectly, is considerably higher up on the metal bat. It makes you feel disoriented. Maybe it's psychological because the bat is made of metal but you feel you can't get through it at normal speed. Somehow I felt as if all my energy was being dissipated. It was noticeable, too, that if you didn't get the ball in the middle there was a considerable amount of jarring.' Lillee was not amused. Did the bat have a future? 'Let Lord's make the comments on it. They're the experts.' he said. 'They're the ones who are supposed to know, aren't they?' Alas, within the month, or shortly thereafter, a terse amendment to cricket's Law Six effectively scuppered Lillee's ambitions to become a metal millionaire. Before the end of the winter, Lord's had revised the rules to stipulate that 'the blade of the bat shall be made of wood.'

Since then there have been other attempts to market sensational and quite revolutionary new bats. The first was in 1991 when a Bristol firm introduced a double-faced bat. It was made of willow and conformed to the size and width of a traditional bat. The real difference was that it had as much wood at the toe as it did in the middle just below the splice. Hence the sweet spot was much larger than on a conventional bat. The Bristol bat was approved by cricket's general committee but never really caught on.

The following year the International Cricket Council also declared legal a bat that had a traditional blade but a revolutionary handle. This was also introduced by Australians, on this occasion by Doug Walters and Steve Smith. The handle of the bat bent back away from the top of the blade then hooked forward again, forcing the batsman's hands behind the face as the ball was played. Richie Richardson, the West Indies captain, tried the new bat during practice at the Sydney Cricket Ground and declared, 'It looked a bit strange when I saw it but I thought it could be the bat of the future.' It would seem not. So far the standard shape of King Willow – which once yielded the wood for 1,179 bats from a single tree – has withstood all challenges.

The Days the Records Books were rewritten

Graeme Hick was an England batsman in waiting when he played the greatest innings of the century. The 21-year-old Zimbabwean still had three years to go before he had a residential qualification for England, when in May, 1988, he hit an epic 405 not out for Worcestershire against Somerset at Taunton. It was the highest championship score this century and the second highest ever made in England behind Archie Maclaren's 424 for Lancashire in 1895. By coincidence, Maclaren's innings was also against Somerset at Taunton.

Ian Botham, then a county team-mate of Hick's, described it as the greatest individual innings he had ever seen, comparing Hick and Viv Richards of the West Indies.

Hick was going at a phenomenal speed when Worcestershire skipper Phil Neale declared the innings closed at tea-time, leaving Hick just 20 runs short of setting a record score for all first class cricket in Britain.

This was how the young man achieved world-wide fame by playing only the eighth individual innings above 400 in cricket history. His first 100 came in 153 minutes off 126 balls and included 13 fours. The second 100 were scored off 151 balls, took 189 minutes and included a six and 11 fours. The third century came off 134 balls in 142 minutes and included two sixes and five fours. The last, stunning hundred that took him to 400 came off 58 balls in 71 minutes and included eight sixes and six fours.

Since he had arrived in England, Hick had made a stunning impact. In 1986 he had completed his 50th century in all cricket before his 20th birthday. At 20 years and 112 days he became the youngest to score 2000 runs in a season. The following year he scored hundreds in three successive championships innings but nothing equalled that 405.

Hick didn't mind missing Maclaren's record. 'I didn't even know it existed. I just kept going. Getting the highest score I've ever got is a great achievement. I gave a few chances and I enjoyed a bit of luck when I started to tire after getting 300.'

Two years later there was another innings that matched the splendour of Hick's. England captain Graham Gooch scored 333 against India in a Test at Lord's. It was the third highest largest individual total by an England batsman, surpassed only by Len Hutton's 364 in 1938 and Walter Hammond's 336 not out in 1933. Afterwards Gooch was as humble as ever. 'Graham,' said a journalist, 'how does today rank among all the days of your life?' The England captain paused and looked into the distance. 'It was all right,' he replied. 'Yeah. All right.'

The spectators thought it was more than that. Long after play had ended, people were queuing for replica scorecards, to be produced in later years to prove that, yes, they were there. Gooch batted all the first day and most of the second before he was out. At precisely five o'clock, just when the cricket world was believing that he could sail past Gary Sobers' Test record of 365, Gooch tried to drive Prabhakar and the ball nipped back between bat and pad, taking leg stump. Gooch had been at the wicket for ten and half hours, collecting 43 fours and three sixes along the way.

As he trudged back to the pavilion, the weariness and fatigue in his body clear for all to see, he must have felt a damned sight older than his 37 years. There was a time in the 200s when Gooch seemed to be continually sweeping at the Indian spinners and missing. On 278 he drank a whole bottle of tonic water and at tea he was one short of his 300. When he left the field, his helmet remained in the middle. As one journalist wrote, it was if Gooch was saying in the words of an American general: I shall return.

Return he did only to fall just short of those other mammoth scores. Patrick Collins of the Mail on Sunday wrote that Gooch had revealed the finesse of a surgeon and the beefy belligerence of a nightclub bouncer. It was a notable triumph of sublime technique and crippling concentration. 'Yeah,' Gooch repeated. 'It was all right.'

GOLF

Renton Laidlaw

Few words are mis-used more often in sport than sensational except perhaps those dual imposters-disastrous and tragic. It is never a disaster when Seve Ballesteros misses a two-foot putt just costly or disappointing; neither is it a tragedy if Sandy Lyle misses a half-way cut. This is just his bad luck on the week – embarrassing, perhaps, and costly in terms of prize-money but not to be compared with loss of life in a motorway crash or train smash.

So it is with sensational, a word that has been cruelly debased because of its association and use to describe really quite ordinary sporting occurrences. Yet how does one decide whether a person's performance, an incident or a happening is exceptionally noteworthy or not? What are the guidelines to decide which golfer is a sensation, which win a sensation?

As far as I am concerned for something or someone to be sensational he or she must have performed so commendably as to have appeared almost god-like or for the incident or shot to be so incredible or so unusual in character and deed as to take everyone – even the golfing afficionados – by surprise.

People, performances and shots are the three categories I shall address, limiting myself to the past 30 years and even then not attempting a comprehensive review. In golf some players in whatever generation have been giants from Harry Vardon, J.H. Taylor and James Braid through Walter Hagen, Gene Sarazen, Bobby Jones and Henry Cotton to Byron Nelson, Ben Hogan and Sam Snead.

In the past 30 years you could say Jack Nicklaus, Arnold Palmer and the man-in-black Gary Player, who only started wearing black because he wanted to be different from everyone else and realised that everyone noticed the villanous cowboy in western films because he was normally dressed in black, fit the bill as does Severiano Ballesteros. What each one of them has done in their careers is nothing short of sensational. Although Tony Jacklin was an inspiration to thousands of young golfers in Britain when he was at his peak, although Johnny Miller sparkled for a time in the early 70's and quiet-mannered Tom Watson won five Opens in nine years and although Lee Trevino joked his way through an incredible career and Greg Norman played his part in advancing the popularity of golf, none of them can match the worldwide impact produced by the Big Three a few years ago and more recently Ballesteros, darling of the crowds wherever he plays around the world.

We have seen the best of the Big Three and maybe even Seve, the man Norman admits gave him the confidence he needed to become a world-beater. Maybe 35-year-old Seve will not win another major but no-one will deny the contribution he made to world golf with his sometimes adventurous and always exciting play so reminiscent of Palmer in his heyday.

Arnold Palmer

Palmer, the golfer who has become a folk-hero and legend in his own lifetime, started the modern boom marching the fairways of the world with his own army of fans, smaller today but still as loyal to him as they were when he burst on the scene in the late 50's to transform the game to what we know it today. His warmth and homespun talent, learned as a boy at a club in Pennsylvania which he now owns, his power-play, his dynamism, his outgoing personality, his honesty, his integrity and his readiness to meet with and talk to his fans, was an early indication that he was made for stardom. He could handle with ease the pressure of stardom albeit that pressure was less then than it is now. The modern golfing millionaires owe a massive debt of gratitude to Arnie whose winning ways attracted expanded television coverage, new sponsors putting up more prize-money while convincing thousands to take up the game, with the result that more courses needed to be built. These days Palmer is a multi-millionaire, his earnings wisely invested by Mark McCormack who carved out his own millionaire career as an entrepreneur, manager, promoter and wheeler-dealer out of shrewdly realising that, in any golfing boom, the golfers, especially Palmer. Player and Nicklaus, needed to be managed. What a job he made of it. Today McCormack flies the world thriving on a strict schedule of business meetings before breakfast, after it, through lunch and before, during and after dinner. He would not want it another way. He is a workaholic who has built an empire on the back of Arnold Palmer, who was shrewd enough himself to see, when McCormack first approached him, that they could do business together.

It was charismatic Arnold Palmer with his sheer power off the tee, and a swing easily recognisable because of its distinctively high finish, who captured the imagination of the fans. It was never difficult to know where Palmer was on the course. It was where the crowds were, where the cheers were coming from. So loyal was his army that when a then chubby Jack Nicklaus, a much less warm, outgoing personality than Arnie, came along to challenge him in the early 60's Arnie's fans did not like it one little bit!

Throughout his career Palmer has had the magnetism of the Pied Piper without having to tootle a pipe. Just being on the course with Arnie, who at one point was being encouraged to move into politics – he does sometimes play with George Bush and hopefully, quietly, is giving the President a lesson or two – was and is exciting even today! Arnie, like Ballesteros who came to match

59

him, wears his heart on his sleeve. Just as you can when following Seve, you could suffer and celebrate with Palmer, whose craggy visage and bearing now gives him the look of a John Wayne and similar legendary popularity. Palmer came from a humble, honest background and had his most productive spell from 1955 and 1973 when he won 61 titles including two Open Championships, four US Masters and a US Open although that should have been two had he not blown a big lead over Billy Casper at the Olympic Club in San Francisco in the final round in 1966 and lost the subsequent play-off.

Losing that title that year might have been Palmer's saddest moment in major title golf had there not been two other disappointments – never winning a USPGA Championship and, unlike Gary Player, Jack Nicklaus, Gene Sarazen and Ben Hogan, never completing a Grand Slam, and not winning the 1960 Centenary Open at St Andrews, the first year he came to Britain to play in it.

Palmer can be credited with breathing new life into the Open to the point where it is now well-established again as the world's Open. Americans had become conspicuous by their absence until Palmer came along to give the Championship his support and, with his backing, other Americans started crossing the Atlantic to compete.

In 1960 he had come to St Andrews having won the Masters and the US Open. In 1930 Bobby Jones had completed what was then termed the Grand Slam – victories in the US Amateur and Open and the British equivalent in the same year. In 1960 Palmer was bidding to win the modern Grand Slam – victory in the Masters, the US Open, the Open and the USPGA. He had captured the first two legs but lost out sensationally, by a shot, to quiet Australian Kel Nagle, fancied as a winner by no one – except his Australian World Cup partner Peter Thompson. Palmer won a year later using his massive power to harness the cruel winds that lashed the Royal Birkdale course and again the following year when he beat Nagle with ease in superb weather at Troon followed for the last time by thousands – fans were roped off after this – but neither of these wins could compare with what a win in 1960 would have meant to him.

Almost as sensational as his runaway win at Troon was the part he played in the late 'Champagne' Tony Lema's victory in 1964 at the Old course, St Andrews. It had long been felt that it was not possible for someone to turn up a day and a half before a Championship at St Andrew's, play one practice round and win because of the subtleties of the course, but Lema proved the critics wrong with the help of the absent Arnold Palmer's trusty caddie 'Tip' Anderson. Lema hit the ball where he was told to, hit the headlines with the story of his sensational triumph and the picture pages, too, enjoying a glass or two of bubbly with the pressmen who had said victory was not possible! Tragically Lema would die two years later in a plane crash – a tragedy (in the true sense) that left golf all the poorer.

If Palmer rejuvenated the Open, there had been the sensational performances earlier of South African Bobby Locke with four wins between 1949 and 1957. In 1949 he beat the late Harry Bradshaw who at one point had had to hit a ball lodged in a broken bottle lying in the rough – and in 1957 he won despite replacing the ball on the wrong mark on the final green – a mistake spotted only later by studying television pictures. It was first time the cameras had been there! Then there was Australian Peter Thomson who matched Harry Vardon's five wins in a 12-year run from 1954 later to be equalled by Tom Watson's even more impressive five victories between 1975 and 1983 including the never-to-be-forgotten duel in the sun he had with Jack Nicklaus at Turnbery in 1977 when his 65 and 65 in the final two rounds of the Championship beat Nicklaus' 65 and 66 by a shot. So big were the crowds that year the players were unable to spot those landmarks on the course that helped them judge distance and direction.

Trailing Watson by a shot, Nicklaus, who had won in 1966, 1970 and would again in 1978, kept up the pressure right to the end holing a 36-foot roller-coaster of a putt across the 18th green for a birdie 3 leaving Watson to hole his 18-inch one for victory. Watson, knowing Jack, had geared up to the realisation that he would need to hole his birdie putt to take the title after a battle in which these two giants of the game earned everyone's respect and impressed each other too. Watson, the Huckleberry Finn of golf, could be the last man to dominate the game in America the way Hogan and Snead, Byron Nelson, Palmer and Nicklaus had done. Now there is simply too much talent around to allow anyone to top the US money list four years in a row as Watson did. Like Palmer, Watson has not won a USPGA but Watson's demeanour, his bearing and sportsmanship has made him one of golf's most loved personalities despite being the man who removed Nicklaus from his kingly throne!

The Golden Bear

No curriculum vitae can compare with that of Nicklaus. When Johnny Miller finished in an unheard of 63 to win at Tucson and Phoenix in successive weeks in 1975 and when he beat Seve Ballesteros at Royal Birkdale for the British title to emulate his idol Tony Lema, he was creating sensational headlines and threatening to outdo Nicklaus, but he faded. Watson came closest in the States but to 'doing a Nicklaus' but Jack's career record remains inviolate. None can compare with that of the Golden Bear, golfer of the century in America ahead of Hogan, Palmer and Jones. Nicklaus has, quite simply, been incredible. No player in any sport has remained so solidly at the top as long as he has. With natural caution I respectfully suggest no one will better his list of achievements.

Whether overweight as he was in the early days before disciplining himself to eating sensibly, or slimline, as he is now, Nicklaus has conquered everything in golf. His record is simply sensational. All told he has won 20 majors – six Masters between 1963, when he was 23, and 1986, when he was 46: four US Opens between 1962, when he had the temerity to beat Palmer at Oakmont and 1980, when he beat Isao Aoki by a shot preventing the Japanese player from becoming the first Far Easterner to win a major. He won two of his three Opens at St Andrews coming from one behind with three to play to triumph in 1978 and packed his five title wins in the US PGA Championship into the 18 years between 1963 and 1980. Add in two US Amateur Championship titles and all Nicklaus is missing is an Amateur Championship win in Britain. Even more incredibly he has had 19 second place finishes in majors and nine third places! His 30-year career scoring-average in the States is 70.96! Still as enthusiastic about playing because he does still believes he can win, he even averaged 69.79 in Senior Tour golf for the Over 50's in 1991, the year he won a record 310,000 dollars in a Senior Skins game . . . as if he needed the money!

Like Palmer he has diversified, making much more now of his course designing and building career than Arnie. Nicklaus has always been a more difficult man to get to know. He does not have the natural charm of Palmer, with whom he is inevitably always compared, and his grass roots popularity has suffered as a result but the world of golf to a man admires what he has achieved. Where there is warmth for Palmer there is respect and plenty of it for Nicklaus who re-wrote much of golf's record books and set tough standards for others to aim at.

For over 20 years any young golfer turning pro has wanted to do even better than the Golden Bear – a brilliant name coined for Nicklaus by distinguished Australian golf writer Don Lawrence, who was rewarded with a couple of shirts! Very quickly they found out that that goal was unattainable. Tony Jacklin, despite his sensational 1969 win at Lytham when he became the first British winner of that title since Max Faulkner 18 years earlier, and despite his even more spectacular 1970 US Open victory accomplished in splendid style at Hazeltine, had begun to realise by then that he could not out-score the magnificent Nicklaus and when Lee Trevino chipped in at the 17th in the 1972 Open at Muirfield to beat the British player, when he had looked a winner all the way, Jacklin's dream was finally shattered. Jacklin's drive and enthusiasm was never quite the same. Realising he could not be the best came as a blow to his morale as it did to dozens of others ready, willing and believing themselves able to show Nicklaus a thing or two!

Nicklaus' dedication has remained constant. His desire to win burns as strongly today as it did when he beat Charlie Coe one up to win his first US Amateur title in 1959. Not always easy-going off the course, Nicklaus has preferred to do most of his talking with his clubs and more recently with his pen on the golf course design board. The legacy he wants to leave golf is a series of courses that have enhanced the game by providing a stiff but not too severe test, a thought-proving but not impossible challenge if the resort developer will allow!

The Man in Black

So much for Palmer and Nicklaus. Gary Player completes the Big Three. How much more might he have achieved had he been based permanently in America but, as a proud South African, he refused to move to the US and consequently became the most travelled golfer of his generation. He has circled the globe over 60 times, travelled well over seven million miles and spent, he reckons, nearly three years sitting in airline chairs – a fact pointed up in his book 'Golfers Begin at Fifty'. During his illustrious career Player has hit seven million balls and spent more hours on the practice range and in the gymnasium than any other golfer.

Throughout his 130-win career he has been a fitness fanatic. Indeed but for his fitness he would never have been able to maintain the schedule that made him a crowd-puller wherever he played. He won three Opens in three decades – 1959, 1968 and 1974. He won three US Masters including the one in 1978 when he came from seven behind with a round to go to win with a then record 64, two USPGA championships and a US Open victory in a play-off with Kel Nagle of Australia in 1965 at Bellerive. That gave him tremendous satisfaction in that it enabled him to beat Nicklaus to a Slam – victory in all four majors at least once. Small of stature but big in heart, Player won the South African Open 13 times, the Australian Open seven times and, at the height of the anti-apartheid movement's most active period, he could only play with the help of an armed guard. A great match-player he made the World Match-play Championship his own for a time, winning five of the first 11 tournaments at Wentworth and finishing runner-up on another occasion. In that time only Arnold Palmer, twice the title-holder, won more than once.

In Match-play finals he beat Peter Thomson, Jack Nicklaus twice, Bob Charles and Graham Marsh round the famous Burma Road and not always without controversy. Hale Irwin beat him 2 and 1 in the 1974 final when Player was going for his sixth success. Yet of the 41 matches he played round Wentworth one stands out more than the others – his match in 1965 with Tony Lema. The matches are over 36-holes and after 19 holes Player was seven down to the American who had covered the last eight holes in the morning in 29 shots to turn a one hole deficit into a six hole lunch-time lead that had Player stirred but not shaken . . . not even after losing the 19th. No-one ever wrote off Player who made more birdies towards the end of rounds or tournaments than anyone else in golf, but even his loyalist supporters were biting their nails that day. Then Player birdied four holes in a row winning three of them to reduce his deficit to four. The Wentworth course is not jut a demanding golf examination; it also tests a player's fitness and concentration.

Having lost another hole before the turn Player was up against it – five down with nine regulation holes to play. The stage was set for a vintage Player comeback. He won three holes quickly, curling in a 10-footer for an eagle at the long 13th, the 31st of the match, after Lema had sunk a 30-footer for a birdie. Two down now, then one down when the troubled Lema hooked into the trees to lose the 34th hole. With one to play Player was still one down but he birdied the last to square matters and won at the first extra hole when he hit two glorious woods onto the green and Lema, bunkered in two, could not get down in two more to keep the game alive. Player was so exhausted he nearly fainted and had to be assisted back to the clubhouse as Lema tried to work out just what had happened. Their match remains one of the most sensational in the history of an event packed with drama.

There was Jacklin v. Trevino in 1972 in a repeat of the battle Trevino had won for the Open at Muirfield. Jacklin, silent and not responding to Trevino's chatter, was four down at the lunch-break but trimmed monster Wentworth to just 63 shots in the afternoon . . . and sensationally still lost. There was the spectacular scoring produced by Sandy Lyle and Tsuneyuki Nakajima in 1986. On the card both were round in 65 in the morning and both in 64 in the afternoon but Lyle won by two holes in match-play.

Super Seve

If Gary Player dominated early World Match-play tournaments Severiano Ballesteros dominated the event between 1981 and 1992 emulating Player's five wins and, to date, never losing a final. Ben Crenshaw, Sandy Lyle, Bernhard Langer twice, and Mark McNulty were Seve's victims in the finals, the last in 1991 probably being his most satisfying success coming in a year when he silenced those critics who had dared to write him off by winning the European Volvo Tour Order of Merit for a record sixth time. He holds a very special position in the history of the game from the moment as a raw teenager who had learned golf by hitting shots in a field beside his house close to the Royal Pedrena Club at Santander, he burst on the scene at rainy Venice in 1974 and almost beat established Peter Oosterhuis and Johnny Miller. It was Miller who was involved in another sensational duel with him in 1976 at Royal Birkdale. Miller won the Open that year but for long enough it seemed as if the ex-caddie who spoke little English and could read none at all, was going to score, at age 19, a most dramatic victory in the oldest Championship in the world. With a round to go he was sensationally two shots clear of Miller but his youthful enthusiasm and willingness to lash at the ball when a more cautious approach might have been more fruiful, took its toll. By the turn on the final day he was behind and when he lost five more shots quickly by finding the thick rough, it looked as if he would tumble off the leader board.

Amazingly, he rallied, picking up four shots in five holes from the 13th, eagling the 17th in the process. He knew a birdie would tie him for second with Jack Nicklaus even if he could not win and he achieved that with a third shot played at the last with all the poise and control of a seasoneed veteran. The shot convinced John Jacobs, renowned TV commentator, top worldwide coach and the man chosen to make the European PGA tour work in the early 70's, believe that Seve was a genius. He was right. That pitch had been played, from skimpy rough to the left of the green to a pin cut just seven yards on a slick-surfaced green. He could not have stopped the ball anywhere near the stick had he lofted the ball over the two big traps which stood between him and the hole and he needed to get down in two to tie Nicklaus. Instead he hit a low 9-iron which skipped between the traps and rolled softly down to the pin. A week later Ballesteros won his first tournament in Europe when he took the Dutch Open. Today he has won over 60 in Europe and 20 more worldwide.

For 12 years in tournaments other than the majors and frequently in them, too, he has started favourite, expected by his adoring fans to win. In majors until most recently he has been the man to beat winning two Masters, including the 1980 tournament in which he sensationally took a 10-shot lead into the final round! He has never won a US Open or a US PGA Championship but he zig-zagged his way to a first Open triumph in 1979 at Lytham, hit a glorious 6-iron to the heart of the Road Hole (the 17th) in the final round and then birdied the last to edge out Tom Watson and Bernhard Langer in 1984 and, in 1988, played some of his gutsiest golf to break the heart of runner-up Nick Price of Zimbabwe who must have felt the way Tom Weiskopf felt when he admitted he had played as well as he possibly could in the 1975 US Masters and still finished tied with Johnny Miller behind Jack Nicklaus.

At Lytham in 1988 Ballesteros, world star, was at his majestic best encouraging comparison again with the bravest performance by the charismatic Arnold Palmer. When Mark McCormack brought the pair of them together in a first round 18-hole match in the 21st World Match-play Championship the fans did not want either to lose! Palmer came to the last one up and looking like making a birdie but Ballesteros, equal to the drama of the moment, holed his pitch-and-run for an eagle and despatched his grey-haired opponent at the third extra hole to wrap-up one of the most emotional ties in the 32-years history of the event.

Sensational performances

So much for golf's personalities who, throughout their careers, have provided enough sensations to satisfy the most discriminating fans. In recent years, however, there have been victories by others which have created a sensation on both sides of the Atlantic, not least in the majors. In the Masters there was Larry Mize's 1987 victory and Sandy Lyle's incredible wire-to-wire success a year later and Tony Jacklin's 1969 victory in the Open and Bill

Rogers' triumph at Royal St George's in 1981 followed by his equally sensational disappearance from the scene. There were there surprise victories of Lee Trevino, Orville Moody, and Jacklin in three successive years at the US Open and wins by Bob Tway and John Daly in the USPGA at Inverness, Toledo and Crooked Stick, Indiana in 1986 and 1991.

Mize, the only Augusta-based golfer on Tour, had been a part of the Masters for several years before he won. The slim young American, not a regular Tour winner, had worked the huge scoreboards and marvelled at the performances of those players whom he dreamed of joining later when he earned his Tour card. The Masters ticket is the most sought after and most difficult to come-by but when Mize started qualifying to play in the Masters many of his friends, because they were local, had tickets and came to watch. In 1987 they saw him tie after 72-holes with Ballesteros, already a double winner and rated something of a course expert, and Greg Norman who had muscled his way to an impressive win in the 1986 Open at Turnberry when the Championship committee set up the course at its most difficult with fearsome rough. That was the year he had led with a round to go in all four majors. At the time Norman was hot.

In the play-off Ballesteros three-putted to lose out at the 10th, traditionally the first extra hole, and at the 11th Norman looked favourite to join the elite in the small but exclusive champions' locker room in the huge white-painted clubhouse which overlooks the course. The Australian was on the green in two. Mize had missed the putting surface finishing on a bank to the right of the green. His ball lay some 30 yards from the pin and his chance of stopping the shot from the rough on the slick green sloping away from him was, to say the least, a long-odds chance. Norman stood by quietly as Mize, in the gathering gloom, set himself up for a shot that would create as much noise around the world as Gene Sarazen's 3-wood into the hole for an albatross, a double-eagle as the Americans call it – in the 1935 Masters. Mize's ball bounced on the green and began to gather speed. It seemed certain to run off the other side when incredibly it hit the stick and disappeared like a rabbit down the hole. For a split second Mize himself could not believe it before he jumped in the air and performed a winner's dance. Norman, shattered, missed the putt to keep the play-off alive!

Although Nick Faldo in 1989 and 1990 would win the title at the same second extra hole against Scott Hoch and Ray Floyd, he was not the first Britain to be fitted out with a Green Jacket. That went to his great rival Sandy Lyle, who had beaten him to an Open win in 1985 at Royal St George's although now 2-1 down following Faldo's remarkable parring of hole-after-hole to win in the rain and mist at Muirfield in 1987 and his much more impressive victory in 1990 at St. Andrews when he ripped the heart out of Greg Norman with whom he was paired in the final twosome by shooting a third round 67 to the Australian's 76.

In 1988 at Augusta, however, it was Lyle who was walking tall among the huge pines that gives the place such an awesome cathedral-like atmosphere. Coming to the last with Mark Calcavecchia in the clubhouse on 282, Lyle knew he had to birdie to win. It has not often been done at the Masters. Doug Ford had holed a bunker shot in 1957 to collect a Jacket and Arnold Palmer had sunk a birdie putt for one of his four successes which came in seven years from 1958. What Lyle needed to do with his final drive was avoid hitting into the trees on the right or going into one of two cavernous bunkers on the outside of the dog leg on the left as it winds its way punishingly up the hill. Lyle, who had had control on the final day, lost it and caught the second trap. He had 147 yards to go – a 7-iron shot. He needed nothing less than the shot of his career. He needed to swing perfectly and needed, too, that little bit of luck that every winner seems to get along the way.

He conjured up a majestic shot. The ball hit above the pin and screwed back down the slop to finish 10 feet above the hole. On Augusta's greens it would be possible to three-putt in those circumstances but, looking composed, even if inside he was in turmoil. Lyle took several deep breaths, decided on the line, forgot about that and concentrated then on judging the pace of a putt he knew would make golfing history.

On the green where Hogan, Palmer, Nicklaus, Player, Ballesteros and Watson had all triumphed, sometimes more than once. Lyle coolly judged everything to perfection. The ball never looked like going anywhere else. Sensationally he had won the Masters.

Unlikely Winners

Years earlier in 1955 Jack Fleck had created a sensation by winning the US Open by beating the great Ben Hogan, a sensation of a different age, in a play-off by three shots. Fleck ran two public courses in Davenport, Iowa and had prepared for the Championship at the Olympic Club that year by turning up a week early and playing 44-holes practice holes a day! He ended up a golfing David whipping the then Goliath Hogan and there were similarities in 1969 when ex-Army sergeant Orville Moody won the title. A year earlier Lee Trevino, with a swing described by the leading writers of the day as agricultural and more appropriate for scything hay than hitting a golf ball, had confounded his critics by proving that his method was best for him by beating Jack Nicklaus by four shots at Oak Hill, Rochester in New York State, tieing Nicklaus' one-year-old winning aggregate record in the process! Two years earlier, Robert Sommers recalls in his history of the US Open, Trevino had been cleaning clubs, polishing shoes and picking up range balls at a club in El Paso and had only played in the 1967 Open because his wife had, unbeknown to him, mailed in his entry. A year earlier he had stayed in a cheap motel, eaten frugally, drunk beer with a Baltusrol member and finished behind Nicklaus. Trevino, one of gold's most extrovert characters, has entertained fans around the world with his golf and his one-liners, collecting in the process not one but two US Open titles, two Opens in Britain and two USPGA victories, but he never won a Masters.

The officials had hardly got over the surprise of the Trevino win when along came an even more unlikely winner – Moody, whom many still consider the worst putter ever to win the US Open. Later in life on the Senior Tour he would pioneer the broomstick putter that Arnold Palmer and the purists in golf so detest. In 1969, backed by a lawyer, a retail clothier and a mystery man he knew from his army days, Moody was not considered a title threat although Trevino, a pal of his on Tour, had mentioned in a pre-Championship newspaper preview that he thought Moody might take the title from him.

Everyone laughed but Trevino and Moody had the last laugh as the man they nicknamed 'Sarge' showed incredible nerve to shoot 281 and win by one from Bob Rosburg, a distressed Jerry Barber and Deane Beman who would later become chief executive of the US Tour. Moody shot 71, 70, 68 and closed with 72 to create the biggest surprise in major golf until another unknown John Daly came along 22 years later to win the USPGA.

Trevino and Moody had created something of a stir by winning the national Championship in successive years and there was a further surprise a year later when Tony Jacklin, leading from start to finish, added the US Open crown to his 1969 Open win at Royal Lytham and St Annes. Unlike the two Americans who had just won the title before him, Jacklin was well enough known when he came to Hazeltine, the much criticised 1970 venue, lacking, as Nicklaus said, definition. Dave Hill was particularly scathing. 'They ruined a good farm when they built this course,' he sneered and his mood was little better at the end when Jacklin had become the first British winner of the title since Ted Ray in 1920!

What was so sensational about Jacklin's success was the manner of it – 71 on a first day when almost half the field had shot 80 or worse in the wind that had swept across the plains, and then three 70's. He putted superbly, maybe as well as he ever did in his illustrious career, to beat Hill by five shots. For just over a month Jacklin held both the British and American titles but he never won another major, although unlucky not to pick up two more Opens at St Andrews in 1970 when Doug Sanders lost to Jack Nicklaus in a play-off after missing a curling two-and-a-half footer for victory at the 72nd hole, and 1971 when Trevino edged him out at Muirfield. Hazeltine was probably Jacklin's greatest golf achievement. Jacklin, the trailblazer who helped create the PGA European Tour with John Jacobs and Ken Schofield before retiring at 40 disillusioned, in some respects, with the game, recently had a lengthy taxi-ride in London. At the end the driver refused to take his fare. 'Listen, mate,' he said.' You've given me so much pleasure watching you over the years that I could not possibly charge you for the ride!'

Since 1970 there have been some surprise winners of the US Open but none to compare with Trevino, Moody and Jacklin over 20 years ago.

There was Miller's record-breaking closing 63 which allowed him to come from six behind to win in 1973 at Oakmont with a total of 279 – four better than Nicklaus and Palmer had shot 11 years earlier. Miller's round over a soft course with receptive greens was sensational but for many its still ranks below Palmer's closing winning 65 at Cherry Hills in 1960. Nicklaus's last round 65 at Baltusrol in 1980 and Hogan's 67, the lowest score of the week, in the final round of the 1951 Championship at Oakland Hills where he, unlike Miller, had had to handle hard, fast greens.

The 1977 US Open at Southern Hills, Tulsa, was memorable because of the sensational shot Jerry Pate played at the last hole when needing a birdie to beat Tom Weiskopf and Al Geiberger, the first man to shoot 59 on the US Tour at Memphis in 1977, although that has since been equalled by Chip Beck at Las Vegas in 1991. Pate, who had handled the challenge of John Mahaffey, his playing partner for the day, hit his final drive into the rough. He needed to play a recovery over the water if he was going to try for his birdie. The safe shot was to lay up, pitch on and make sure of a play-off but Pate, whose career was later to be seriously affected by neck trouble, played one of the most spectacular shots in golf – a winning 5-iron to three feet. It would have been anticlimatic had he missed the putt.

Headline Making

The events of the final day rather than the golf was what made the Championship memorable the next year. It featured Hubert Green, who was leading at Southern Hills when police received a call from a woman indicating that three men with guns were on their way to kill the golfer. The clubhouse was closed, police were drafted in to protect Green, who was playing that year some of his best golf. He was told but decided to carry on and, under the most enormous pressure, won a US Open unrivalled for suspense off and on the course.

A tree made the headlines in 1979 at Inverness in Toledo when, overnight, the USGA planted a 24-foot high spruce with a 26-foot branch span to prevent players doing what Lon Hinkle had started – namely driving down the 17th to shorten the way to the green at the adjacent eighth hole! In mid-June it looked incongruously like a big abandoned Christmas tree and was christened the Hinkle-berry. After the Championship had been won by Hale Irwin, scoring the second of his three victories, it was removed.

In 1982 the Championship went to Pebble Beach, that delightful course on the Pacific where Tom Watson learned his golf and where Mark O'Meara has won four AT&T Championships. The engrossing on-course duels between Watson and Nicklaus were a feature at this time and it looked as if Big Jack would take the honours on this occasion. Playing ahead of Watson he was in the clubhouse – or rather the scorer's tent – on 284 after a closing 69. Nicklaus, chasing a fifth US Open title, watched anxiously on a TV monitor as Watson, tied with him, came to the difficult short 17th.

The shot back towards the ocean was a 3-wood or 2-iron. Watson elected to hit the iron but he pulled it catching the left edge of the green before bouncing into the thick collar of rough between two bunkers. The ball lay 18-feet from the pin but fortunately on top of the grass and not buried in it. To get it close to the hole, however, needed delicate precision because it was downhill, but Watson had practised the shot many times. His caddie, Bruce Edwards, whispered to him just to get it close. Watson, in an amazing burst of super confidence, retorted, 'I'm going to make it.' Judged to perfection the ball hit the collar of the green, ran down, hit the stick and disappeared for an unlikely 2.

Like Nicklaus had the 16th one year at Augusta after holing a birdie putt en route to victory or Irwin would years later when he holed across the last green at Medinah to make it into a play-off for the 1990 US Open, Watson leaped around the green waving his club above his head. It was a sensational shot and it won him the Championship. After making a birdie at the last to win by two. Watson was met by a disappointed Nicklaus. They shook hands. 'You little son-of-a-bitch, you're something else. I'm proud of you.'

In that moment the sportsmanship that is so much a part of golf was revealed again – a reminder too of that magic moment at Royal Birkdale in 1969 when with the Ryder Cup result hinging on the then Open champion Tony Jacklin's game with Nicklaus they had come up the last all square. Jacklin had holed across the green to win the 17th and as they walked up the home hole on which so much depended. Nicklaus asked the young Britisher if he was nervous. Jacklin nodded and Nicklaus admitted he was too. Minutes later after Nicklaus had holed out, he conceded Jacklin his two footer to halve the hole and draw the match grabbing his arm and whispering, 'You would not have missed it.'

Sadly Bernhard Langer missed the six footer that would have given the Europeans a draw and enabled them to hold on to the Ryder cup at Kiawah in 1991. Captain Bernard Gallacher indicated no-one should have had to face up to such pressure at the end of three engrossing days of competition against an American team whipped up into a nationalistic fervour by their captain Dave Stockton. Langer does not shoulder the blame for leaving the Cup in America. A lesser player would never have got as far against the inspired but tiring Hale Irwin, whose shorter putt the German had graciously conceded. The tension round that final green was incredible and when Langer's putt slid past the hole the eruption of delight and relief from the Americans that they had won might have been heard in Charleston several miles away!

The Europeans, with Nick Faldo and Ian Woosnam not at their most brilliant, had battled with dignity and probably deserved a draw, but victory in a play-off a week later in the German Masters indicated Langer had not been scarred by the experiences at Kiawah in a match as sensational as the 1985 European triumph at The Belfry, the European success at Muirfield in 1987 when Jack Nicklaus and his team had proved a trifle over-confident, or the 1989 draw which produced Christy O'Connor's classic 2-iron second shot to three feet at the last to win a crucial point by beating Fred Couples who had gone in with a 9-iron.

There have been more surprise winners of the US Open than in the Open in Britain but the 1981 Championship at Royal St George's produced a shock – an American, who had only been persuaded to travel to England by Ben Crenshaw, took the title. Bill Rogers was a slight, mild-mannered player who loved the famous links and even more the historic surroundings of Sandwich where there are houses 500 years older than America itself. Although he had won the World Match-play title two years earlier and been joint runner-up to David Graham in the US Open a few weeks earlier, he certainly did not start favourite at the course in the south-east of England where in 1975 Arnold Palmer won his last big title – the British PGA by five strokes with a brilliant last round 71 in a gale.

At half-way Rogers, gaining in confidence all the time, led by one from Crenshaw with Tom Watson four behind. On the third day Rogers fired 67. Crenshaw 76 and at the 54-hole mark the unfancied American led by five from Britain's Mark James and Langer, who was making such an impact not just in his native Germany but throughout Europe with his fine play. Coming to the turn on the final day after a virtually sleepless night, Rogers' lead had been cut back to one by Langer but, surviving this crisis, the American, sensing he did have the guts to win an Open, was four ahead with five to play and then with one to go.

As he strode forward to the green he was engulfed by the crowds and at one stage, a local policeman, clearly not a golf fan and believing the unprepossessing Rogers to be a member of the gallery, pushed him back. 'I'm only trying to finish,' said Rogers politely and he did to become a worthy champion. Later he would drift from the scene – a victim of burn-out but not before he had enjoyed a World Tour as champion, being cheered in places he never knew existed and which he could not always find on the map. Later Rogers would insist that winning the Open really did mean being the World's champion but, although he won seven times in 1981, he had only one more victory in America after that. Now the man who conquered Royal St George's in 1981 seldom plays a Tour event. He had his moment, he had his year but the jet-setting lifestyle of a top star was not for him.

Around this time Tom Watson was the dominant figure in Open golf. If it could be argued he rather backed into his 1982 triumph at Royal Troon, where the 1932 champion Gene Sarazen, then 71 years of age, made a final appearance and holed in one at the Postage Stamp 8th on the first day and

71

holed a bunker shot there for a 2 on the second day! Watson certainly did not back into his fifth open at Royal Birkdale. There he hit a career-best 2-iron to the last to clinch a glorious victory over a great course. Yet it would be the same club that ended his hopes of equalling Harry Vardon's six Open victories record at St Andrews a year later when he and Bernhard Langer, still chasing an Open success, lost out to Ballesteros. In the final round the three were locked in a grim struggle. Ballesteros, playing ahead of Watson and Langer, had hit the 17th green with a 6-iron but Watson, with about the same distance to the flag, elected to tempt fate and go again with the club that had won him the title a year earlier. A 2-iron was far too much and the ball bounced over the green, over the road after which the hole is named and nestled against the wall. In that moment Watson had lost as up ahead Seve, who would go on to win again in 1988, holed for a closing birdie to give himself a two-shot cushion. That week on the slick at Andrews greens Seve had putted superbly. That year he dedicated his victory to his mother who had watched from a nearby window as he won, but for Watson the disappointment of losing was almost as great and had almost as significant an effect on his career as Jacklin's defeat by Trevino at Muirfield in 1972.

Watson may disagree and may yet equal Vardon's record but since 1984, troubled by his putting, practising less and spending more time with his family, he has not been the power he was in the late 70's and early 80's when he and Ballesteros could be said to have ruled the world of golf between them. Watson's reign at the top was shorter than Seve's who would go on to win another Open in a nail-biting finish to the 1988 Championship in which his victims included Nick Price, Nick Faldo and Sandy Lyle. That year he clinched his win with as delicate and beautifully executed little pitch from the side of the final green as you could hope to see. He was unlucky not to see it drop! That week in July he won with as controlled a golfing performance as his 1979 victory over the same course had been wild.

The least impressive of the four majors is the USPGA, packed with club professionals and, until very recently, run by the PGA of America whose commitment has always been to serve American professionals rather than ensure a truly international field. As a result the impact of the event worldwide has been much less than the Masters, the US Open and the Open. The image of the Championship, held in mid-August, has been hurt too by an apparently uncontrollable desire by the officials to hold it in some of the hottest, most tiring spots! Yes, there has been excitement, drama and even a sensational win or two in recent times not by foreigners who seldom do well on courses designed for US-style target golf, although Australian Wayne Grady took the title in 1990 beating, in the run-in, Fred Couples who would later emerge as a compulsive and exiciting winner. In recent years two winners of the title come readily to mind – Bob Tway and John Daly.

Tway is remembered for holing the bunker shot at the last which finally killed off Greg Norman, who had had the 1986 Championship won half a dozen holes from home, while Daly's triumph at respected Crooked Stick was a real-life example that fairy-tales still do happen.

Daly's Day

John Daly was not originally in the USPGA Championship. Nor was he first, second or third reserve. He was ninth alternate and only got the call when Nick Price from Zimbabwe, whose wife was expecting their first child, pulled out at the last moment. Officials could not make contact with the seventh and eighth reserves but made it through to Daly, who with his fiancee Bettye Fulford, drove up from Memphis to arrive just hours before the tournament began. He used Price's caddie and set off in his first major without a practice round but without any fears about a course everyone described as a tight, stern test.

Daly, with long straggly blond hair and a less than athletic figure, is a phenomenon. As a youngster he learned to play golf at Dardanelle, Arkansas with borrowed men's clubs far too heavy for him. When he got to the top of the back swing he could not hold it there with the result that he developed a swing so full that it would seem he must have back problems! He does not. He hits his driver on average 315 yards, a 3-iron 245 yards and a 9-iron 165 yards. He carries the ball 290 yards.

No-one believed that without a practice round he would make the half-way cut at Crooked Stick but after 36 holes he led with rounds of 67 and 69 and held a three shot lead at 54-holes after adding another 69, but could it last? Surely he was bound to crack?

He never did. While the big names trailed – Greg Norman was 13 adrift at the end. Nick Faldo ten back and Tom Watson, Jose Maria Olazabal and Ian Baker-Finch, troubled by a back injury, missed the cut – Daly just strode like a veteran to a gloriously unpredictable win showing no apparent sign of nerves. Daly's name went on the silver trophy along with his hero Jack Nicklaus, whom he had watched so often on televison, Gary Player, Sam Snead and Walter Hagen. It was for him a dream come true but his three-shot victory on 12 under par was an indication of how well he had played on one of architect Pete Dye's masterpieces. A year earlier Daly had been just another competitor, albeit a long hitter, on the Hogan Tour. His rise to stardom had been truly meteoric.

Over the years other US Tour victories have made the headlines. The wins of amateurs Scott Verplank at the 1985 Western Open and left-hander Phil Mickleson at Tucson in 1991 had been as remarkable as the win of Robert Gamez who hit a 7-iron into the hole to beat Greg Norman at Bay Hill in 1990 but nothing compares with what Daly achieved that week in Indiana.

The victories of Britain's big hitter Laura Davies and Sweden's Liselotte Neumann in successive US Women's Open at the end of the 80's were almost but not quite as incredible as that of French amateur Catherine Lacoste's sensational 1967 success in the event when she became the youngest, the first amateur and first European winner of the title and so it goes on.

There was Gary Player's sponsored black protege Vincent Tschabalala winning the French Open at le Touquet in 1976 after having had some mealie-mealie sent from his home in South Africa because he did not care for so much rich French food!

What is certain is that in the unpredictable world of golf sensations are an integral part and parcel of the scene and every now and again – Trevino claims every 10 years – a new golfing sensation bursts on the scene. There is so much to look forward to.

HORSE RACING

Christopher Poole

Attempting to compare the merits of great performances achieved during differing eras is futile and yet nothing attracts more heated debate whenever horseracing fans gather. Is Lester Piggott a greater jockey than Fred Archer or Gordon Richards? If Sea Bird, Nijinsky, Mill Reef and Shergar had met in same Derby which would have won?

Opinions differ widely, theories and counter theories are proclaimed without having to withstand the burden of proof. But some facts stand absolute, even in a field of sporting endeavour where divergence of views has always been accepted as commonplace.

For example, only a dedicated controversialist would argue that Arkle was not the greatest steeplechaser of the post-war period; that Red Rum's record in the Grand National is supreme and that Piggott's comeback to race riding constitutes the biggest Turf sensation for a generation.

Other sub-headings in this chapter are more open to question but each, in its own way, represents the kind of story which lifted horseracing coverage to the front pages by the perception that they had far broader appeal for newspaper readers than normal.

What follows is a glimpse at the big events and the major personalities, equine and human, that made those sensational headlines. The choice is strictly personal with no attempt at comprehensive analysis. Others might have chosen differently and reached conclusions far apart from mine.

But this sport has always thrived on disagreement. It is fundamental to the very nature of racing since every time horses run against each other the formation of a betting market is dependent on a diversity of views as to which contestant will reach the winning post first.

The Shortest Knight – a giant of the Turf

I was 15 years of age when Gordon Richards, the first and still the only jockey to have been awarded at knighthood, rode Pinza to win the Coronation Derby of 1953. It was the little man's 28th – and final – Derby ride, thus providing a suitable climax to a fabled career in the saddle which had established the miner's son from Shropshire as a folk hero.

It also happened to be the first Derby I watched live on Epsom Downs and the experience proved indelible. Richards, perhaps the greatest professional sportsman of his day and certainly the most consistently successful, had triumphed in just about every worthwhile race on the calendar but for the Derby.

His desire for that supreme Turf achievement had reached obsessional levels, matched only by common cause among his legion of admirers. As Pinza swept into the lead with two furlongs left to run, there was a split second when Epsom's throng seemed to hold a collective breath only for a wild cheer to supplant the silence as his mount galloped home four lengths clear of the Queen's colt Aureole.

Sir Gordon held so many records. Champion jockey 26 times, he was to partner a total of 4870 winners by the time injury forced retirement upon him the year after Pinza's victory in the premier Classic. But that single Derby victory counted for more.

They called him The Shortest Knight but this idol of the public stood tall in terms of respect and admiration.

The Unlikely Comeback

The riding careers of Sir Gordon Richards and Lester Piggott overlapped for a period of seven years, from 1948 until Richards retired. The two men, it is reasonable to say, were not close friends. In fact, they were the keenest of rivals.

Piggott, who was to win the first of his nine Derbys and record haul of 30 Classics – to date – just 12 months after Pinza carried Richards home in triumph, has outscored the old champion by partnering more than 5300 winners worldwide, despite a riding weight in maturity of rarely less than 8st 6lbs, some half a stone heavier than that of Richards.

That he became the greatest rider of his era is unquestionable, that is he the greatest of all time certainly arguable.

Unlike Richards, who had no family background in racing, Piggott was born into a distinguished and long-standing Turf dynasty which stretches back more than two centuries. His great-great-great-great grandfather, John Day, was the top trainer of the mid-1700's and passed on his gifts to a namesake son who rode 16 Classic winners and trained a further 10.

Ernest Piggott, Lester's grandfather, was a jump jockey of great renown who rode three Grand National winners while Lester's own father, Keith, trained a winner of the celebrated Aintree steeplechase. Ernest Piggott married Margeret Cannon, daughter of champion jockey Thomas Cannon and sister to another title holder, Mornington Cannon, and Lester's mother, born Iris Rickaby, was the daughter of Frederick Rickaby who rode three Classic winners and sister to Lester Frederick Rickaby who rode five before being killed while serving in France during 1918. The great jockey of today was named in his memory.

Lester Piggott is instantly recognizable to millions not just as a famous sportsman but as one of the country's most newsworthy celebrities. Yet he has never sought public attention, claiming to dislike it. However, the man now riding on into his 58th year, has undergone something of a personality change since being freed from prison after serving part of a sentence for tax evasion and returning to the saddle.

Far more relaxed, talkative and frequently smiling, he has gained admiration from a new generation of racegoers while retaining the devotion of older followers.

Piggott's decision to stage a riding comeback after retiring from the saddle to train just before his 50th birthday and subsequently going to jail, really was sensational. But he lost no time in showing that, if his once awesome strength as a jockey had diminished somewhat, the matchless skill remained.

I was fortunate enough to be at Belmont Park, New York, in November, 1990, when Piggott crowned his 'second coming' by winning the million-dollar Breeders' Cup Mile on Royal Academy, trained by Vincent O'Brien, his great mentor. It was, perhaps, the most emotional occasion on any racecourse since Gordon Richards won his only Derby, 37 years before.

The Triple Crown Colt

Lester Piggott's Classic record at Epsom is unmatched. In addition to his nine Derby victories, the great jockey has ridden six Oaks winners on the tricky Surrey course.

Perhaps the greatest of all his 25 big-race Epsom triumphs was that when partnering Nijinsky in the 1970 Derby which formed the middle leg of that horse's Triple Crown, inaugurated by landing the 2,000 Guineas and completed by success in the St Leger. Nijinsky thus became not only the first Triple Crown colt for 35 years but set a standard for Classic versatility no contender has rivalled since.

Like three other of Piggott's Derby heroes, Nijinsky was trained at Ballydoyle in Co. Tipperary by Vincent O'Brien and it was on the magnificent gallops there that I first saw the bold-eyed son of Northern Dancer early in 1969.

For years I have kidded myself that at a glance Nijinsky's potential as a champion was evident. Alas, it was not, at least to my eye. But Piggott, not only an outstanding jockey but also a wonderful judge of horseflesh, is reputed to have jumped down from Nijinsky's back after his first gallop on the big bay colt and announced: 'He'll do for me.'

That much-quoted remark may well be apocryphal but Nijinsky and Piggott formed a brilliant association and were at their combined peak on Derby day in 1970, sweeping majestically to a memorable win. Nijinsky was a greatly gifted racehorse but slightly neurotic, his temperament soon reached boiling point. Seeing Piggott switch the colt off throughout the

Derby until asking for his mount's effort as the winning post loomed, was to watch a master tactician at work. Sadly, Nijinsky's faultless record was ended by defeat in the Prix de l'Arc de Triomphe and his racecourse career finished in anti-climax with another defeat in Newmarket's Champion Stakes, a race he should never have contested at the end of a long and exacting season.

But his reputation for excellence remains high, not least since he returned across the Atlantic for a successful stallion career in the Bluegrass country of Kentucky.

It was there that I last saw him, late in 1991. An old gentleman of 24, looking rather burly and stiff in his joints, he nevertheless carried his handsome head high, still well set on that arching neck. Nijinsky, champion racehorse and sire of champions, retained that look of eagles. I felt proud to be on visiting terms with him.

The Shergar Saga

It was 11 years after Nijinsky's Triple Crown triumphs that Shergar won the Derby by a record 10 lengths in the colours of the Aga Khan. Trained at Newmarket by Michael Stoute and ridden by 19-year-old Walter Swinburn, Shergar's effortless Classic victory earned him widespread acclaim.

Hindsight has tempered that enthusiasm somewhat and it may well be that Shergar did not rank among the top postwar Epsom winners but, having gone on to also take the Irish Derby with Piggott in the saddle as deputy for Swinburn, sitting out a careless-riding ban, the Aga's homebred colt was certainly flavour of the moment among many experts.

Less impressive in Ascot's King George VI and Queen Elizabeth Diamond Stakes, Shergar flopped as an odd-on favourite for the St Leger, where certainly his stamina and possibly his wider limitations were exposed. He did not make it to Longchamp for the Arc de Triomphe.

Nevertheless, when Shergar was dispatched to the Aga's Ballymany Stud near the Curragh racecourse in Co. Kildare following a £10 million syndication deal involving many other leading Thoroughbred breeders, hopes were high that he could be a top-level sire. His book of mares included the names of many top matrons in European racing.

Shergar's stallion career was, of course, to be shortlived, ending in tragedy and infamous sensation.

Just after 8.30 on a dark February night in 1983, a group of armed and masked men drove through the imposing gates of Ballymany Stud, located on the outskirts of the little town of Newbridge. No guards prevented their arrival, no passers by noticed them come.

Two of the men knocked at the front door of the house where Jim Fitzgerald, Ballymany's head groom, lived with his family and it was opened by Bernard, Fitzgerald's 21-year-old son. He was bundled back inside at gun

78

point and Fitzgerald senior forced to take one intruder to the stallion barn while the other threatened his family.

Having identified which horse was Shergar, Fitzgerald was obliged to help load the Derby winner into a box. The stud groom was then forced to lie face down on the horsebox floor as the kidnappers drove back through the gates and it was some four hours later before he was set free on the roadside near Naas, only some seven miles from Ballymany.

Shergar was never to be seen again. But plenty more was spoken and written about his abduction.

Within 48 hours a £2 million ransom demand had been received by Ghislain Drion, the French manager at Ballymany. Police confirmed that M. Drion had received a telephone call heavy with menaces but that was the last detail to be given despite an international clamour for information concerning Shergar's disappearance.

The Aga Khan and his syndication partners reached a decision, presumably unanimously, that they could not and would not respond to threats. No ransom money was to be paid. A police investigation, under the command of Superintendent Jimmy Murphy, lasted many months but it soon became all too clear that the Garda had no worthwhile clues to the whereabouts of the horse.

In the decade since Shergar's shameful snatch many rumours and theories have been voiced within the Turf's close-knit community but no hard news has ever been forthcoming to end the mystery. It is widely assumed that the IRA or members of some splinter movement with similar aims attempted to raise a donation by kidnap and blackmail.

But the perpetrators might just as easily have been common criminals with no terrorist affiliations. In any case, they were clearly not horsemen in the view of Mr Fitzgerald and may well have found that attempting to conceal and control half a ton of Thoroughbred stallion was beyond them.

The likelihood is that they killed and buried the unfortunate Shergar within a few hours of taking him from Ballymany, perhaps even before they discovered that the Aga and his co-owners had no intention of paying blood money for Shergar's return.

There is, thankfully, no comparable case involving a horse of this fame and ability in the annuls of racing history in the British Isles and, by refusing to meet the kidnappers' demands, the breeding syndicate almost certainly assured there will be no repeat.

But, as Colin Turner wrote in his definitive book 'In Search of Shergar,' the unthinkable actually happened. 'In horse-loving Ireland, the super horse simply vanished.'

The Sparkle of Arkle

Ireland's connection with producing, nurturing and racing horses is timeless and that verdant country's renown as a cradle of steeplechasing stands supreme throughout the world. In fact, almost all jumping's greats were bred there including the peerless Arkle, unquestionably the out-standing National Hunt horse of modern times.

It is a measure of Arkle's total dominance that he was unable to be contained within the normal handicap scale so that officials were obliged to form two handicaps for races in which the great horse was entered – one to include him and another should trainer Tom Dreaper decline to saddle his champion. Arkle's three commanding and consecutive Cheltenham Gold Cup victories in 1964-65-66 form the plinth on which his fabled career stands. The three victories, by an aggregate of 45 lengths, mark him as the most gifted steeplechaser ever to look through a bridle. None stand comparison.

By Archieve, hardly a fashionable stallion, out of an elderly mare named Bright Cherry, Arkle was a freak. But Dreaper, who always claimed that champions are made in heaven and not produced as the result of breeding programmes, saw some glimmer of future glory when he paid 1150 guineas for Arkle as an unraced three-year-old at the Ballsbridge Sales in August, 1960. He was bidding on behalf of Anne, Duchess of Westminster.

Arkle's early efforts in 'bumper' races were a long way short of spectacular and Pat Taaffe, that celebrated Irish horseman who was to become the champion steeplechaser's regular jockey and most devoted fan, recalled years later that he was unimpressed when he first looked at the future triple Gold Cup hero. 'He was thin and moved so badly behind you could have driven a wheelbarrow between his hindlegs,' Taaffe said. But if he was surprised that the Duchess had bothered to buy Arkle, he was to be much more shocked when, on a bleak January afternoon at Navan two years later, Arkle gained his first victory.

Taaffe was riding strongly-fancied stablemate Kerforo who started favourite. But it was Arkle, unconsidered at 20-1, who came home in first place. 'He came cruising past as though he had just jumped into the race, with Liam McLoughlin on his back and grinning like a clown,' Taaffe said.

Arkle was beaten in two further hurdle races that season but 'chasing was always going to be his real game.

Faced with a worthy rival in Mill House, who would have been considered a great champion on his own right but for the misfortune of being Arkle's contemporary, this most brilliant of steeplechasers stamped an absolute authority on the winter sport, being beaten by only four other horses in the span of five seasons.

Arkle was a sporting sensation all right. We shall never see another to match him.

The Grand National

Anne, Duchess of Westminster would never risk her pride and joy in the

Grand National although Pat Taaffe always claimed Arkle would have jumped Aintree's fearsome fences without so much as turning a hair. But Liverpool's world-famous race provides sensations every year.

Having covered 34 Nationals as a racing journalist and seen a total of 40, I find it difficult to decide just which were the most sensational during my experience. Red Rum, who was to Aintree almost what Arkle had been to Cheltenham a decade earlier, certainly deserves his place as the most outstanding specialist in the event's long history.

On the other hand, nothing in racing is every likely to match the emotion generated by the 1981 victory of Aldaniti and Bob Champion. A patched-up old horse ridden by a jockey who had survived cancer. Pure Hollywood. Pure Grand National. But the most memorable of them all must be Foinavon's 100-1 fairytale back in 1967. He had no more chance of winning than a rocking horse but for an intervention from a quirky parton saint of lost causes.

As the survivors approached the 23rd fence that year, by a supreme irony the smallest and least formidable of all National jumps, a loose horse with the singularly appropriate name of Popham Down, took it into his head to career right across the takeoff side. One rival after another fell, stopped, was baulked or knocked over.

That fine Irish commentator Michael O'Hehir, whose son Tony is calling the horses to this day, worked his tonsils into overdrive trying to name all those who had come to grief before startling listeners with the memorable words, 'God, they've all fallen.'

For once O'Hehir was wrong. Just jumping the previous fence – Becher's Brook – came that plodder Foinavon, about a furlong behind but still going strong. Somehow John Buckingham steered him wide of the battlefield and he just staggered over the obstacle in the furthest corner.

In his wake were being enacted the most amazing scenes ever witnessed on any racecourse. Frantic jockeys ran after their bewildered horses. At least one rider re-mounted the wrong runner. Josh Gifford, the man who would one day train Aldaniti, managed to get back on Honey End only for the big-race favourite to fall a second time.

Considering that Honey End was eventually to finish second, beaten by only fifteen lengths, he must count as the most unlucky National loser of them all. But meanwhile Foinavon, head down and oblivious, just kept running at his one pace. Not one in 100000 had backed the blinkered no-hoper but racegoers, stunned by the pile-up one minute, were raising a cheer for this least likely hero and his flabbergasted jockey the next. Racing folks are generous like that.

John Buckingham got his due share of back-slapping, Foinavon himself made every front page in the country and beyond. The bookmakers, of course, were delighted and the crowds melted away from Aintree that evening knowing they had seen the most unpredictable Grand National of them all.

The Sport of Kings and Queens

An association between horseracing and members of the Royal Family has permeated British social history for centuries.

King Henry VIII, when he could spare the time from getting married, falling out with the Vatican, building up what was then the world's most powerful navy and refining the rules of lawn tennis, enjoyed a day at the races; so did his daughter, the first Elizabeth.

Charles II ran his court from Newmarket, insisting that ambassadors make the 60-mile coach journey from London into the wilds of rural Suffolk to conduct official business while the King devoted himself earnestly to such country pursuits as hunting, cockfighting, a staggering and ever-changing list of Royal mistresses and racing. Not for nothing did he become known as the Merry Monarch.

Queen Anne, so historians claim, was grossly fat and stultifyingly dull but she too was a racing fan and gave permission for the course to be constructed on Ascot Heath where, to this day, is staged the great sporting and social occasion known as Royal Ascot, still commanding patronage from the present Queen. Edward VII, who first registered the now familiar Royal colours of purple, gold braid, scarlet sleeves with black velvet cap and gold fringe in 1875, was a great man of the Turf, winning the Derby three times.

His enthusiasm was outspokenly criticized by some narrow-minded subjects but aroused demonstrations of loyalty and affection among the majority.

Of course, Edward VII shared other enthusiasms with Charles II and it was the encouragement of Lady de Bathe, formerly Lily Langtry, which fired the King's love of the Turf, a pastime considered far too disreputable to attract the patronage of his mother, Queen Victoria.

She would certainly not have been comfortable among the violent 19th century racecourse crowds or in the company of raffish members of the nobility hell bent on ruin via the betting rings. Edward, on the other hand, devoted to the pleasures of both table and bedchamber, was quite at home in this decidedly mixed company and found racing very much to his taste.

However, he never claimed to be an expert on bloodstock which the present Queen most certainly is. Her first involvement in racehorse ownership came during 1949 when she took a share with her mother in the steeplechaser Monaveen. The new Royal ownership team made an ideal start when Monaveen won at Fontwell Park on his first outing for them.

He was to win three further races in addition to finishing fifth behind Freebooter in the 1950 Grand National but broke a leg later that year and while the now Queen Mother kept her interest in steeplechasing with happy results, the Queen herself decided to concentrate on Flat racing, a passion for which had started when she saw her father's filly Hypericum win the 1946 1000 Guineas.

On her accession, the Queen took control of the Royal Studs and gained her first outright success as an owner when Stream of Light carried off the Lancashire Oaks. Aureole's second place in the Coronation Derby of 1953 has already been mentioned in the passage devoted to the exploits of Sir Gordon Richards but, sad to relate, no horse belonging to the Queen has ever come as close again to landing the premier Classic. However, Her Majesty has enjoyed a distinguished career as breeder and owner of horses, her first Classic success coming with Carrozza, ridden by Lester Piggott, in the 1957 Oaks. That was a great season for the Royal colours, Almeria, another of the Royal fillies, winning four races including the Yorkshire Oaks and Royal Ascot's Ribblesdale Stakes. Overall there were 30 successes in the Royal colours and Her Majesty finished that season as leading owner in prizemoney terms.

The following year she won the 2000 Guineas with Pall Mall and in 1959 achieved other notable victories with Agreement in the Chester and Doncaster Cups backed up by Pindari (King Edward VII Stakes) and Above Suspicion (St James' Palace Stakes) for a double at Royal Ascot.

But then the Royal racing fortunes hit a major slump and it was not until 1965 that the Queen's runners began landing big races again, Canisbay getting home in that season's Eclipse Stakes and Apprentice, a five-year-old maiden, giving her another success in the Yorkshire Cup at odds of 33-1. To prove it was no fluke, Apprentice and his jockey, Stan Clayton, went on to score again in the Goodwood Cup.

The 1967 season proved frustrating for the Queen. Her best colt, Hopeful Venture, won four races but finished second to Ribocco in the St Leger and was then disqualified from first place in the Prix Henry Delamarre at Longchamp. That verdict was, to say the least, unfortunate as Hopeful Venture was the Queen's first runner in France. English jockey Brian Taylor lodged an objection on behalf of runner-up In Command, a course of action which might well have cost him his head back in the days of Henry VIII, but the Longchamp stewards agreed with his version of events.

But success in France for the Queen and, indeed, Hopeful Venture was not long delayed. The next season this colt followed wins in the Ormonde Stakes at Chester and Royal Ascot's Hardwicke Stakes by landing the valuable Grand Prix de Saint-Cloud and relations between English and French racing, somewhat strained by the Longchamp incident, were fully restored. In fact, French racecourses were to prove happy hunting grounds for the Royal horses from then on. Albany won the Prix Psyche and Example the Prix de Royallieu in the Queen's silks during 1971 and Example returned across the Channel the following season to capture the Prix Jean de Chaudeney.

83

But it was in 1974 that the Queen achieved her biggest overseas triumph when Highclere, supplementing a victory in the 1,000 Guineas at Newmarket, stormed home in the Prix de Diane (French Oaks) at lovely old Chantilly.

No filly had ever completed this particular Anglo-French Classic double and the expert and friendly Chantilly crowd gave Highclere and jockey Joe Mercer a reception which might, I suppose, have rivalled even those accorded at Epsom when Her Majesty's great-grandfather was leading in his Derby winners at the turn of the century.

In 1977, the Queen's Silver Jubilee year, came another revival with Dunfermline, ridden by Willie Carson, winning both the Oaks and St Leger. The Royal filly's Doncaster effort was specially deserving of praise since she beat Alleged in a driving finish to the St Leger and that colt was to go on to win the European championship in the Prix de l'Arc de Triomphe both that season and in 1978, the first back-to-back scorer in Longchamp's fabled event since the unbeaten Italian champion Ribot in 1955-56.

But as all breeders and owners of bloodstock tend to discover, notable victories tend to be followed by periods in the wilderness and Her Majesty's trainers had little enough in the way of big-race winners to delight their patron for much of the 1980's.

The Queen had a useful filly in Height of Fashion who won three good races during her 1981 juvenile season and the following year took the Lupe Stakes at Goodwood and Newmarket's Princess of Wales's Stakes.

The Queen might so easily have kept Height of Fashion as a broodmare but it was decided to sell the daughter of Bustino to Sheikh Hamdan Al-Maktoum. This proved to be regrettable decision, at least so far as the Royal Stud was concerned, since Height of Fashion, having bred the high-class Unfuwain, then produced Nashwan, the 1989 2000 Guineas, Derby, Eclipse and King George VI and Queen Elizabeth Diamond Stakes winner. Hamdan Al-Maktoum's great good fortune and foresight in buying such an influential mare for his rapidly developing stud empire was certainly the Queen's loss and she remains without that crowning achievement of owning a Derby winner.

But at least the decade ended on another high when Unknown Quantity, the first horse owned by a member of the Royal Family to race in the United States for 35 years, won the valuable 1989 Arlington Handicap in Chicago. Jockey Jorge Velasquez still boasts about the day he rode a winner for the Queen of England!

MOTOR RACING

David Smith

Man against man; machine against machine – there is something unique about the excitement generated by a motor race.

The demonstration of speed, skill and courage can quicken the pulse of both competitor and spectator alike. The fact that this is a sport which tests to the limit the bounds of human and mechanical abilities merely adds to the tension and the drama.

The history of motor racing is littered with examples of successful technical innovation or driving of a supreme nature. In this chapter we have cast our net far and wide with the aim of capturing the spirit of the sport in its many facets.

Thus we read of triumph and tragedy; method and emotion; talent and sheer audacity.

The common thread binding each story to its neighbour is that each, on its day, was a sporting sensation.

Mike Hawthorn and the 1953 French Grand Prix

It was called the 'Race of the Century'. Now the French are, of course, exponents of the art of extravagant exaggeration, but on the balmy evening of 5 July 1953, when a fusillade of champagne corks popped in celebration of the first World Championship race to be won by an English driver, it must surely have seemed as though no Grand Prix would ever again reach the dizzy heights of excitement, courage and drama enacted out over the 5.157 miles of public roads that made up the Reims circuit.

Certainly, on the morning of the race, few observers expected Mike Hawthorn to take the chequered flag. It was accepted that Hawthorn possessed a rare talent behind the steering wheel of a racing car. After all, Enzo Ferrari had offered him a place in his famous Italian team just two years after the former mower mechanic had made a competition debut in the Brighton Speed Trials.

But in this pioneering age of World Championship Grands Prix, Hawthorn remained a babe surrounded by men. He was 24-years-old. His Ferrari team-mates – Italians Alberto Ascari, Giuseppe Farina and Luigi Villoresi – were respectively 35, 47 and 44.

Ranged against the cars bearing the badge of the Prancing Horse were the faster but slightly less nimble Maseratis of the great Juan-Manuel

Fangio (42), Froilan Gonzalez (31), Felice Bonetto (50) and 'Pinocho' Marimon (29).

Also on the grid were a pair of young Englishmen by the names of Stirling Moss and Peter Collins. But their time had yet to come. This day was to belong to Hawthorn.

Ascari claimed pole position round the roughly triangular Reims circuit with Hawthorn starting from the middle of the third row. But it was Gonzalez, driving a tactical race by starting with half-empty fuel tanks in the hope of pulling clear prior to a mid-race top-up, who set a scorching pace beneath the clear blue sky.

After 20 laps, one-third of the race distance, Hawthorn had hauled himself up to second place although he, Ascari and Villoresi were playing a tactical game themselves and were keeping the flying Maserati in check by slipstreaming each other down the long straights. First one Ferrari would lead, then another would leap-frog ahead through the 'hole' in the air to take up the chase.

It was team-work at its finest, but the individual brilliance of Fangio meant that the former world champion was in amongst this triumvirate when, one lap before half-distance, Gonzalez roared into the pits for fuel.

The next time round, lap 30, Fangio led from Hawthorn and Ascari with less than a second covering the three cars.

Inch by inch, Fangio and Hawthorn began to draw clear as first one man and then the other clawed his way into the lead: Fangio, the Argentinian, distinctive in tee-shirt and goggles; Hawthorn, the blond Brit, distinguished in his bow-tie and windcheater.

He recalled the battle: 'We would go screaming down the straight side by side absolutely flat out, grinning at each other, with me crouching down in the cockpit trying to save every ounce of wind resistance.

'We were only inches apart and I could clearly see the rev counter in Fangio's cockpit. Once . . . he braked harder than I expected and I shunted him lightly, putting a dent in his tail.

'That shook me . . . I thought it would take some living down. But he showed no resentment at all; he just kept on fighting every inch of the way, according to the rules, in the way that has earned him the admiration and respect of everyone in motor racing.'

Fangio was to remark later that he tried every trick in the book to shake off the Ferrari. But there was a wise head on Hawthorn's young shoulders. For as the race wore on into a third hour, he deduced that the Maserati had lost first gear.

On a high-speed circuit like Reims this should not have posed too much of a hinderance. But the corner leading on to the long, long start-finish straight was the first-gear Thillois hairpin. It was here that the race was to be won and lost.

Over the line to start the last lap, Hawthorn led Fangio in a blur of red. Almost in their wheeltracks Gonzalez clung to third place from the pursuing Ascari.

The huge French crowd loved it!

Out into the gently rolling countryside, Hawthorn maintained his advantage. But on the long run down to Thillois Fangio wrung every last ounce of power out of the wailing Maserati to inch ahead. But, of course, he had no first gear, and the Ferrari was just that shade sharper on the brakes.

Hawthorn plunged down the inside of his rival as the two cars hurtled towards the hairpin. It was a close run thing, but he scrambled round on the cobbles to lead as Fangio slid slightly but decisively sideways.

Now Hawthorn gave his Ferrari its head and he raced across the line with Fangio just one second behind after 309.4 miles and 161 minutes of enthralling competition. In a blanket finish Gonzalez took third place just half a second behind Fangio, with Ascari fourth.

Hawthorn was to win the French Grand Prix again in July 1958, the year he claimed the World Championship title. A little over six months later, now retired from the dangers of motor racing, Hawthorn was killed driving his Jaguar saloon car on the Hog's Back, a stretch of road between Farnham and Guildford.

The 1955 Le Mans Disaster

Death has always been an omnipresent shadow chasing those involved in motor racing, especially in the years leading up to the Second World War and during the formative World Championships of the 1950s.

Perversely, death was almost a way of life to those who drove racing cars in an era when a bone-dome helmet was the extent of any protection in the event of a crash.

There was little protection for spectators either. Huge crowds often stood within feet of the track with only earth banking and a few straw bales separating them from tons of high-speed metal.

In 1952, 13 people were killed when a car left the track at Weyberg in the German Rhineland. Nine years later, 15 died, including Ferrari driver Wolfgang von Trips, during the Italian Grand Prix at Monza.

But by far the worst disaster to befall motor racing occurred on the evening of 11 June 1955. Over 80 men, women and children died and another 100 were injured when a Mercedes sports car plunged into a packed spectator enclosure during the Le Mans 24 Hour endurance event.

The French marathon was, and still is, one of the world's most famous motor races. Legends evolved around the likes of the pre-war 'Bentley Boys', racers who kept their cars going to the line despite mechanical failures and accident damage, and often under the most daunting of conditions as rain and mist made the early hours on Sunday a treacherous trial of blind faith and courage.

There was the Le Mans 'start' too, in which, on the stroke of four o'clock on Saturday afternoon, the drivers would sprint across the track and jump into their machines before engaging in battle.

It was to witness this unique spectacle, and to savour the carnival atmosphere which bubbles throughout the race, that a crowd of 250,000 made their way to the circuit marked out on public roads a mile or so to the south of the town of Le Mans.

The 23rd running of Le Mans was expected to feature a major confrontation between the crack German Mercedes team and the British Jaguars. And so it proved as, for the first two hours, Mike Hawthorn's Jaguar and the Mercedes of world-champion Juan-Manuel Fangio battled for the lead.

It was not only a duel between two fine drivers, but there was technical interest too. The Jaguars, distinctive with their tail fins, were fitted with what were then innovative disc brakes. The silver Mercedes made do with huge drum brakes, but these were augmented by an air-brake flap which pivoted up behind the drivers' head at the end of the long straights.

By the 42nd lap, the cars were beginning to make their first pit stops for fuel. Fangio, partnered by Stirling Moss, was chasing Hawthorn, co-driven by Ivor Bueb, as the two cars approached the start-finish straight. Ahead of them, being lapped, were the Mercedes of Pierré Levegh and the slower Austin Healey of Lance Macklin.

Fangio later described what happened next. He recalled, 'What I saw as we approached the pits after about two hours' racing . . . was Hawthorn's Jaguar overtaking Macklin's Austin Healey on the left and then his brake light going on as he pulled across to the right to stop at his pits for the first refuelling.

'Macklin then had to dodge to the left to pass the slowing Jaguar. Levegh was just in front of me and I was about to lap him when Macklin moved into his path.

'I saw him throw up his left hand as he moved across towards the left side bank, trying to squeeze through. He was doing maybe 125mph and me 135mph and he just ran straight up the sloping tail of the British car and crashed onto the top of the left-side bank. The engine and the front end of his car broke away and went through the crowd.

'I saw Macklin's car bouncing off the pit wall on the right and in a split-second I was through and it was all behind me. On my next lap . . . I looked across the inside of the circuit and could see the smoke. I began to shake. But even then I had no real idea of the magnitude of the disaster when I was signalled in to hand over to Moss.'

In fact, when Levegh's car hit the banking, it had burst into flame and burning wreckage had whipped through the close-packed crowd like shrapnel from an exploding bomb.

Horrifying reports from the scene spoke of decapitated children lying in a scene reminiscent of a battlefield. Levegh was one of those who perished as, for some 60 yards, the sandy ground was drenched in blood.

But still the race went on.

While priests mingled with rescue workers, Fangio and Moss led the event as darkness descended and the headlights on the cars twirled like lighthouse beams around the circuit.

There was reason behind this apparent madness. For the organisers knew that if the race was stopped, a mass exodus would hamper the rescue effort. It was not until two o'clock in the morning that Alfred Neubauer, the Mercedes team-manager, received orders direct from Germany to pull his cars out of the race as a mark of respect.

Victory, if it can be called that, thus went to Hawthorn and Bueb. But the repercussions for motor racing were enormous. Mercedes withdrew from the sport at the end of the season, and were not to return until 33 years later.

Several races were cancelled in the wake of the disaster, and motor racing was banned completely in Spain, Mexico and Switzerland.

Today, a chicane has lowered speeds along the start-finish straight at Le Mans. There is a wide, purpose-built pit lane protected by a concrete wall. On the other side of the road, two walls and a high wire fence protect the spectators who still come, every June, in their tens of thousands.

Stirling Moss and the 1961 Monaco Grand Prix

There was something intensely menacing about the appearance of the Grand Prix Ferrari. Its bright red nose cone tapered to a central point, revealing two large flared 'nostrils'. Some likened the look of the car to a shark, and indeed Ferrari were expected to swim unhindered around the harbour of Monte Carlo when the 1961 World Championship opened on Sunday 14 May down on the Mediterannean coast.

The little blue minnow of a Lotus to be driven by Stirling Moss was certainly considered by the Italians to be of no great threat. But on a sun-baked afternoon in Monaco, this was the one that got away!

The race was significant for the fact that it was the first to be run under new regulations restricting the size of engines to 1500cc. Between 1954 and 1960, engines could be built to a more powerful 2500cc capacity, but a sharp increase in speeds allied to the switch from front-engined cars to more nimble rear-engined machines forced motor sports' governing body, then called the CSI, to act in a bid to maintain some margin of safety.

The major British teams fought against these new rules and there was even talk of a break-away championship. When they eventually came into line, it was too late to prepare truly competitive engines for the start of the season. Coventry Climax and BRM laid plans to make engines to the new formula, but at Monaco most of the British teams would have to make do with comparatively outdated in-line four-cylinder engines.

Ranged against them were the fuel-injected, air-cooled, flat-four Porsches, and the purpose-built V6 Ferraris. Indeed, Ferrari had two new engines ready for Monaco, a 60-degree V6 developed over two years in Formula Two, and a more potent 120-degree V6. The advantage to the Italians was some 20 horsepower, and the race was expected to be a romp for the cars bearing the badge of the Prancing Horse.

The first sign that the race might not go entirely to the Ferrari plan came in practice when Moss whipped round the 1.95-mile track in 1min 39.1secs, good enough to secure pole position by two-tenths of a second from Richie Ginther's Ferrari and Jim Clark's striking new Lotus 21.

This small, streamlined car made the year-old Lotus 18 driven by Moss appear positively antiquated. Entered by Rob Walker, the blue 18 with its white nose band had won at Monaco with Moss behind the wheel 12 months earlier. But then it was fitted with a 2.5 litre engine. Now, modified to take a 1.5 litre engine, its box-like shape seemed out of place next to the latest Lotus and Ferraris.

Ginther made the running from the start, rounding the Gasometer Hairpin ahead of Clark and Moss with Dan Gurney (Porsche), Tony Brooks (BRM), Jo Bonnier (Porsche) and Phil Hill (Ferrari) in close pursuit.

After 14 of the scheduled 100 laps, Clark was out of the running with a broken fuel pump and both Moss and Bonnier had forced their way past Ginther. But it appeared as though the Ferrari 'sharks' of Americans Ginther and Hill, and their German team-mate Wolfgang von Trips, were merely marking time before they attacked.

Sure enough, by lap 24, Hill had moved up to lead the attack on the flying Moss. But the British driver responded magnificently. The stopwatch told the story. Up the hill towards the Casino Square, Moss would lose more than a second to the more powerful Ferraris. But he would claw it back while plunging down to Mirabeau Corner and Station Hairpin.

Driving with the side panels removed from his car to aid cooling, Moss even found time to wave to the enthralled crowds lining the streets and filling the balconies on the flats and hotels overlooking the tiny Principality.

Later, Moss would reveal his game-plan. 'I said to myself: well, I may only have 80 per cent of the Ferraris' power behind me, but let's make them go; make them go the whole race . . .'

With Bonnier retiring with a dead engine and von Trips losing touch in fourth place, it was left to Hill and Ginther to chase the Lotus. On the 77th lap Ginther, in the very latest 120-degree V6 car, forced a way around his team-mate and set about reducing the five-second gap to Moss.

After 85 laps the gap was down to three seconds. With their cars on the very limit of adhesion, the two men made nonsense of the practice times with a joint fastest lap of 1min 36.3secs. By this stage, Hill was out of contention in third place and von Trips, fourth on the leaderboard, was lapped.

Now there was no time for a friendly wave. Moss was concentrating 100 per cent on the road in front as the distinctive nose of Ginther's Ferrari would appear as a threatening red dot in his mirrors.

With 10 laps to go, Moss extended the gap to five seconds. With four laps to the flag Ginther recovered half a second and was relentlessly closing again. Into the last lap and the two cars were separated by just four seconds as the crowd rose to its feet.

Down through the Station Hairpin for the last time, onto the sea-front and through the tunnel, round the Tabac corner and Moss took the chequered flag by just 3.5 seconds from Ginther. It had been a masterful display by the Master of Monaco.

So far as the world championship was concerned, the writing was on the wall and Phill Hill went on to claim the title after von Trips was killed at Monza. Moss, of course, was to become known as the greatest driver never to lift the world crown. Indeed, within a year his career was finished by an accident at the Goodwood circuit.

Jim Clark and the 1965 Indianapolis 500

At first, America did not take to Jim Clark. And Jim Clark did not take to America. 'Indianapolis would be fine without Americans . . .' he would say.

This mutual disrespect was hardly surprising. In 1963, Clark and the Lotus team were perceived as foreign marauders come to rob the native drivers of their richest pay-day. For his part, Clark, the quiet Scot with a remarkable talent for driving anything on four wheels, found the hype and hysteria associated with motor racing on the other side of the Atlantic hard to handle.

Yet he and Lotus boss Colin Chapman found the challenge of Indy to be a compelling one. For this was a race quite unlike anything in Europe.

The Indy 500 ranks alongside the Le Mans 24 Hour sports car marathon and the Monaco Grand Prix as one of the world's three most famous motor races. Run over a banked oval track 2.5 miles in length, it is an event which attracts huge crowds who come to witness a spectacle of speed, colour and drama as the competing cars shave the concrete retaining wall at quite fearsome speeds.

The race actually counted as a round of the World Championship between 1950 and 1960, but was dropped when European teams failed to get to grips with the specialised cars and techniques demanded by the 'Brickyard.'

But this inner-sanctum of American motor racing came under threat in 1963 when Lotus, backed by Ford of America, brought their nimble little rear-engined machines to do battle with the huge front-engined Indy specials.

Those who cherish the memory of the great Jim Clark argue to this day that he should have won Indy first time out that year.

The organisers had insisted before the race started that any car dropping excessive oil would be ordered in to the pits.

91

Thus, when the leading Offenhauser-Special of Parnelli Jones began to leak oil with Clark a few lengths back in second place, the Lotus team rightly expected the American to be 'black-flagged'.

It never happened, and Lotus were left to curse their inexperience and naivety as Jones won with Clark second.

Lotus returned in 1964, but the team suffered a humiliating defeat with a series of tyre failures despite Clark having started from pole position. In addition, the deaths of drivers Dave McDonald and Eddie Sachs in a huge pile-up had served to underline the dangers of the race.

It finally came right the following year in a race which made headlines around the world. Clark chose to compete in the United States at the cost of gaining possible World Championship points from the Monaco Grand Prix which that May clashed with the Indy 500. But starting from the centre of the front row he led for all but a handful of laps.

A crowd of 350,000 forgot past animosities and hailed the Scot's victory. Later that year, Clark clinched his second World Championship title. He was killed while competing in an insignificant Formula Two race at Hockenheim in April 1968. But the memories of his courage and skill live on.

Nigel Mansell and the 1986 Australian Grand Prix

There is little room for emotion in the cool, technical world of modern Grand Prix motor racing. A winning driver may punch the air as he takes the chequered flag, and then there is the scripted ritual of spraying champagne from the victory rostrum.

Just occasionally tempers may boil over. But always outside of the car. Most drivers are only too aware that a red mist decending over a visor during the heat of battle could impair judgement with disastrous consequences.

For the most part, though, success is acknowledged with little more than a smile and disappointment is met with a simple shrug of the shoulders.

Nigel Mansell's shoulders are broader than most, and they have carried more than the odd burden or two during a long career amongst the Grand Prix elite. But on the afternoon of Sunday 26 October 1986, not even Mansell could contain his feelings. Despair was engraved upon every feature of his face and his eyes surrendered all trace of colour and sparkle.

In one cruel explosive second, fate had robbed Mansell of the World Championship. The hurt and the hardship had been for nothing. The dream had become a living nightmare as a hunched figure walked slowly away from his broken racing car.

Yet it had been all going so well. Mansell had arrived in Adelaide for the final round of the title chase, the Australian Grand Prix, knowing that third place would make him the first British winner of the World Championship since James Hunt's triumph in 1976.

But the prospect of earning motor racing's highest honour meant more to him than that. For Mansell had cleared the most daunting hurdles to come this far. He and wife Rosanne (has a woman ever devoted more love and support to the pursuit of her husband's ambitions?) plunged their savings into a second hand racing car only for Mansell to suffer a serious neck injury in a crash at Brands Hatch. With Rosanne's blessing, Mansell then sold their flat to finance a drive in Formula Three, the proving ground of future world champions.

Even when the engineer from Birmingham finally made his Grand Prix debut for Lotus in the 1980 Austrian Grand Prix, he was forced to endure searing pain from burns inflicted when high octane petrol was accidentally spilt inside the cockpit.

Mansell never won a race in five years with the Norfolk team, though it was not for the want of trying. The turning point in a chequered career came in 1985 when Frank Williams signed him as a solid number two, nothing more, to former world champion, Keke Rosberg. Mansell repaid Williams by scoring his maiden Grand Prix triumph at Brands Hatch, and followed that up by winning in South Africa.

The victories kept coming the following year in Belgium, Canada, France, Britain and Portugal. Through hard graft and single-minded perseverance, Mansell had established himself as one of the world's top drivers. Now only two men stood between him and the title: Williams team-mate Nelson Piquet and McLaren's Alain Prost. But one of them had to win the race with Mansell out of the top three for the unthinkable to happen.

Mansell rose to the occasion, claiming pole position ahead of Piquet, Ayrton Senna and Prost. He then lost the initiative at the start of the 82-lap race and for a while it looked grim as the Williams slipped to fourth place behind Rosberg (now McLaren), Piquet and Prost.

Then Piquet spun and Mansell was through into that vital third position. Now came the decisive chapter in the tale. On the 32nd lap Prost dived into the pits to replace a punctured tyre. All four wheels were changed and the worn rubber carefully examined by Goodyear technicians. They decided that the tyres would have lasted until the end of the race.

This news was passed on to the Williams pit crew. They had a choice: let Mansell run to the end on the same set of tyres, or risk losing time with a pit stop for fresh rubber. They chose to let Mansell race on.

A little after half-distance, Rosberg led from the fast recovering Piquet with Mansell clinging to his precious third place ahead of Prost, who was motoring at record speeds on his new tyres.

Then Rosberg's right rear tyre failed. The Finn, in his last Grand Prix, parked his lame McLaren by the side of the track. It was an ignominious end to a glorious career.

Now the alarm bells began ringing in the Goodyear camp. Piquet, leading, and Mansell, who had been taken by Prost, must come in for new tyres.

There were 18 laps – 42 miles – to go before the chequered flag came out. A Goodyear advisor was on his way to the Williams pit when Mansell accelerated on to the long Brabham Straight.

Dawn was breaking back in Britain, yet millions of enthusiasts had set their alarm clocks to watch the live broadcast on BBC television. Suddenly, the screen was full of sparks and flailing rubber as Mansell's left rear tyre exploded.

Instead of the cameras focusing on a driver fighting for the World Championship, they now zoomed in on a man fighting for his life.

The wounded car, still racing at over 150mph, twitched this way and that as Mansell corrected each spasm with lightning reflexes. Ahead lay a sharp right-hand corner. But Mansell could also spy the sanctuary of an escape road. The Williams plunged on beyond the bend and, in one final act of defiance, veered right and smote the concrete wall. Not hard enough to injure the driver, but a front wheel was forced back off its mountings.

The crazy ride was over. After 16 races around the world, the championship challenge was in tatters. Prost won the race and the title. He said, 'I am sorry, honestly, for Nigel.'

Mansell made his way back to the pits where Rosanne was waiting. They embraced each other as the world looked on. No-one could fail to have been moved by the emotion of the moment.

When he had gathered himself, Mansell said: 'It has been a long, hard season and you think of all the things you've gone without – companionship, friendships, your children. Rosanne and I have got to get together and get to know each other again.

'It makes it all rather hard to swallow. It will take time to get over it but I will, although at the moment next year seems a long way away.'

Nigel Mansell and Ayrton Senna in the 1991 Spanish Grand Prix

There are those who question Grand Prix motor racing's claim to be classified as a sport. They point, with some justification, to the technical nature of Formula One which bestows one driver with a certain advantage over another which has little to do with talent or skill behind the steering wheel.

But every now and again circumstances arise in which the human element comes to the fore. These are the moments when the destiny of a race is dictated by the actions of the driver, rather than the input of a designer or engineer.

One such moment arose during the Spanish Grand Prix at the new Circuit de Catalunya just outside the Olympic city of Barcelona.

It featured a duel between Nigel Mansell and Ayrton Senna down the long start-finish straight which, in real time, lasted barely 12 seconds. But to appreciate the drama, it is necessary to go back to the 1989 World Championship campaign.

In Portugal, Mansell and Senna had collided in controversial circumstancs. Then, in Japan, the destination of the title was decided in favour of Alain Prost when he and Senna – they were McLaren team-mates, remember – ran into each other at the Suzuka circuit's tight chicane.

Twelve months later and the two men crashed into each other again. This time the outcome, in so far as the championship was concerned, favoured Senna. But the nature of the incident, in which the Brazilian's McLaren ran into the back of Prost's Ferrari at the first corner of the first lap of the race, left a bitter taste in many mouths.

So we come to the 1991 Portuguese Grand Prix. At the start, Mansell surprised title rival Senna with an audacious swerve on the grid which hardly endeared him to the McLaren driver.

But then, as he led the race, Mansell came in to the pits for a routine tyre change. For once, the Williams team botched the job. The right rear wheel was not secure when Mansell was signalled away, and it fell off a matter of yards down the pit lane.

Mansell eventually resumed, but was disqualified for infringing the rules regarding pit lane safety. Second place gave Senna a commanding lead in the championship. Mansell had to win in Spain to keep his challenge alive.

It did not help when, in a pre-race football match, Mansell hurt an ankle. He limped to the drivers' briefing on the Sunday morning and there was jostled by Gerhard Berger, once a team-mate at Ferrari but now number two to Senna at McLaren. It may have been meant in jest, but Mansell was in no mood for fun and games.

The tension heightened further when the briefing degenerated into an abusive squabble over driving standards with clear reference to Mansell's explosive start in Portugal.

Bear in mind the observation of one team manager immediately following that briefing, as he said, 'If the race is anything like that, make sure you find somewhere very safe to watch from – and make it a long way from the track!'

Remember, too, the intimidatory nature of Senna as demonstrated in Japan, and the need for Mansell to win the race to retain any hope of the championship. Thus it was surely a case of light the blue touch paper and retire when, at the start of the fifth lap, Mansell's Williams whipped out from behind Senna's leading McLaren as the two cars crossed the finishing line.

The television cameras caught the moment perfectly. On and on they came down the straight, touching 200mph as the wheels of the McLaren, on the left side of the track, and the Williams drew closer and closer until barely a couple of inches separated them.

Ahead lay a sharp right hand bend. Someone had to give way.

On and on the two cars sped until, at the very last moment, Mansell squeezed through on the inside of his rival.

It was, without a doubt, a perfectly fair overtaking manoeuvre and at no point had either driver transcended the bounds of sportsmanship. But it remains one of the great moments of modern motor racing.

Mansell went on to win the race, but he lost any hope of the championship when he spun off in Japan. Reliable machinery helped Senna retain his title, but the question remained: who, that year, was the better driver?

Sensational Sprinter! Has there been a finer
athlete than the great Jesse Owens? His modern
counterpart, Carl Lewis, was inspired by a
childhood meeting with the great man.

▲ **Sensational Split Seconds!** The first man to run a mile in less than four minutes, Roger Bannister, flanked by his pacemakers, Chris Brasher (left) and Chris Chataway, in May 1954.

◀ **Sensational Seb!** After an unexpected defeat by team-mate Steve Ovett in the Moscow Olympic 800 metres final, Sebastian Coe turned the tables in the 1500m race.

▶ **Sensational Centimetres!** Bob Beamon suddenly jumps so far in the 1968 Olympics Long Jump competition that he lands beyond the range of the measuring equipment!

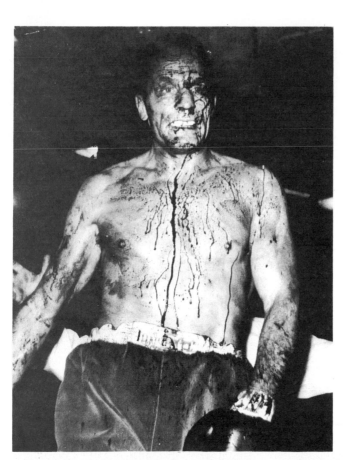

◄ **Sensational Sight!** Fragile scar tissue around his eyes left Henry Cooper damaged and bloodied after almost every fight including this bout, one of his two against Muhammad Ali. The boxer's left hook, 'Enry's 'ammer, floored many opponents, including the champion.

► **Sensational Stoppage!** The 'unbeatable' Mike Tyson is counted out after being knocked down by 'no hoper' James 'Buster' Douglas.

▼ **Sensational Speaker!** Cassius Clay – the 'Louisville Lip', who, as Muhammad Ali, resumed a remarkable boxing career after an enforced lay-off caused by his refusal to serve in the Vietnam War. Surely the possessor of the fastest feet and hands of any heavyweight boxer, Ali 'talked up' his fights like no-one before him, but also usually made his prediction come true.

◄ **Sensational Scorer!** Seen here with David Sheppard, now Bishop of Liverpool, Len Hutton, whose 364 against Bradman's Australians remains one of cricket's greatest innings, walks to the crease with typical good humour and relaxation.

▼ **Sensational Centurion!** Graeme Hick's incredible innings of 405 for Worcestershire was described by those who witnessed it as flawless, frightening and phenomenal.

◀ **Sensational Star!** The great Arnold Palmer, whose cavalier style and awesome ability brought the game new stature and increased attendances at all tournaments he appeared in throughout the world.

▶ **Sensational Slip!** The classy swing of Bernhard Langer whose missed putt at the 1992 Ryder Cup brought a dramatic last day to a truly sensational end.

► **Sensational Sparkle!** Perhaps the greatest steeplechaser ever – Arkle – whose jumping acumen would bring gasps of disbelief from seasoned race-goers.

► **Sensational Steeplechaser!** The frightening fences of Aintree and the 'cavalry charge' of the Grand National were taken in his stride by the remarkable Red Rum, whose record in the race will surely never be equalled.

◄ **Sensational Sir!** Gordon Richards brought sensation to Epsom Downs in the Coronation Year of 1953 when he won his first Derby at his 28th and last attempt.

▲ **Sensational Speedster!** With the looks of a matinee idol and daring of a comic strip hero, Mike Hawthorn – with Stirling Moss – was a trailblazer for the British motor racing stars who have followed.

◄ **Sensational Seconds!** Three extra seconds of play caused sporting sensation at the 1972 Olympic basketball match between the USA and Soviet Union. In those extra moments the Soviets turned defeat into victory.

▶ **Sensational Sweetheart!** Olga Korbut, here at Montreal in 1976, captured the hearts of television audiences worldside and stimulated a generation of young children to take up her sport.

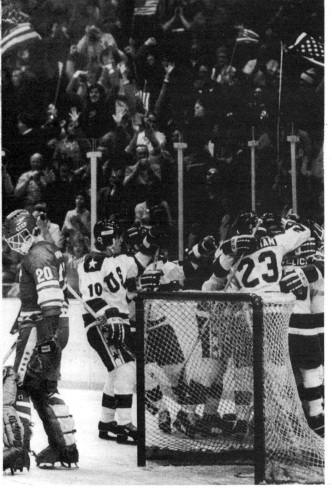

◀ **Sensational Stars and Stripes!** The USA v USSR ice hockey match at the 1980 Olympics took on all the dramas felt during the Cold War years.

▲ **Sensational Sorrow!** Paul Gascoigne cannot hide his tears at England's World Cup defeat in 1990. The young Geordie, having waited for his chance in the national team, was a great success in the finals.

▲ **Sensational Stanley!** Not only was the 1953 Cup Final at Wembley a sensational match, with Blackpool coming from behind late in the game to defeat Bolton 4-3, but the architect of that rally was Stanley Matthews, England's star winger and a great favourite with fans countrywide.

Sensational Senor! 'Pancho' Gonzales featured, with Charlie Pasarell, in the longest Wimbledon match on record where, despite being much the older man, he came out on top after 112 games.

Sensational Saint or Sinner! After 20 years at the top of one of the most exciting sports, Jimmy Connors is still capable of sensational performances and delights in staging unbelievable comebacks.

▲ **Sensational Silver Jubilee!**
With exquisite timing, Virginia
Wade chose the Royal Jubilee
year to finally win the Ladies
Singles at Wimbledon.

◀ **Sensational Snooker!** Yes! Yes!
Yes! Dennis Taylor celebrates his
1985 World championship win
over Steve Davis after potting the
final black of the final game.

▶ **Sensational Skier!** The
outstanding downhill skier of the
1980s, Franz Klammer poses
below the famed Hahnenkamm
Slopes at Kitzbuehl, scene of
some of his most flamboyant
performances.

Sensational Sailing! Admirals Cup yacht, Kookaburra III, rounds a buoy with the world's media watching every manoeuvre to an unprecedented degree.

THE OLYMPICS

Mick Dennis

Mark Spitz and The Magnificent Seven

The Munich Olympics of 1972 will always be remembered for the savage act of terrorism which defiled them. Arab terrorists infiltrated the Olympic village, kidnapped and then murdered members of the Israeli team.

With that sombre backdrop, sporting achievements seem trite and trivial, but in fact those Munich Games produces some of the greatest Olympians.

Mark Spitz, for instance, was the ultimate Olympic sensation. He amassed the greatest ever personal accumulation of gold medals; an unprecedented and almost incomprehensible haul of seven at Munich to go with the two golds he had collected four years earlier in Mexico.

Just think about that. Consider the dedication, determination, discipline and sheer talent which Steve Ovett, for instance, needed to win one gold medal.

Spitz won seven at one Games, and with each of the seven golds in Munich came a new world record. No competitor had ever annihilated the opposition so comprehensively. Nobody had ever dominated an Olympic arena so completely. Nobody had displayed such a devastating amount of natural ability, honed into an unmatched competitive edge by years of unstinted application.

Spitz learned to swim at the age of two when the family lived in Hawaii, but he was nine when his grace and pace in the water first really impressed people. By then the family had moved to Sacramento, California, and his father, Arnold, was doing well as the manager of a scrap iron and steel business.

Mark started training at the Arden Hill swimming club, and by the time he was ten he held seventeen national age-group records. The boy was good.

When people started telling Arnold Spitz that his son had a special talent, Arnold started to listen, and decided that if there was a chance of little Mark achieving something with his swimming, then he would get every possible help. Arnold and his wife used to take it in turns to get up at 5 am to take Mark training, and when their rabbi complained that swimming was interfering with the youngster's Hebrew lessons, Arnold replied, 'Well, even God likes a winner.'

Eventually it became clear that to ensure that Mark continued winning, his remarkable talent needed special tuition. So the lad joined George Haines, the

US men's Olympic coach, at the swank Santa Clara Swim Club. 'From the first time I saw him, I knew he was a potential champion,' said Haines.

The Spitz family moved across Sacramento to a neat house near the club, and Mark transferred to Santa Clara High School. He was still at the school when he first started breaking world records and the newspapers dubbed him 'The Human Torpedo'. People called him other things as well, and not all of them were laudatory. The most frequently used adjective was 'arrogant,' but then Spitz had a lot to be arrogant about.

It must have been infuriating for his rivals to hear it when the 17-year-old Spitz told reporters, after smashing another record, 'It felt really easy'. But it was true. It *WAS* easy for Spitz, who had grown into a tall (six feet), slim (11st 6lbs) young man. Of course the training was physically demanding. He was in the pool for 20 hours a week and swam a minimum of 26 miles each week flat out. There was little time or energy left for any sort of social life away from the pool, but the actual swimming still came easy to Spitz.

Haines said at the time, 'He has this great, natural rhythm. With many swimmers there is a danger of tying up in the shoulders or getting cramp, but Mark's rhythm means that, even if he's not in top condition, he can go flat out without worry of tying up.'

He also had outsized hands, which pulled huge amounts of water out of his way, and strange joints which allowed him to flex his legs slightly forward from the knee and gave his kick extra zip. He also had an obliging metabolism so that the young Spitz was able to say, 'I guess I'm lucky with my weight. I don't diet. I eat pretty much anything I like.'

Not all of his comments were so innocuous, however.

Those close to him found his personality engaging enough, and there were some warm friendships but, perhaps because the swimming and the winning was easy, young Spitz continually said things which sounded brash.

As he prepared for the 1968 Olympics in Mexico he said, 'People say I don't like losing, but does anybody? I keep being asked whether I'm the best swimmer in the world, and I have to say that if I'm not, then I am certainly striving to become the best.'

Worse still, although he denied having said anything so categorical, were reports of an extravagant prediction that he would be first in six events at the Mexico Games.

A year earlier, in the 1967 Pan-American Games, Spitz had won five golds and it did not seem unreasonable to assume he could do at least as well in Mexico, especially as he was going to the Olympics backed by a plethora of astonishing statistics. In the two years before Mexico he had won 22 national and international titles, broken 28 US records and set ten world records.

So expectations were high in Mexico. In the 100 metres butterfly, for example, Spitz, the world record holder, lined up alongside compatriot Doug Russell in the final. The two young men had raced many times before and although Russell always took the early lead, the result was always the same. Spitz always won with a strong finish.

But in the Olympic final, Spitz decided, inexplicably, to go faster from the start and not leave so much for his finish. Russell, separately and privately, decided to start off more slowly than usual and save some energy for the last 25 metres. The two rivals had, unknown to each other, reversed their tactics, and the result was that Russell powered past Spitz at the finish to beat him for the first time.

More disasters followed. Spitz picked up two team relay gold medals, but that was all. In his last final of the games, exhausted by a week's racing and drained by the unexpected and unaccustomed experience of defeat, the 18-year-old Spitz finished last in the 200 metres butterfly. His time of two minutes 13.5 seconds was more than eight seconds slower than his own world record.

Years later, Spitz recalled the reaction of the American press and public. 'People were ready to write me off as an arrogant brat who could not do the business when it came to the big ones. Maybe they were right about my being a bit of a brat, but I was determined to prove they were wrong about the other thing. I knew I could win the big ones.'

But there were noticeably fewer predictions as Spitz prepared for the Munich Olympics of 1972, and he seemed visibly nervous when he stood on his blocks for his first final in Munich; the 200 metres butterfly, the event with which he had finished his depressing stay in Mexico four years earlier.

This time, once Spitz hit the water, the old, easy rhythm came back and so did the power. Spitz led from the gun and finished a clear winner, only seventh tenths of a second outside the magical two minutes mark. His time was a new world record and Spitz leapt high out of the water with his arms aloft in triumph, but it was only the beginning.

A few hours later that same evening came the first relay final, the 4x100 metres freestyle. The USA team was so strong that they had entered two second choice swimmers for the qualifying round and still set a world record. For the final, Spitz and John Murphy replaced Dave Fairbank and Gary Conelly. Spitz swam the last leg, and touched home in three minutes 26.42 seconds. It was another world record and another gold medal.

The very next day, Spitz took his third gold of the Games, overhauling team-mate Steve Genter in the last length of the 200 metres freestyle and shaving a fraction of his own world record. On the medal podium, he gleefully waved his shoes at the crowd . . . and at the cameras. Surely the gesture was just exuberance and not motivated by any commercial consideration? The International Olympic Commission held an impromptu inquiry, Spitz assured them he had not been paid to display his trainers, and the Commissioners believed him.

So the victory parade continued. Two days later, in the 100 metres butterfly, Spitz won by more than half a second from Canadian Bruce Robertsoon. Gold medal number four, and another world record. One hour later the incredible Spitz was back in the water, swimming the anchor leg of the 4x200 metres freestyle relay. The USA team were already well in front when he dived in, and Spitz ploughed on to the finish to make sure of another world record. Even those who had delighted in the cocky teenager's failure four years earlier had to applaud 22-year-old Spitz now. He had won five gold medals in four days.

Spitz was entered for two more events, the 100 metres freestyle and the medley relay. The relay was almost certain to bring another gold, but the sprint race was not a formality. Another American, Jerry Heidenreich, was a genuine threat and Spitz was beginning to think it might be a good idea not to take part in a race he might lose. That way he would leave Munich undefeated. His new coach, Sherm Cavoor, had other views, however. If Spitz did not face Heidenreich, he would be considered a coward, and, besides, he could beat Heidenreich.

Spitz was persuaded, but looked sluggish in the heats and was only the third fastest qualifier for the final. Then came one of those Spitz tactical switches. Instead of saving himself for a last gasp spurt, Spitz went flat out from the gun in the final and built a lead. Hendenreich kept in touch, however, and suddenly Spitz began to tire and that famous rhythm disintegrated. Somehow, from somewhere, Spitz found the resilience to battle on and he fingertipped the wall a fraction ahead of his rival. Gold medal number six and world record number six, but for once it had been anything but easy.

And so to the medley relay, in which each team has four competitors, each of whom uses a different stroke to complete two lengths of the 50 metre pool. The East Germans started well, with backstroker Roland Matthes setting a new world best. Then Britain got a brilliant breaststroke leg from David Wilkie, but all eyes were on Spitz, who was waiting to swim the butterfly leg. He had some work to do, but it was soon apparent that he was back at his breathtaking best and the watching worldwide television audience was agog as he handed over a lead to Jim Montgomery. Would the Americans win again?

Yes. World record number seven and gold medal number seven. Spitz had made history.

Olga Korbut, The Munich Munchkin

Even in 1972, the year of her Olympic triumphs, there were better gymnasts. But there has only ever been one Olga.

Born in Belorussia, the youngest of four children, she was 17 at the time of the Munich Games, but had the pre-pubescant body and apparent innocence of a 12 year old. She was just 4ft 11ins tall, weighed just six stones, and, with her sharp features, looked like a pixie. Often her face was tense with concentration, but when she smiled, her entire face lit up.

'For me,' she said, 'gymnastics is an expression of my inner soul.' When she smiled, you believed her.

Olga charmed her way into the hearts of the world, and as the Games unfolded, taking her on a roller coaster ride of success, failure and glory, we all suffered and rejoiced with her. Her performances in Munich instantly popularised a sport which had previously had a very limited appeal. Schoolgirls who had viewed PE lessons as a form of torture suddenly queued to join gymnastics clubs, eager to put on leotards and emulate Olga. In Britain, membership of the British Amateur Gymnastics Association doubled in the two years after Munich, and most of the new members were girls aged between three and 16.

Yet Olga very nearly did not compete in Munich. She was originally picked as a reserve for the Games and only earned a place in the Soviet line-up because a team-mate became ill. But Olga made the most of her good fortune.

Olga and her coach, Renald Knysh, had always realised the value of her impish appeal. Women's gymnastics is, after all, part dance, part theatrical performance (particularly the floor exercises) and Knysh and Olga had devised a programme which utilised her abnormally flexible spine; a programme full of flourishes and graceful gestures – and full of Olga's beguiling smiles.

The smiles were on prominent display as she made an immediate impact with a spectacular routine on the parallel bars. The audience loved it and their reaction was so enthusiastic that TV producers were alerted and shuffled their schedules to introduce Olga, the smiling elf with the child-like innocence, to the world.

But the next day Olga's smiles were replaced by genuine tears. She made a complete mess of her uneven bars programme. From start to finish it was a disaster. Her timing had gone and she was still weeping when the judges scored her 7.5. That ended her chances of becoming all-round champion, and she finished seventh with the gold going to the great Lyudmila Tourisheva.

Two days later Olga was back for the separate competitions for the championships on the four individual apparatuses, and the world was hoping the magical Munchkin would strike gold.

At first, it seemed that Olga and her growing army of fans would be denied. The judges marked her second on the uneven bars, and the crowd kicked up bedlam, stamping their feet, whistling and booing. The judges were not moved, but the demonstration by the crowd was a remarkable testament to Olga's appeal.

On the balance beam, however, she needed no help from the audience. She was magnificent, and the gold medal was a formality.

101

She also shared a team gold, but it was the individual gold she gained with her floor exercise, or rather the performance which earned it, which took gymnastics into a new era. The programme included dazzling back somersaults and other traditional but devastatingly delivered ingredients, but it also had elan, unashamed cheek, showmanship and showbiz. It finished with that pointed chin tilted upwards as the famous smile exploded onto her face and onto millions of television screens.

Four years later 14-year-old Nadia Comaneci of Rumania, took centre stage at the Montreal Olympics by scoring seven perfect tens. Olga, the Soviet captain, finished fifth over-all and was even outshone by her team-mate Nelli Kim, who also managed a couple of perfect tens.

But then Olga had never claimed to be perfect. Just unique.

The team who didn't want their medals

The 1972 Games also produced a sensation on the basketball court, when the USA, winners of the seven previous Olympic tournaments, lost in the final amid some of the most controversial scenes ever witnessed at a sporting contest.

From the time basketball was introduced to the Olympics in 1936 in Berlin, the United States had dominated the sport. They won all their four matches in Berlin, where the games were played outside on clay tennis courts. Their team included a centre called Joe Fortenberry, who was six feet eight. At the next Games, in London, in 1948, they had a seven feet tall centre (Bob Kurland) and won all their eight matches. The scene had been set: the Americans were the giants of the sport.

In 1952 in Helsinki, where the volatile Uruguayan team contributed to the entertainment by assaulting the referee in one match, the gold medal again went to Uncle Sam's boys. The USA beat the USSR 36-25 in the final.

Four years later, in Melbourne, the USA won all their matches by at least 30 points and again beat the Soviet Union in the final. In Rome in 1960 the Americans averaged more than 100 points every game, and, once more, took the gold with the silver going to the USSR. Yet again, the story was repeated in 1964, in Tokyo, where again the Americans were undefeated and again they beat the Soviets in the final.

In Mexico in 1968 the sequence was broken, because it was Yugoslavia and not the USSR who finished second. The winners? America, of course. Their victory in the final meant that they had won all 62 of their matches in Olympic history.

In Munich in 1972, the Americans continued on their all-conquering path, and duly progressed to a final showdown with the Soviets.

But the USSR surprised everyone by scoring first and staying ahead throughout the first half, which ended with them 26-21 in the lead. Astonishingly, as the second half edged towards its climax, the Soviets remained ahead. The Americans battled on with increasing desperation and whittled away at the Soviet lead. With six seconds left on the clock the Americans were just one point behind.

The intense pressure finally told and the Soviets made two bad blunders. Firstly, Sasha Belov's poor pass was intercepted by America's Doug Collins, and secondly Sako Sakandelidze, struck by panic, deliberately fouled Collins to stop him getting a scoring attempt.

Now it was the turn of Collins to feel the pressure as he braced himself to take the two free shots awarded for the foul. He took a deep breath . . . and sank them both. America were ahead for the first time in the game, 50-49.

But the USSR had called a 'time out' after the first Collins shot and so the game should have been halted. Now the Soviets protested furiously and argued that, although the clock showed only one second remaining, they should be allowed more time.

William Jones, the British Secretary of basketball's ruling body, agreed and decreed that the clock should be put back two extra seconds, so that three seconds remained to be played. History has decided that he was wrong to do so, but that was the decision he made.

So the Soviets had the ball and had three seconds to score. Ivan Yedeshko threw a pass almost the length of the court. Sasha Belov caught it, spun around, sprinted between two opponents and scored. The Soviet Union had won 51-50. The USA had been beaten for the first time.

Or had they? They filed a protest claiming, with considerable justification, that the clock should not have been put back and that the Belov score should be disallowed. A five-man committee was convened. Two members (representatives of Puerto Rico and Italy) voted in favour of ruling out the Belov score. Two members (from Communist Poland and Communist Cuba) voted in favour of allowing the score to stand. The casting vote went to the committee chairman, Terrence Hepp of Hungary. He decided that Belov's score should stand.

So that was it, the USA had lost for the first time; by one point in the dying seconds of an extended match, and then by on vote in the committee room. The USA team declined to accept their silver medals.

God bless America

International sporting contests frequently become vehicles for jingoistic nationalism (although whether they should or not is not a topic for debate here). Sometimes, at certain moments in a country's history, sport becomes a metaphor or substitute for more bloody conflicts. For instance, when Argentina beat England in soccer's World Cup in 1986 (with help from Diego Maradona's 'Hand of God'), the people who took to the streets of Buenos Aires to celebrate carried banners referring to the Falklands War between the two countries four years earlier.

103

The ice hockey match between the USSR and the USA at the 1980 Winter Olympics at Lake Placcid was another contest which symbolised much more than mere sporting issues to the combatants and to the millions of their compatriots who watched, and to understand the passions the game aroused, it has to be put into its historic contest.

The United States was undergoing an identity crisis in 1980, and perceived itself to be losing stature and status on the world stage. President Jimmy Carter was considered by many to be a weak leader, powerless to help the American hostages who were being held in Iran and offering only bluster and rhetoric to counter the threat to world peace posed by the Soviet invasion of Afghanistan.

The Soviets, as shown by their disregard of world opprobrium at their Afghanistan intervention, were a menacing superpower able to ignore American disapproval. Cartoons showed the Russian bear toying with the American eagle.

Carter had taken one decisive step. As a protest about the Soviet invasion the President had decided that the USA would not send a team to the 1980 Summer Olympics in July and August in Moscow. But that meant that the Winter Games, on American soil (or rather, snow and ice), assumed even more importance. The Winter Games, in the February before the Summer Games, were to be the only opportunity for American sportsmen and women to show their prowess; the only chance for the American people to exorcise their national chagrin . . . if there were any American winners.

It was in that emotive setting that the USA met the USSR in the decisive match of the Olympic ice hockey competition.

The two teams had met 20 years before (when the Olympics had also been in America) and the USA had won, but, for the most part, the Soviets had enjoyed almost 30 years of world dominance of this spectacular, sometimes violent sport.

Just before the 1980 tournament, the young American team played a 'friendly' warm-up match against the USSR team and lost 10-3, and when the Olympic tournament proper got under way, the omens did not look good for the millions of Americans watching their TV screens. The USA team had an average age of just over 22 and there was considerable concern that the coach, Herbie Brooks, had picked almost half his squad from the university of Minnesota, where he worked.

In the first match against the highly-rated Swedish team, the USA fell behind in the first half and were still trailing 2-1 in the dying seconds. Then coach Brooks, a charismatic if dictatorial leader of his troops, gambled on a bold ploy. He took off his goalkeeper, Jim Craig, and sent on an additional out-field player in his place. It worked. With less than 30 seconds left, Bill Baker hit a long-range shot which slithered in and earned the USA a 2-2 draw.

104

In the next match, against second favourites Czechoslovakia, the Americans again conceded an early goal but battled back once more to score a quite astounding 7-2 triumph and suddenly the folks in their homes across the nation were sitting up and taking notice of this ice hockey team, who continued to achieve exciting, almost theatrical triumphs. Against Norway, the USA inevitably conceded an early goal but then collected five late goals to win 5-1. Against West Germany, the USA conceded TWO goals before grabbing a 4-2 victory and only against Rumania did the home team score first (on their way to a 7-2 win).

Now the USA were in the second round of matches, along with Sweden, Finland and the Soviets, although under the complicated procedure adopted for the tournament, the Swedes and the USA did not have to play each other.

Instead, early in the evening of Friday, February 22nd, the USA and the USSR faced each other on the ice. An ice hockey match consists of four periods, each of ten minutes, and there are many people in America who can recount in detail the events of those 40 minutes that day.

The Soviets, generally accepted as the best team in the world, went into the match having scored 60 goals and conceded just 13 in the tournament. The USA record was a far less impressive 25 for and ten against, and so it was to the surprise of absolutely nobody when the USSR scored first. Buzz Schneider equalised, but the Soviets scored again and only when Mark Johnson snatched a second equaliser with the very last shot of the first period did it become apparent that this American team was capable of giving the Soviets a real contest.

The Soviets scored an impressive third goal, but it was the only score of the second period and now the tension in the air was tangible. Eight more scoreless minutes ticked away, and still the Soviets only led by a single goal and must have been wondering whether it would be enough. Then Mark Johnson took control of a loose puck, sped beyond a defender and slapped in a shot from close range. As the puck hit the back of the net, an entire nation went berserk. It was 3-3, with 12 minutes left.

Lifted by the incredible noise in the stadium, and surely sensing their destiny, the young Americans pressed forward again, but, although the mighty Soviets began to look vulnerable, it seemed they would survive until the end of the third period and then be able to launch an assault in the last ten minutes. But, almost at the moment the third period was ending, Mike Eruzione, the USA captain, scored the goal of the match. He deliberately let a USSR player get between him and the goal so that the goalkeeper's view was obscured and then fired a magnificent shot from 10 yards. It was 4-3 to America.

The final period was played out in a deafening cauldron of noise as the sell-out crowd screamed encouragement to the young men who, rightly or wrongly, at that moment symbolised the free world taking on the might of a brutal, totalitarian regime. The Soviet players may have been bemused by scenes they could scarcely comprehend, but they did not cower. Instead they too were lifted by the excitement of the occasion and added a new determination to their resolute insistence that they would not lose. The USSR went forward in wave after wave of breathtakingly fast and powerful play.

But Jim Craig, in the USA goal, was inspired, blocking shot after shot after shot and his team-mates fought a brilliant, unyielding rearguard action in front of him. The clock was ticking on. The noise and the tension were almost too much to bear. And then it was all over. The USA had won, and unprecedented scenes of rejoicing followed, amid which, it should be remembered, the Soviets made a point of congratulating their victorious opponents.

Many people cried, including, it is said, most of the policemen on duty in the sports hall. Herbie Brooks locked himself in the toilet for half an hour as he struggled in vain to come to terms with what his team had achieved, and in the changing room the 20 men of the USA squad sang 'God Bless America' until their throats were hoarse.

Eventually the rejoicing abated and coach Brooks faced up to the daunting job of getting himself and his players ready for their last game. After the exhilarating euphoria of beating the USSR, nothing else seemed to matter, but the fact was that the Americans still had to play Finland. If they lost it was possible that the USSR would still take the gold medal.

So it was that two days after the match against the Soviets, the USA took on the Finns and found themselves 1-0 down after one period and 2-1 down after two. Once more the crowd began to produce deafening support, and once more the Americans responded, equalising two minutes into the third period, moving ahead four minutes later and scoring a fourth goal four minutes from the end of the match.

Mike Eruzione, the captain who had scored the winning goal against the Soviets, collected the gold medal on behalf of his team.

RUGBY UNION

Chris Jones

The back-to-back Slams!

For those unlucky enough to have witnessed England's awful exit from the inaugural 1987 World Cup with a defeat against Wales in a rain-soaked quarter-final in Brisbane, the idea that five years later that same country would record the first back-to-back Grand Slams since 1924 would have been laughable. England returned from Australia desperately needing a new direction and purpose and within months they had been forced to make an appointment that would take them to the World Cup final of 1991 and successive Grand Slams.

Mike Weston, England's 1987 World Cup team manager, resigned when the Rugby Football Union refused to sanction his choice of coach for the coming season. Into team managership came Geoff Cooke in October 1987 – the day the Great Storm which decimated large areas of England. His arrival was to be just as devastating for those unwilling to move with the times and accept new fitness programmes and demands on their time and commitment to England's national squad. Cooke had a number of key players on which to base his new regime including Wade Dooley, Dean Richards, Rob Andrew and Rory Underwood. He also chose to make Will Carling, then 22 and the youngest member of the team, captain with the belief he would be good enough to carry through to the 1991 World Cup.

A win over Australia in 1988 signalled the start of the revival and it proved that English players could compete with the Southern Hemisphere by running the ball and dominating up front. It was a watershed for the players and Cooke's new regime and suddenly Twickenham was echoing to the sounds of sell-out crowds captivated by regular victories at the home of English rugby.

It was not all plain sailing. There were tour defeats in Australia and Argentina and then a Grand Slam that got away in 1990 when Scotland walked out onto Murrayfield and exposed a weakness in England's armoury – the ability to win under the extreme pressure of expectation. Carling and his players examined the reasons for their failure and vowed to make amends by becoming ruthlessly efficient with their forward play to such an extent that the opposition was sucked into a war of attrition they could not win.

It started in Cardiff with England's first win in Wales for 28 years and suddenly the 1991 Five Nations championship looked set fair for the first English Grand Slam since 1980. Revenge over Scotland at Twickenham maintained the momentum and a hard fought win by the forwards in Ireland plus a Rory Underwood try secured the Triple Crown. Bring on France!

The French came to Twickenham also aiming for the Slam and stunned the sell out 60000 crowd with one of the great tries of all time. It started under their own posts and finished with Philippe Saint-Andre diving to score under England's after a mesmeric blur of magical running and kicking. England, fuelled by another Underwood try, used their magnificent pack to stay just ahead of France and emerge 21-19 victors. The Twickenham pitch was engulfed by delirious supporters who carried their heroes shoulder high from the field. As he was hoisted up, someone removed Carling's boots from his feet as souvenirs of a day that proved that England could be winners, and their pack, which had been the backbone of the 1989 British Lions in Australia, was unmatchable. The question now was; Could England repeat the achievement or would they follow the example of the 1980 side and break up and lose the ground gained?

England were good enough to reach the World Cup final later that year but the strain was beginning to tell and suddenly injury robbed them of Mike Teague, the Gloucester flanker, and Paul Ackford, the brilliant Harlequins lock, announced he was retiring. How could England replace those two key elements from the pack and win another Grand Slam?

The answers came from the squad that Cooke, the team manager, had worked to so hard to mould and train up to the standards of fitness and commitment shown by Australia and New Zealand. Into the void left by Ackford came another policeman, Martin Bayfield, who at 6ft 10ins was the tallest lock to represent England. Mick Skinner, after a great World Cup, proved he was still hungry for work after being confined to the replacement's bench in the 1991 Slam campaign.

Cooke and Carling decided to continue with the more open style of rugby that had been used in the World Cup final. It was obvious that England had the pace and skill to run teams ragged but needed to play consistently in this fashion. Dick Best, an advocate of running rugby, took over as coach from Roger Uttley, and into the team came Tim Rodber, a young No 8, who was rated better than the experienced Lion Dean Richards at the start of a season that was to see Richards return halfway through and give the team someone who could retain possession and clear up the loose line out ball resulting from the loss of Ackford. The second Grand Slam was won with style and a hat-full of points. Scotland were beaten by a record score on their own pitch and Ireland suffered their greatest beating at Twickenham. It was all too much for the French who were so intimidated that they eventually were routed with two players sent off as they had no answer to the North Hemisphere's top team. All that was needed for a second successive Slam was the execution of Wales.

England defeated Wales 24-0 without having to reach any great heights. It brought criticism that the 1992 Slam was devalued because the opposition had been poor. That was dismissed by England and their delirious supporters who once again invaded Twickenham to celebrate the first back-to-back Grand Slams since 1924. Two seasons of magnificent triumph under Will Carling and the promise of more to come.

The Lions in the All Black Den

New Zealanders simply called him 'The King'. To British rugby supporters he was Barry John of Wales and the Lions. The clean cut outside half was the magician whose rugby spells enabled the 1971 British Lions to become the first touring team to win a series in New Zealand and enter the record books as legends. The names roll off the tongue, Edwards, Gibson, McBride, Pullin, Davies, Duckham, JPR Williams and so may more.

When they had arrived in New Zealand, a country that had inflicted severe beatings on Wales in 1969, the Lions manager Doug Smith, of Scotland, gave the locals a good laugh by predicting his squad would win two tests and draw another to take the series. He was proved to absolutely right and like John, was given a new name – 'Witchdoctor Smith'! The tour record read P 26 W 23 D 1 L 2. Barry John's own points haul proved how vital he was to the team with 191 made up of 7 tries, 31 conversions, 28 penalties and 8 drop goals.

The tour party contained very experienced men from each of the four Home Unions and they were intelligently led by John Dawes, of Wales, who engendered a team spirit that was to ensure the Lions bounced back from a comprehensive second test defeat and overcome the violence of Canterbury which left three players with serious injuries.

But, the man who really masterminded the success of this tour was a chain-smoking Welshman. Carwyn James was the first 'master coach' and his tactical brain and ability to mould the best of British into a Lions team capable of great deeds cannot be underestimated. He deeply understood the game as it was in 1971 and knew the All Blacks would rely heavily on their rucking technique.

James realised he had a pack of forwards that could compete up front and win enough ball for a back division of pace and vision led by John who had been part of a Grand Slam winning Welsh side that season. With young JPR Williams at full back the Lions had the ability to counter attack with an alacrity the All Blacks did not have the wit or capability to match. Their most dangerous man was scrum half Syd Going whose play forced the Lions to change the make up of their back row during the series. Derek Quinnelll, the uncapped Wales flanker, came into the test side to shackle the troublesome Going. Again it was an example of the flexibility and tactical appreciation of James.

To establish the scenario for a Lions test series win it was decided to concentrate on getting the scrummage right and Ray McLoughlin, of Ireland, making his second Lions tour to New Zealand, was the vital cog. He would have played in the test matches but like Sandy Carmichael, the other leading prop, was punched out of contention in the Battle of Canterbury. This came before the First Test in Dunedin. The Lions defeated Canterbury 14-3 but lost McLoughlin, Carmichael (multiple cheekbone fracture) and Mike Hipwell, the Ireland scrum half. The Lions went into the first test with Ian 'Mighty Mouse' McLaughlan and Sean Lynch in the front row with hooker John Pullin and Gareth Edwards nursing a hamstring injury. McLaughlan scored a try after charging down a kick and the front row did its job helping the Lions secure a vital 9-3 win but Edwards did not make it past the 10 minute mark. He was replaced by Chico Hopkins, of Wales, who had a tremendous match. John kick two penalty goals and the All Blacks realised they had real battle on their hands. Ian Kirkpatrick, the All Black forward scored one of the great tries of the series as his side bounced back with a comprehensive 22-12 second test win in the Christchurch mud.

The 'Going Question' had to be solved before the third test in Wellington and it was decided to play a back row of Quinnell, Mervyn Davies and Fergus Slattery. However, Slattery, of Ireland, dropped out through illness and John Taylor, of Wales, returned to play an important part in the 13-3 victory that ensured at least a share of the series.

The Lions stunned the opposition and the huge Wellington crowd of 50000 by taking a 13-0 lead. John kicked a drop goal, converted Gerald Davies's try from the touchline and then added the extra points to his own try made by Gareth Edwards' tenacity. They did not score again but defended with calm assurance and John and Edwards repeatedly cleared the lines.

Now, came the final test in Auckland and the Lions would have to draw to give manager Smith his predicted series outcome. By the final whistle the Lions had secured their coveted series win with a 14-14 draw that earned Smith his new title of 'Witchdoctor'. New Zealanders agreed it had been the finest rugby team to ever visit their land and John was 'The King'. It had been a tremendous battle to tie the final test after the All Blacks raced into an 8-0 lead with Wayne Cottrell scoring a try that Laurie Mains converted and then followed with a penalty. It seemed that even the 'King' was going to be denied as he missed with a drop goal and two penalties before finding the posts with another penalty. England's David Duckham was forced into touch near the All Blacks try line and after Edwards had darted for the line he passed to Peter Dixon, of England, who crashed over for the try. John added the conversion and suddenly it was 8-8.

Shortly after the restart it was the boot of John, with his final points of the tour, who gave the Lions the lead for the first time. The All Black response was a try from a line out by Tom Lister, a flanker, but Mains could not convert. Once again the match was tied, this time 11-11 and then something unusual happened. JPR Williams collected the ball 45 yards from the posts and proceeded to drop an amazing goal to recapture the lead. There was still time for Mains to level matters with a penalty at 14-14 and the series had been won just as the team manager had predicted. The tour party received an unprecedented welcome on its return to London Airport the following Tuesday. They had achieved something remarkable with a squad of players that had scaled the greatest heights spearheaded by 'King' (Barry) John.

Hancock's greatest day

England 3 Scotland 3, Twickenham, March 20, 1965

Andrew Willam Hancock, a wing, only played three times for England and managed a single try. But, that one moment of glory was so extraordinary that it entered English rugby folklore. The try covered 95 yards hugging, for the early part, the West Stand touch line as England, trailing 3-0 to Scotland, launched a desperate late counter attack when the ball suddenly squirted out of a ruck deep in English territory.

Mike Weston, the England stand off, had passed to Hancock believing the wing would kick to touch and bring an end to a game that had entered its dying minutes before a crowd including Her Majesty, the Queen. It was to be the longest run for a try ever seen in international rugby ending with an utterly exhausted Hancock diving in at the north-west corner of a ground that rose to acclaim a new rugby hero.

Hancock was 25 years old when first capped on the right wing in 1965 in the 9-6 England win over France at Twickenham but was then moved to the left for the Calcutta Cup meeting with the Scots the following month. He stood five feet nine inches and weighed 12 stones and had started his rugby career at Framlington College in Suffolk and then entered London University where he read estate management for his B.Sc. degree. He was to amass a long list of clubs and counties and it read like this at the end of his career; Framlington Coll, London Univ, Sidcup, Cambridge, Northampton, Stafford, Wasps, London Counties, Staffordshire, Eastern Counties and the Barbarians.

A town and country planning officer, he was given an England debut in that French match when Edward Rudd was injured. Hancock is unusual in that his try scoring exploit was hailed because it was a match saving moment rather than a match winning piece of individual brilliance.

Both teams in the 'Hancock Match' were desperate to win the Calcutta Cup to brighten a season that had seen both come to the game with bottom place in the Five Nations table an ominous possibility. A draw would be enough to save England from sharing bottom place and the game featured the allowable unrestricted kicking to touch. The half backs took the brunt of this work moving their respective forwards up and down the touchline. Stewart Wilson, the Scots captain, and Mike Weston both missed penalty opportunities and it was Scotland who eventually took the lead thanks to a drop goal from David Chisholm, the Scots outside half from the Melrose club.

England were then under assault from the rampaging Scots and Gwynne Walters, the Welsh referee, controversially denied Chisholm a try which he appeared to score despite being covered by a number of English tacklers. Then scrum half Alex Hastie, also of Melrose, was recalled by the referee after he had crossed the English try line with the final minutes ticking away. That incident compounded the view that England were going to lose the match and the Scots would finish on the attack and threatening the first try of the contest. How wrong everyone was!

Hancock had spent the entire game on the wing waiting to be given a chance to run. Scotland's second half play meant he was left with nothing but defending to occupy his talents. With time about to be whistled by the referee, the ball bounced towards Weston who moved it straight away to Hancock before taking a heavy tackle from a Scots forward. Hancock realised there was no point kicking as the next stoppage would be the end of the game and so he set off in the hope of somehow creating an attack from a very unpromising position 95 yards from the Scotland line and with little room to manoeuvre along the West Stand touchline.

The wing takes up the story; 'I tried to find an opening to start a passing movement. By accelerating towards the touchline I managed to pass a number of Scots who appeared to be taken by surprise. It was dangerous running so close to the touchline and I decided to move inside to gain more room. This allowed me to glance inside and see the Budge Rogers (the England flanker) was coming up and I attempted to pass to him but realised he was too far back.

'As I turned inside again I saw another Scot blocking my path. I was touched but managed to maintain my stride and there was now no more blue shirts ahead of me but the line was still a long way off! My lungs and legs were hurting but I dared not slow down because someone was running behind me (a Scots centre) and I did not know whether it was Budge Rogers or a Scottish defender, but the chance to score drove me on and I got there for the try.'

Those watching from the West Stand saw Hancock go desperately close to the touch line and some Scots suggested he had put a foot on the line. However, film of the run proves he managed to keep his feet inside the line as he crossed the England 22 and evaded a despairing Scottish tackle. By the time Hancock came level with the Royal Box on half way, he had swerved in-field seven metres to give himself room to attack the touchline again as Wilson, the full back, sped across in a last ditch attempt to halt the winger. The full back's tackle was not good enough and although Hancock was forced to check his stride coming out of the full back's grasp, he did not lose too much momentum. 'I was really puffed by now and all I can remember seeing was the line which became blurred as I got nearer. I simply flung myself across. I had no feeling of elation when I had made it because I was. just too tired:' said Hancock.

His comment after the match that 'I don't suppose I shall ever score another try like that, as long as I live' proved to be absolutely correct. But, he could hardly complain as that one run had put him firmly into the record books.

That Most Celebrated of Tries

Barbarians 23 New Zealand 11, Cardiff, January 27, 1973.

There is nothing more sensational in rugby union than a try that covers the entire length of the field. France proved this fact with their marvellous long range strike initiated by Serge Blanco behind his own posts and finished off by Philippe Saint-Andre under the England posts in the 1991 Grand Slam decider.

That try did not bring ultimate victory but a try of similar length did play a significant part in winning one of the great rugby matches of all time. The Barbarians met the victorious 1973 New Zealand side at Cardiff to round off an All Blacks tour that had proved the Southern Hemisphere men had bounced back from the series defeat by the British Lions on New Zealand soil in 1971.

The 1972-73 New Zealand touring side had played a dour game and, in fact, there had been nasty moments during their visit. Their nine-man rugby had only offered fleeting glimpses of the running power their squad contained. They decided to signal the end of the tour by throwing off the shackles and taking on the Barbarians with the ball in the hand. That is why the match had such a frenetic opening and saw Bryan Williams, the strongly built All Black right wing, with the ball in his possession in the fourth minute. He reached near to half way before opting to put up a high kick that fell deep inside the Baa-baas 22 and bounced low before rolling end on end towards the Baa-baas line at the Westgate End of the famous stadium. Phil Bennett the Welsh outside half, raced back to recover the ball but found himself without meaningful support and a stream of All Blacks looming ahead.

What happened next has become rugby legend and the most repeated footage of a rugby match ever shown on television. Rugby men and women around the World can reel off the names of those who took part in arguably the greatest try ever seen. Bennett, a hero of Llanelli's famous victory over the All Blacks at Stradey Park in the third match of the tour, ignored the kick to touch option and produced a series of side steps that left four All Blacks wrong footed and clutching at air.

Bennett was still a long way from his own players who were sprinting back in an effort to offer the little outside half someone to pass the ball to. It was JPR Williams, the full back, who was the first 'friendly' face Bennett saw and he chose to pass to his Welsh colleague even though both players were still only yards from the Baa-baas line.

Williams was immediately tackled around the neck by his name sake Bryan, but the full back somehow managed to take the blow and still feed the ball onto John Pullin, the England captain and hooker who was one of three who were now forming up on the left side of the Baa-baas half, close to touch. Gareth Edwards was also in the vicinity but he, like the opposition, was caught out by the decision to run the ball rather than kick to touch. Edwards got out of the way as Pullin passed to John Dawes, the Wales centre and Barbarians captain. Edwards, at that point was facing the wrong way and had to turn and follow Dawes who bypassed two All Blacks with a marvellous dummy barely 10 feet from the touch line. He angled his run inside to link up with those who were now able to run in support. Tom David, the Welsh flanker, was on his right and took the pass on the Baa-baas 10 metres line and did not release his one-handed pass to Derek Quinnell, the Welsh lock, until he had reached the All Blacks half.

Quinnell did remarkably well to pick up the pass which was shin high from David and he immediately looked to find John Bevan, the Wales left wing, who had room to exploit along the touchline.

As far as Quinnell knew, the only option he had was Bevan and his pass floated towards the wing. Suddenly onto the scene sprinted Edwards who had been desperately trying to catch up with play and he could not have timed the intrusion better. By the time Edwards intercepted the pass to Bevan he was at full speed and that momentum took him clear of the would be tacklers and now it was a question of keeping the legs pumping for 40 metres to the left-hand corner.

Only Grant Batty, steaming across from the other wing, could get near Edwards and the scrum half sensed the approaching danger. He decided to cover the final yards in mid-air launching a dive for the line that negated Batty's tackle. The crowd went crazy, the All Blacks trouped back in stunned silence and Edwards trotted back to half way taking in enormous gulps of air. This sensational score had come only minutes into a game which most believe to be the finest match ever televised.

It sparked an open game that featured five more tries including a bewildering series of raids that ended with JPR Williams taking a pass from Fergus Slattery, the great Irish flanker, and barging over the try line. By the final whistle the try had already been repeated numerous times and its majesty will never be lost.

SOCCER

Michael Hart

This is a subject almost designed to provoke arguments. For a start what constitutes a 'sensation' in football? Is it a 'sensation' because the newspaper headlines tell us so, or is there a finer, purer, underlying element that is essential before a goal, a match or an individual player can be elevated to 'sensational' status?

I doubt, for instance, that many would dispute that Pele was a sensational player. But was Maradona? He was certainly outstandingly talented, but I believe that his life style, his questionable behaviour on the field of play and some extravagant media coverage played a significant role in establishing a global image that could be described as sensational.

Was the 2-1 defeat of defending League champions Arsenal by the Fourth Division outcasts of Wrexham in the third round of the FA Cup in January 1992 more or less of a sensation than the triumph of Hereford, then of the humble Southern League, over mighty Newcastle in a third round replay in February 1972?

For me one of the most inexplicable results in the history of the game came in Belo Horizonte in the 1950 World Cup when England, among the favourites to lift the trophy, were beaten 1-0 by the United States. That was a sensation. Newspaper offices in London, refusing to believe the result as it chattered over the wires from Brazil, demanded clarification. Once confirmed, it was a scoreline that needed little embellishment by the media. It was a 24-carat gold sensation in its own right.

The bigger the stage and the bigger the players, of course, the more dramatic and sensational the headlines. The World Cup, therefore, inevitably provides the international game with a Who's Who of sensational players, epic deeds and dramatic matches.

But it is Wembley and the FA Cup that have combined to enhance the domestic game in England with a rich and fascinating history of spectacular achievement, glorious triumph and embarrassing defeat.

The 'White Horse Final'

Since Wembley first staged the FA Cup Final in 1923 – itself a quite sensational event – the world's oldest and most enduring knockout tournament has rarely ceased to astonish and surprise.

116

The excitement generated by the first final at Wembley provided fairly emphatic evidence of the popularity of a tournament that had started in 1872.

The Empire Stadium was itself an attraction; the largest in the world at the time and the first part of the 1924 Empire Exhibition Complex to be completed. It was designed to hold 127000 spectators but as West Ham United and Bolton Wanderers waited to kick-off that afternoon, 200000 fans were estimated to be in the ground with further thousands locked outside.

Milling fans on the pitch numbered around 10000 and caused the kick-off to be delayed by 45 minutes but the arrival of mounted police – including Officer Storey on his famous white horse – helped avert a disaster. By the end of the match, which Bolton won 2-0, 1000 spectators had been treated for injuries.

Six of the Best

The FA Cup Final at Wembley was to become the showpiece stage for the great players, but not all of them had the privilege of appearing in a final. George Best, the most talented British footballer in my time as a sports writer, played at Wembley for Northern Ireland but never played there in an FA Cup Final.

That was a pity because the FA Cup Final was his kind of occasion . . . full of charisma and intrigue, larger than life, an occasion that, in itself, was sufficient to build a reputation and secure a place in the game's folklore.

After all, who would remember Everton's Mike Trebilcock but for the two goals he scored against Sheffield Wednesday in the 1966 final; or West Ham's Alan Taylor who scored two against Fulham in the 1975 final.

Best? Well he's remembered for mesmerising skills, a playboy image and a career of quite awesome potential cut short by his own destructive life-style off the pitch. But he was a sensational player and I was privileged to see him produce a sensational performance in the FA Cup.

It was in February 1970 on a mud heap of a pitch at the County Ground, home of Northampton Town. The place was packed with 21000 fans eager to see whether the local heroes from the Fourth Division could oust Manchester United and the likes of Bobby Charlton, Paddy Crerand, Brian Kidd and Best and steal into the quarter finals for the first time. They held out for 27 minutes before Best hit his stride.

He was playing his first game following a four week Football Association suspension yet moved across a flooded pitch like a clipper ship in full sail. He was unstoppable from the moment he swept in at the back post to give United the lead, heading home a centre from Kidd. By the time he had finished he had scored SIX goals – a quite irresistible performance in United's 8-2 victory.

No footballer made a greater impact on life in Britain than Best. He was a man of his time, a spindly kid from East Belfast who had a wonderful talent, good looks and long black hair. You couldn't ask for much more in Britain of the Swinging Sixties.

117

He was christened 'El Beatle' by the media after possibly the most sensational performance of his career. That was in March 1966 in the European Cup quarter final second leg in Benfica's Stadium of Light. United took a slender 3-2 lead to Lisbon where Benfica were considered invincible.

Although Manchester United didn't win the European Cup until two years later, this was the match that established Best's reputation in Europe. Fireworks lit the sky and a 96000 crowd made a noise that chilled the blood as Benfica's legendary Eusebio was presented with his European Footballer of the Year award before the kick off.

Best was just 19. In the sixth minute he rose brilliantly to head in a free kick from Tony Dunne. Six minutes after that he received a pass from David Herd on the halfway line, swept beyond the lunges of two defenders and finished with a low drive into the far corner of the net. Two minutes later Best combined with Denis Law to provide John Connelly with a third goal . . . three in the opening 14 minutes.

Manchester United won 5-1 and, although they went out of the European Cup to Partizan Belgrade in the semi final, Best's sensational contribution that night in Lisbon has never been forgotten.

The Matthews Final

No argument about who is the greatest British Footballer will end with unanimity but, for me, such argument must start with Best. Older observers, of course, would probably chose Sir Stanley Matthews as their point of reference. I didn't see Matthews play though I am prepared to accept that he, the Wizzard of Dribble, was a sensation.

Matthews' career cannot be recounted briefly, because, unlike Best's, there was nothing brief about it. It lasted 33 years and ended five days after his 50th birthday. Best's career in the First Division lasted just 11 years and was followed by five years of roaming between Fulham, Hibernian and California.

Matthews played nearly 800 first team games for Stoke and Blackpool, including three FA Cup Finals, between 1932 and 1965. Those are the nuts and bolts of the legend. The real story was to be found in the impassive face, the spare body and the quick feet. With a sway of the head or a drop of a shoulder Matthews would tempt opposing defenders to commit themselves and, once they had, he wriggled out of range and his pace carried him away from trouble.

It was in the tangerine jersey of Blackpool that he enjoyed his greatest triumphs though he had to wait until he was 38 before a coveted FA Cup winners medal was his. It was 1953 – the Year of Coronation, the ascent of Everest, Gordon Richards' Derby – and Blackpool were through to their third final in five years. In 1948 Matthews and Blackpool lost 4-2 to Manchester United and in 1951 they lost 2-0 to Newcastle.

By this time in his career Matthews was a national institution and he received thousands of letters from well-wishers in the weeks immediately before the 1953 final. What the public didn't know was that four days before the final Matthews pulled a muscle in training. He needed a pain killing injection on the morning of the match and, even then, in the days before substitutes, there was doubt about whether he should play.

But play he did . . . and with 20 minutes remaining it looked as though an FA Cup winners medal would elude him once again. Bolton were leading 3-1 when Matthews dramatically, sensationally, took the game by the scruff of the neck. Inviting tackles, he dismissed his opponents with sleight of head, shoulder and foot and with a sudden change of pace and dazzingly accurate crosses completely unhinged the Bolton defence. Stan Mortensen was the man who capitalised on the brilliance of Matthews. He scored a hat-trick – the first in an FA Cup Final – his third goal coming with three minutes remaining.

The teams were level at 3-3 when Matthews produced his final flourish. He picked his way along the right flank, cut inside and lay on the winning goal for Bill Perry. Blackpool 4 Bolton 3 . . . a sensational finish to a match known for all time as 'the Matthews final.'

'The Battle of Highbury'

Nearly twenty years earlier, when Matthews was just 19 and still learning the basics of his trade with Stoke City, he was selected to play for England against Italy at Highbury. It was his second appearance for his country and was to be one of the darker episodes in England's international history. It certainly produced sensational newspaper coverage around the world at the time.

The game at Highbury in November 1934 was labelled as the unofficial 'Championship of the World' because Italy had just won the World Cup. England had never entered the competition and looked upon it rather disdainfully as a trivial irrelevance for the entertainment of foreigners. As football's mother country, the English in those days considered themselvees automatically superior.

The Italians, in the throes of a new Fascist era under Mussolini, considered themselves to be superior on merit – not merely on reputation. The English decided there was no better way to settle the issue than by beating the Italian upstarts at Highbury.

For the Italians the game had some political significance. Mussolini saw a victory as a triumph for Fascism and offered the players remarkable inducements, including exemption from military service.

The English Football Association realised just how seriously the Italians were taking this friendly when they objected to the German match referee. Dr. Pecos Bauwens spoke good English, but no Italian. Eventually the Italians agreed to a Swedish official, Otto Olsen, who spoke neither English nor Italian.

The Football Association selected seven Arsenal players for the England team and, not surprisingly, more than 50000 spectators were at Highbury for the match. In the first minute they saw an incident that was to shape the entire game.

Luisto Monti, an Argentinian-born defender who played for Juventus, lunged at Ted Drake and, in so doing, broke a toe. As he limped off the pitch he accused Drake of crippling him and this set the tone for the rest of the game.

For the next 15 minutes the Italians kicked and hacked at everything that moved and Arsenal full back Eddie Hapgood had to leave the field with a broken nose – the legacy of an Italian elbow. But the loss of their discipline and self-control, plus, of course, the departure of the injured Monti in the days before substitutes, allowed England to exploit the defensive vulnerability of the Italians. England led 3-0 within 15 minutes and, when Hapgood returned after treatment, it seemed a foregone conclusion that the inevitable defeat of FIFA's world champions would simply confirm the English as the greatest footballing nation on earth.

But at half time the Italians regained their composure and, with just ten men, played some superb football in the second half, scored two goals through the graceful Meazza and, in the end, were narrowly defeated 3-2. England, having just held on to their victory, maintained their unbeaten home record but the long held conviction that they were the best in the world was beginning to crumble.

The Clown Prince

Stanley Matthews was perhaps football's first superstar. The growth of the media and particularly the new fashion for personalising news and creating villains and heroes provided a colourful stage and vast audience for the gladiators of sport. Professional footballers had long featured on the back of cigarette cards or in grey columns of newsprint but, in the years after the Second World War, new, racy tabloids and, ultimately, television elevated the great players to superstardom.

Just as is the case today, some like Matthews, Tom Finney or Billy Wright were propelled to stardom purely by their footballing skill. Others, perhaps less talented, still found stardom because they had charisma or enjoyed one sensational achievement that catapulted them into the game's folklore.

Len Shackleton came into that category. There is no doubt that he was a masterful inside-forward but, more than that, he had a presence and personality that charmed the birds from the trees. A one-time Arsenal groundstaff boy released for being 'too frail', he joined Bradford Park Avenue but after just seven games, and four goals, Newcastle United signed him for £13000. That was a lot of money in 1946 – the third highest fee in history at the time.

120

Three days after he signed 52137 turned up at St. James Park to watch Shackleton make his debut for Newcastle in a Second Division match against Newport County. It was a quite sensational match and it immediately established Shackleton as one of the most vibrant characters in the game.

He scored six goals in Newcastle's 13-0 win. The crowd adored him. He waltzed disdainfully through tackles, sat on the ball and clowned around for the crowd. He was the Paul Gascoigne of his day.

'Everything I tried that day against Newport worked,' he recalled. 'I could have scored with my eyes shut. But had I dreamed about the perfect debut for my new club I would not have come up with six goals. In a way it was the worst thing I could have done. There was just no way I could follow that.'

Shackleton was right. The following season he was sold to Sunderland where he spent 10 years, scoring 97 goals in 320 League matches. He became a Roker Park folk hero known nationally as the Clown Prince of Soccer – the title of his autobiography. In his book, one chapter was entitled 'The average director's knowledge of football.' The title appeared at the top of the page, but the rest of the page was blank.

At his peak he was regarded as one of the most creative and unorthodox attacking players in the country but he paid for his irreverance by being awarded only five England caps between 1948-54.

England 0   USA 1

England were still regarded as one of the great powers of football when they travelled to Brazil in 1950 to play in the World Cup for the first time. The squad of players who travelled to Rio included some of the biggest names in the game – Williams, Ditchburn, Ramsey, Wright, Dickinson, Milburn, Mortensen, Mannion, Finney and Matthews.

The four British Associations had returned to FIFA in 1946 and the World Cup organisers had somewhat indulgently designated the British Championship a qualifying tournament . . . for two nations. The Scots announced that unless they won the British Championship they wouldn't travel to Brazil . . . and they didn't. England won with maximum points and travelled to Brazil as joint favourites for the World Cup with the host nation.

Although by now England had a full-time coach in Walter Winterbottom there remained an 'officers-and-men' aspect to all team matters. The final word on team selection went to the Football Association selection committee.

Such was the optimism in the England camp that the FA sent Stanley Matthews and Jim Taylor, the Fulham centre half, with a touring party to Canada, planning to fly them down to Brazil just before the World Cup.

Matthews and Taylor arrived in Rio after a 15 hour journey just before England's opening match against Chile, a team that had only one full time professional, Newcastle's George Robledo. Neither Matthews nor Taylor was included against Chile who caused England problems in the 200000-capacity Maracana stadium before finally losing 2-0.

It was a far from convincing England performance and may have had something to do with the poor quality of the England team hotel and the fact that most of them were living on a diet of bananas. Winterbottom wanted to play Matthews in England's next match – a formality against the United States.

Mr Arthur Drewry, the FA's sole selector on the trip, had other ideas. He wanted to keep the team that had just beaten Chile, so Matthews was again on the sidelines.

The United States, who had lost 3-1 to Spain in their opening game, were considered no-hopers. Their star player was Scottish-born wing half Eddie McIlvenny, whose greatest claim to fame was seven games for Wrexham in the Third Division North. Their intention was simply to keep the scoreline respectable.

The match was played in Belo Horizonte, an hour's bumpy flight from Rio. The team stayed as guests of a British mining company and the conditions and hospitality were a vast improvement on Rio. But the stadium was small, the pitch rutted – the British community's concrete cricket wicket had to be torn up to accommodate the soccer pitch – and the changing facilities primitive. When England arrived at the stadium they were already wearing their match strip.

The mountain air, by contrast with that in Rio, was invigorating but it was immediately clear that the bulk of the 20,000 spectators in the stadium were supporting the American underdogs.

Although Matthews was sitting among the crowd, this was still an England team littered with big name players – Finney, Wright, Dickinson, Mannion, Mortensen, Ramsey, Bentley.

As expected, England dominated the match. They hit the woodwork on eleven occasions and the American goalkeeper, Borghi, a former baseball player, performed quite remarkably. Once, from Ramsey's free-kick, Mortensen's header crossed the goal line but Borghi dramatically scooped the ball away and the Italian referee, Dattilo, ignored England's appeals. He was similarly dismissive when an American defender punched the ball away from under the bar and refused another England appeal for a penalty when Mortensen was pulled down in the area.

England literally camped out in the American half of the field, but couldn't score. The Americans broke away on only a handful of occasions but one of them, eight minutes before half time, provided the first instance of World Cup giant-killing. A throw in from McIlvenny found Bahr, who shot from 26 yards out. Bert Williams, the England goalkeeper, had the shot covered when it hit Joe Gaetjans, the Haiti-born forward, on the head and flew into the net. Gaetjans claimed he dived to head the ball but some observers believed he knew little about it. Whatever the truth it was irrelevant. The goal was valid.

Despite a furious onslaught in the second half, England couldn't score and within an hour the most sensational result in World Cup history was flashing round the world on the wire services.

Three days later, after a 1-0 defeat by Spain – Matthews was re-instated for this match – England returned home from their first disastrous World Cup adventure.

All the English players, officials and Press men flew back to London. No one stayed to witness and learn from the likes of Brazil, Uruguay, Sweden and Spain in the final group.

England 3   Hungary 6

Stanley Matthews was a one man sensation in his own right. This match against the Hungarians, in November 1953, was almost 20 years after his England debut against Wales in 1934 and he was to continue playing for his country for a further four years. What was so remarkable about this game was not the enduring excellence of Matthews but the fact that it was played at Wembley and represented England's first defeat on home soil by foreign opposition.

The Hungarians arrived at Wembley as the 1952 Olympic champions and were en route to the 1954 World Cup finals where they would score 27 goals in five games. No one questioned the talent of the Magical Magyars. They had not lost an international match for two years and their meticulous preparation for their visit to Wembley included a drawn match against Sweden with an English-type ball a fortnight earlier.

But England had won four of their previous five games against the Hungarians – losing 2-1 in Budapest in 1934 – and were, as all the world knew, unbeatable at Wembley.

England fielded a team of established pedigree – Merrick, Dickinson, Mortensen, Ramsey, Wright and, of course, Matthews, then 38. Matthews' Blackpool team mate Ernie Taylor and George Robb, Tottenham's amateur international, were both making their debuts. They were never to appear for England again.

It was a slate grey November day and few in the capacity Wembley crowd appreciated the artistry of the Hungarians. They had in their ranks some of the world's great players of that era – most notably Ferenc Puskas, their captain, and Nandor Hidegkuti.

The crowd were silenced by Hidegkuti's opening goal in the first minute and then grew increasingly alarmed at England's ineptness. The masters who taught the world to play were now back in the classroom. Hungary played a neat, short passing game that relied on deft ball control and imaginative movement off the ball. The variety of their attacking play simply bemused the England defence.

Hidegkuti had the ball in the net again but the Dutch referee Leo Horn ruled it offside. Then John Sewell, of Sheffield Wednesday, equalised, but it merely gave England a false sense of equality.

Hidegkuti quickly restored the Hungarian's lead and then the mighty Puskas made it 3-1. Soon afterwards Puskas struck again. Mortensen, with his last goal for England, made it 4-2 before Bozsik got on the scoresheet. Hidegkuti completed his hat-trick with a volley from Puskas's lobbed pass.

An Alf Ramsey penalty briefly cheered the Wembley crowd, but it was too little too late. Matthews recalled later: 'It was Hidegkuti who was at the root of our problems. He was playing as a deep centre-forward, in reality in midfield. You can't afford to leave a player of such ability on his own.

'I was sick with disappointment afterwards though there is no doubt they were the better team. The press hammered us and it was even suggested we should go to ballet lessons. Yet Hungary had 11 great players and I don't know who could have beaten them at that time.'

England's domination of the game, so often questioned in the previous decade, was finally buried in the Wembley turf that chill afternoon in 1953. The sensational defeat provoked consternation and debate about the state of the English game and influenced several of the game's leading personalities, including Ron Greenwood, who was later to become manager of West Ham and then England. The Hungarians had shown that strength, courage and endurance – the traditional qualities of the English game – were no longer enough in themselves.

The Hungarians relied largely on imagination, skill and good movement of the ball, virtues they employed once again to devastating effect when they beat England 7-1 in Budapest six months later. For England the years of domination had been brought to a sensational close.

Real Madrid 7   Eintracht Frankfurt 3

The 1960 European Cup Final at Hampden Park secured a place in the annals of sporting excelllence long ago. As a contest, it was probably over by half time but such was the level of skill displayed over 90 minutes that this match has become a collector's item. Indeed, the film of this game is a prize exhibit among the Football's Association coaching aids at Lancaster Gate.

Real Madrid were unquestionably the kings of football in the late fifties. Their emergence and domination of the European Cup had finally demolished the myth of English superiority. They won the European Cup in its first four years and now faced the West German champions on a bumpy pitch in Glasgow. Eintracht had dismissed the local heroes, Rangers, in the semi-final. Their 12-4 aggregate win included a 6-3 trouncing of Rangers at Ibrox and the thought that the German conquerors might end Real's reign attracted the Scots in their droves to Hampden Park. The crowd for the final was 127621.

The star of Real's glittering cast list was Alfredo di Stefano, a balding 33-year-old centre forward who had scored in each of the four previous finals. He was assisted by the ageless Hungarian exile Ferenc Puskas. They also had the benefit of the pace of the Spanish left winger Paco Gento and the creativity and dribbling ability of another Spanish star Luis Del Sol.

Undaunted by Real's towering reputation, Eintracht took the lead through Kress after 18 minutes. Soon, though, Real were level, Di Stefano turning in Canario's centre. When the German keeper failed to hold Canario's shot, Di Stefano reacted quickly to force the ball home and then Puskas hit a fierce left footed shot to give Real a 3-1 lead at half time.

In all Puskas scored four goals, one of them a penalty, and Di Stefano three. At the end the Scottish spectators rose to acclaim the Spanish masters, who were soon doing a lap of honour around Hampden Park. It was the most impressive of their five European Cup Final triumphs.

'We were aware the day was something special, even for us,' recalled Gento later. 'I don't think any of us wanted the referee to end the match and I think that was also true for the crowd.'

England was among the least enthusiastic countries when the European Cup was launched in 1955. But the importance of the competition soon became apparent – largely because of the style and success of Real Madrid.

Their 1960 triumph is now recognised as one of the classics in footballing history and is a symbol of a more innocent age when teams like Real were allowed to perform unmolested.

Tottenham's 'double'

Here in Britain we grudgingly acknowledged the enormous strides made by foreign clubs though the title, 'Team of the Century', was about to be bestowed on one of our own – Tottenham Hotspur.

Rich in history and tradition, Tottenham and their mighty North London rivals Arsenal shared top billing in the capital city for decades. Arsenal had enjoyed more success in the League Championship, but Tottenham had a distinctive style and a reputation for rising to the occasion which had earned them notable triumphs in the FA Cup. They first won the competition in 1901, when they were still in the Southern League.

In 1960-61 they were to achieve what many observers believed impossible in modern football. They won the League Championship and FA Cup in the same season – the first team to achieve the fabled 'double' this century.

Neither Preston North End in 1889 nor Aston Villa in 1897 faced anything like the 49-match programme that stood between Spurs and a revered place in soccer's history books.

Tottenham's £20 a week players included star names like Danny Blanchflower, Dave Mackay, Cliff Jones and John White, tragically killed by lightning in 1964. The manager, Bill Nicholson, was a perfectionist who was to devote 50 years to the club in a variety of roles.

Every match at White Hart Lane that season was packed to capacity with gates of 50000. More than 2.5 million spectators watched Tottenham, home and away, in the days when neither sponsorship nor television money was needed to enable clubs to survive.

Tottenham started the season with a record 11 consecutive wins in the First Division. Asked by reporters if he was feeling the tension, Nicholson replied, 'What tension? It's just a job of work. If you keep losing you get the chop. If you keep winning you win a trophy.

Nicholson was a dedicated, no-nonsense Yorkshireman with a prodigious capacity for hard work. 'A lot of planning and forethought went into that season,' he said. 'It didn't just happen that we recruited a squad of good players and they suddenly became a good team. We worked hard that summer of 1960 on the training ground at Cheshtnut.'

Blanchflower, the Tottenham captain whose outstanding qualities of leadership were rewarded with the coveted Footballer of the Year trophy, recalled, 'I always believed the double could be achieved, and that Tottenham were good enough to do it.'

Tottenham used only 17 players that season. Three played only one game each while Blanchflower, Les Allen, Ron Henry and White played in all 49 games.

For Spurs it was a season of sensational record-breaking. They recorded most First Division wins (31), most First Division away wins (16), most consecutive wins at the start of a season (11) and equalled Arsenal's League Championship record (1930-31) of 66 points (this was in the days of two points for a win).

Their chief goalscorers that season in both the League and FA Cup were: Bobby Smith 33, Les Allen 27, Cliff Jones 19, Terry Dyson 17 and John White 13. Smith and Dyson supplied the goals that beat Leicester City 2-0 in the FA Cup Final at Wembley.

The Cup Final should have been the climax of Tottenham's sensational season but their performance that afternoon lacked conviction or their usual style. As a contest, the game was marred by a 19th minute injury to the Leicester right back Len Chalmers who had to be carried off in the days before substitutes were allowed.

'I felt a slight sense of dissatisfaction,' recalled Nicholson. 'I had wanted us to play well and show how good we were, but the match was not particularly entertaining. I was not conscious of being caught up in any euphoria. In those days you were not mobbed by TV reporters and the Press. I do not remember giving a Press conference, although I did speak informally to some reporters afterwards.'

Nicholson considered it a job well done – no more, no less. It was, nonetheless, a season of legendary proportions for Tottenham – in a sense the yardstick season for the modern domestic game.

Tottenham's great rivals, Arsenal, repeated the 'double' in 1971, ironically clinching the League Championship with a 1-0 win at White Hart Lane in their last game of the season. They also won the FA Cup five days later in the hardest way possible – beating Liverpool 2-1 in extra time at Wembley.

Fifteen years later Liverpool became only the third club this century to achieve the 'double'. It was Kenny Dalglish's first season in charge as player-manager at Anfield and, although he restricted his playing contribution, he scored the winning goal at Chelsea that secured the League title in the final match of the season. He also played at Wembley, helping Liverpool beat their Merseyside rivals Everton 3-1.

Many would argue that Liverpool's feat, achieved when pressures on the modern player were far greater, was the most impressive of the trio of 'doubles' but Tottenham's was the first this century and probably the most stylish.

England 9   Scotland 3

On April 15 1961, with Tottenham already through to the FA Cup Final and just a starlet's eyelash from the League title, two of their most influential players met on opposite sides at Wembley. Bobby Smith, a powerhouse of a centre forward and Tottenham's top scorer that season, faced his club mate Dave MacKay, the barrel-chested bulldog in the heart of the Spurs defence. They met in one of the most sensational international matches staged at Wembley.

England's Home International matches against Scotland dated back to 1872 and had become an essential part of the fabric of the British game. The soccer rivalry between the two nations grew in intensity over the decades and when they met in 1961 the Scots hadn't won the annual battle for ten years.

The Scots were unfortunate to run into an England team at its peak. The players were on top form individually and the whole team was functioning superbly as a unit, thanks largely to the work of coach Walter Winterbottom.

The forward line of Jimmy Greaves (Chelsea), Johnny Haynes (Fulham), Bobby Charlton (Manchester United), Bryan Douglas (Blackburn Rovers) and Smith was in devastating mood. In their previous four matches, against Northern Ireland, Luxembourg, Spain and Wales, England had scored 23 goals.

Scotland, requiring a win for a share of the Home International title, were to leave Wembley totally shell-shocked, with Celtic goalkeeper Frank Haffey most perplexed of all.

Among the 100000 crowd at Wembley that day – the Queen watching her first 'auld enemy' match. The Royal presence inspired England to the highest ever score and the highest ever aggregate score that this match has produced in its long history.

The rout began in the ninth minute when Bobby Robson, an industrious midfield player later to become England manager, opened the scoring. Greaves added two more before half time.

The Scots clawed their way back to 3-2 with a long range drive from Mackay and a diving header from Davie Wilson. But this merely gave them false hope.

The Scots really had no answer to Haynes, who was probably the best passer of a ball in the world at the time. With Robson shouldering the donkey work, Haynes was able to create and inspire from midfield. As the great Scottish striker Denis Law remarked afterwards: 'Haynes and Greaves couldn't believe their luck. We gave them the freedom of the pitch.'

Douglas restored England's two goal lead in the 56th minute and then England really hit their stride, scoring five goals in fourteen minutes: Greaves completed his hat-trick, Smith hit two and the incomparable Haynes drove two long range shots past the hapless Haffey.

At the end the England players carried their proud captain, Haynes, shoulder high around the pitch. Poor Haffey left the field in tears and never played for Scotland again. Scottish goalkeepers have had a tough time ever since!

1966 . . . and all that.

Geoff Hurst's rise to world fame was meteoric. Unknown on the international stage when he made his debut for England in February 1966, he received global acclaim just five months later as the first man to score a hat-trick in a World Cup Final.

Hurst was a modest wing half successfully converted to lethal striker by West Ham manager Ron Greenwood, and his sensational achievement that day at Wembley in July 1966 remains unique.

Born in Ashton-under-Lyne, son of Charlie Hurst, who played for Oldham, Bristol Rovers and Rochdale, the West Ham striker, who played county cricket for Essex, became one of the great stars of the game during the golden age of English football.

For ten seasons Hurst led the West Ham attack with power and cunning. He was a pioneering near-post goalscorer. He ran unselfishly and supplied chances for others.

These were the qualities that persuaded Greenwood to convert him from wing half and the same attributes won him a place in the England side as Sir Alf Ramsey prepared for the 1966 World Cup.

Hurst made his debut in a 1-0 win over West Germany in February 1966 and played in four more warm-up games but was absent when England opened their World Cup programme against Uruguay at Wembley. He missed that goalless draw and the 2-0 wins over Mexico and France.

But Jimmy Greaves, the most prolific goalscorer of the day, was injured against France and suddenly Hurst was required to replace the irreplaceable in the quarter final against Argentina.

This match is remembered not so much for Hurst's goal but for the cynical tripping and body checking of the Argentines, who had already been censured by FIFA for unethical tackling in their earlier game against the Germans.

Hurst and Alan Ball were notable victims of the violence and Argentina's captain, cautioned for a foul on Bobby Charlton, subjected referee Herr Kreitlin to a stream of verbal abuse.

Herr Kreitlin was taking names in his notebook with the zeal of a schoolboy collecting autographs and, when he added the name of Artime, Rattin objected so forcefully that the little referee had no option but to send him off.

Rattin refused to go and for eight minutes the game was held up and pandemomium reigned. Finally, with huge reluctance, Rattin agreed to leave the field and the match re-started.

With just 10 men Argentina showed resilience and skill and their natural talent as footballers posed problems for England. But, in the 77th minute, Ray Wilson hit a pass down the left flank for Martin Peters whose early cross to the near post was met by his West Ham colleague Hurst. He scored with a glancing header and England were through to the semi-finals.

Although Greaves was now fit again, Hurst retained his place in the side against Portugal and Bobby Charlton's two goals put England into the World Cup Final for the first time.

Ramsey chose the same team to face West Germany in the final, denying Greaves the chance to crown his great career on soccer's ultimate stage. With hindsight, who can argue with Ramsey's selection? There must have been some, though, who thought he had got it wrong when Germany took the lead through Helmut Haller after 13 minutes.

A wall-to-wall crowd of 93000 packed Wembley. Prime Minister Harold Wilson rushed back from Washington to be at the match. The shopping centres of England were deserted as the nation tuned in. More than 400 million were watching on television around the world.

Ramsey never wavered in his faith. He had said that England would win the World Cup and his prophecy was back on course just six minutes after the Germans had taken the lead. Bobby Moore, fouled, quickly got to his feet to take the free kick. The England captain played the ball forward to his West Ham colleague Hurst, who headed the equaliser.

It was still 1-1, with just 13 minutes to go of an enthralling clash, when Ball swung over a corner. Hurst's shot cannoned off a defender into the air and dropped at the feet of Peters, who drove in his first goal of the tournament.

Suddenly the Germans swept forward looking for the equaliser, but it was late arriving. In the final minute of normal time Jack Charlton was penalised for a foul on Uwe Seeler on the edge of the box. The free kick was driven into a wall of defenders and the ball was deflected across the face of the goal where Wolfgang Weber stuck out his right foot and squeezed a last ditch shot between Wilson and Gordon Banks.

Ramsey told his exhausted players as they waited for extra time: 'You've won it once. Now go out and win it again.'

After ten minutes of extra time Nobby Stiles found Ball with a magnificent long pass. His cross from out on the flank fell perfectly for Hurst who drove a shot against the underside of the bar. The ball bounced down onto the line and was cleared upfield. The England players immediately claimed a goal. Herr Dienst, the Swiss referee, thought it was a goal. He consulted his Russian linesman and he thought so too. England now led 3-2.

Even today the controversy over that goal still bubbles. Television evidence is inconclusive. Even Hurst himself isn't sure. 'Roger Hunt's reaction at the time is critical,' explains Hurst. 'When my shot came down off the bar Roger was no more than a couple of yards from the ball. It would have been the easiest thing in the world for him to follow it in and push the ball into the net. If he thought there was any doubt that is what he would have done. He didn't. He put his arms in the air and immediately acclaimed the goal.'

Fortunately, Hurst put the issue beyond doubt. Moore, once again taking full advantage of the running power of his West Ham team mate, hit a long ball upfield. Hurst took the ball on his chest and ran towards goal. Only seconds of the match remained. The TV commentator Kenneth Wolstenholme was telling his armchair audience, 'Some people are on the pitch. They think it's all over.'

As he said that, Hurst released an unstoppable shot for his hat-trick. The crowd roared and Wolstenholme added: 'It is now.'

For Hurst it was only just the beginning. In the space of five months he had become England's World Cup winning hero and those three goals changed his life. He was just 24.

He played 49 times for England, scoring 24 goals, and at his peak was the most feared and famous striker in world football. After a career with West Ham, Stoke, West Bromwich Albion and Seattle Sounders he went into coaching, helped Greenwood, then England manager, with the national team and became manager of Chelsea for two years.

The Kings Deposed

England's hopes of keeping the World Cup in Mexico four years later seemed quite substantial. With additions to Ramsey's squad like Terry Cooper, Alan Mullery and Francis Lee they had, if anything, a more accomplished team. Ramsey, by now Sir Alf, had many qualities, but diplomacy was not one of them. He upset his Mexican hosts on numerous occasions and England became the team the Mexicans loved to hate. One local newspaper described Ramsey's side as 'a team of thieves and drunks.'

Bobby Moore's ridiculous persecution for theft in Colombia during England's World Cup warm-up tour had, of course, provided the media with plenty of sensational copy. Moore, accused of stealing a bracelet from the jewellery store in the lobby of the England team's hotel in Bogota, retained an impregnable calm throughout the farcical episode. 'Bob could have bought the entire shop,' remarked Mullery at the time.

Following diplomatic intervention the West Ham and England captain was 'bailed' to play in the World Cup, and he played superbly, while the perpetrators of the hoax were finally charged with conspiracy two years later.

England began their defence of the World Cup with a 1-0 win over Romania, but then lost 1-0 to Pele and the brilliant Brazilian team in Guadalajara. This match was a classic, probably the best played in the 1970 World Cup and produced the memorable diving save by Gordon Banks from Pele. Temperatures were near 100 but the resourceful Mullery marked Pele diligently enough until one pass from the legendary Brazilian, after 14 minutes of the second half, gave Jairzinho the chance to score the only goal.

Ramsey's much-changed team then struggled unconvincingly through a 1-0 victory over Czechoslovakia, Allan Clarke scoring from the penalty spot, to qualify for a quarter final against West Germany in Leon. Sadly, England lost Gordon Banks, acknowledged as the world's best goalkeeper, the day before the match when he was suddenly taken ill; the cause was believed to be a bottle of beer. Whatever, Chelsea's Peter Bonetti had to deputise. It was only his seventh game for England and it was to be his last.

England played spectacularly for an hour, Bobby Charlton shackling the youthful Franz Beckenbauer, and Mullery and Martin Peters providing the goals that looked certain to carry them to the semi final. Then Bonetti, diving late and awkwardly, missed Beckenbauer's half hit shot and the Germans were back in the game.

The arrival of substitute Jurgen Grabowski gave the Germans fresh impetus. He attacked Terry Cooper, exhausted by the killing heat and altitude. Ramsey, inexplicably, took off Charlton and Peters and sent on Norman Hunter and Colin Bell. Suddenly the whole shape of England's midfield changed and Beckenbauer, free of Charlton's attentions at last, began to dominate.

With eight minutes remaining Uwe Seeler, with a looping header over the stranded Bonetti, equalised. Unlike four years earlier, the Germans were stronger in extra time. Grabowski's mastery of Cooper gave Gerd Muller the chance to drive the last nail into England's coffin. Whatever the rights and wrongs of Ramsey's tactical decisions, the fact was that England led 2-0 with 20 minutes to go and lost. England's reign as world champions had ended.

Ramsey's distinguished reign as manager was to last another four years. It was basically the failure to beat Poland in the qualifying competition for the 1974 World Cup in West Germany that cost him his job.

The fact that the Germans had knocked England out of the 1972 European Championship at the quarter final stage hadn't helped Ramsey's position. Nor had his unwavering belief in a negative tactical system or loyalty to several of his older players.

Moore was 32 when England faced Poland in a vital World Cup qualifying tie in Katowice in June 1973. Ramsey left out his best attacking player, the graceful Mike Channon, and the Poles won 2-0, breaking down the England defence with the help of a goal given away by Moore with an uncharacteristic error.

The Poles needed only to draw at Wembley the following October to eliminate England and qualify for the finals. England needed goals and they came in abundance the month before when they beat Austria 7-0 in a warm-up match. It was misleading. Ramsey chose the same side against Poland but, thanks largely to the erratic brilliance of goalkeeper Jan Tomaszewski, England found no easy route to goal.

England dominated the match but their one aberration was ruthlessly punished by the Poles. The uncompromising Leeds defender Norman Hunter, deputising for Moore, rashly tried to dribble the ball past Lato instead of kicking it safely into touch. The Polish winger snatched the ball from Hunter and swept down the wing, crossing for Domarski whose right foot shot went through the legs of Hughes and past goalkeeper Shilton.

Poland held the lead for just six minutes. When England were awarded a penalty for a foul on Peters, Clarke scored from the spot. But England needed to win. Moore, on the substitute's bench, pleaded with Ramsey to send on another winger. Finally, with just two minutes remaining, Ramsey sent on Derby's Kevin Hector for his debut. He had one chance, heading goalward from a corner, but the ball was yet again cleared off the line. England were out of the World Cup. Six months later Ramsey was out of a job . . . sacked after 113 full internationals in which England suffered just 17 defeats.

The hand of God and Gazza's tears

It was to be another 12 years before England even came close to winning the World Cup. In Mexico in 1986, after a disastrous 1-0 defeat in their opening tie against Portugal in Monterrey, Gary Lineker finally discovered his scoring touch and propelled England into the quarter finals with five goals against Poland and Paraguay.

Here England faced the sullen Argentines, who still felt aggrieved at Rattin's treatment in the 1966 World Cup and who, of course, lost the

132

Falkland's War to Britain's task force four years earlier. The Argentines had in their ranks the greatest player in the world at the time – Diego Maradona.

It was he who gave Argentina the lead five minutes into the second half. It was no ordinary goal. Jumping with England goalkeeper Peter Shilton to reach a high cross, Maradona scooped the ball into the net with his hand. Shilton knew immediately that it was handball. Most people in the 114,000 crowd in the Azteca Stadium in Mexico City suspected it was handball. But the Tunisian referee Ali Ben Naceur thought differently. The goal, probably the grossest example of cheating I've seen in a World Cup tie, stood.

Within four minutes Maradona had scored again. This was no ordinary goal either. It was a goal of staggering brilliance. He dribbled at pace through most of the England defence, wriggled past Terry Butcher's lunging tackle, and shot low past Shilton.

Lineker scored – his sixth goal of the competition – but it was too little, too late. England were out and Maradona, describing his first goal, smirked: 'It was the hand of God.'

Four years later, in Italy in 1990, Robson's team went a stage further – to the semi-finals of the World Cup. Their form against the Republic of Ireland, Holland, Egypt, Belgium and Cameroon ranged from indifferent to quite brilliant and when they finally stumbled into the last four of the competition the team awaiting them was the old foe West Germany.

This was a breathtaking match, a footballing classic in an otherwise barren tournament. England had the vastly experienced Shilton in goal, playing his 124th international match, the athletic David Platt and the extrovert Paul Gascoigne in midfield and, of course, Lineker in attack.

But it was the Germans who took the lead in the 59th minute when a free kick from Andreas Brehme struck England defender Paul Parker and looped agonisingly over Shilton into the net.

Then, with ten minutes remaining, a cross from Parker, whipped in by the predatory Lineker, took the tie into extra time. A tense thirty minutes more . . . and still the game was level at 1-1. And so to penalties, a most cruel method for deciding drawn games.

Lineker, Beardsley and Platt all scored. So did Brehme, Matthaus and Riedl . . . 3-3 Stuart Pearce, the Nottingham Forest, left back and a dead ball specialist, ran forward to take England's fourth penalty. Alas, he drove it straight at the German goalkeeper Illgner. Thon scored his penalty to put the Germans 4-3 ahead.

Now everything depended on Chris Waddle. If he missed it was all over for England. He ran forward and powered his shot into the back of Turin's Stadio Della Alpi stadium.

Amid the German jubilation Matthaus found time to console Waddle. Gascoigne, who cried when he was cautioned and realised he would miss the final if England qualified, was now weeping floods of tears.

'In all my time in football I've never known a dressing room like it,' said Bobby Robson afterwards. 'Such desolation. It was like death. There was nothing you could do to bring it back.'

Giant-killers . . . old and new

The biggest surprise of the World Cup in Italy was the first round defeat of Argentina – later beaten in a bitterly-disputed final by West Germany – by the unknown yet highly talented team from Cameroon. The colourful Africans struck a significant blow for the underdogs of football who are beginning to find life increasingly difficult, especially at club level.

The football industry in Europe is geared increasingly for the benefit of the rich and famous. The rich clubs get richer, the poor clubs poorer. In such a context acts of notable giant-killing are all the more worthy and memorable.

The history of the FA Cup is littered with sensations – Third Division (North) Walsall's 2-0 demolition of Herbert Chapman's legendary Arsenal in 1933; Southern League Yeovil's 2-1 defeat of First Division Sunderland in round four in 1949 (81000 watched them lose 8-0 to Manchester United in round five); Fourth Division Colchester's 3-2 fifth round triumph in 1971 over Don Revie's mighty Leeds side; Southern League Hereford's 2-1 victory in extra time over Malcolm Macdonald and Newcastle United in a third round replay the following year.

Twenty years later the gap in class and resources between the bigs guns and the little guys of football is even larger – yet the impossible keeps happening.

In January 1991 Woking, a modest little club from the Vauxhall Opel League, went to the Hawthorns and beat West Bromwich Albion 4-2 in the third round of the FA Cup. An embarrassment for the club, and a costly defeat for the Albion manager Brian Talbot, who was sacked within three days.

A year later Arsenal, the defending League champions and one of the richest clubs in Europe, met Wrexham, the team with only one place to go – up. While Arsenal were winning the League title, Wrexham were finishing bottom of Division Four.

They met at the Racecourse Ground in round three. Arsenal's team cost millions. Wrexham's team cost peanuts and was made up of has-beens, players who had never been anything in the first place and one or two youngsters yet to discover which of the first two categories they would fall in to.

Wrexham won 2-1. 'Two things made it special,' recalled Wrexham's Mickey Thomas, at 38 the oldest player on the field. 'The first was that it was so unexpected and the second was that the opposition were so illustrious, almost on a different planet in footballing terms.'

134

The little Welsh club returned to planet earth in round four where they were beaten in a replay by First Division West Ham. The London club were then beaten in a replay by Sunderland, struggling near the foot of Division Two. In the sixth round Sunderland beat another First Division team, Chelsea, and then beat yet another from the big-time, Norwich, in the semi-final.

It was a series of sensational results for Sunderland with, potentially, the biggest sensation still before them. In the final at Wembley they faced mighty Liverpool, but this time they lost 2-0.

In 1973, as a Second Division club, Sunderland enjoyed a similar charge to the FA Cup Final where they produced one of the biggest surprises in Wembley history, beating the invincible Leeds United 1-0. Then, as now, the beauty of football is its enduring capacity to ridicule the prophets and surprise us all.

TENNIS

Peter Blackman

The Original Rebel

They once called him 'Nasty' but these days the label seems incongruous when he is playing with his young son or when he is chugging around the steep streets of Monte Carlo on his motor bike.

But the hard truth is that Ilie Nastase might well have lit the flarepath for others to follow, like John McEnroe and Jimmy Connors, because for more than a decade the Romanian's on-court behaviour was often outrageous.

In his mid-forties Nastase still has his trademarks: the shoulder-length, slightly greasy black hair, the swagger and that mischievous grin that made officials fume, umpires shout and spectators gasp.

When the bad old days are recalled, and there were many, the former lieutenant in the Romanian Army, who later became the first Eastern Bloc tennis millionaire, shows no sign of remorse.

'I have no regrets at all,' he said. 'When I look back I know that was the way I played my best tennis. That was the way I played the game. If someone didn't like it . . . well, that was too bad.'

Nastase is entitled to his opinion, but the question has to be asked: Did he, in fact, waste his brilliance? The Grand Slams are still the yardstick and he won only two when he was at his peak in the early '70s – the French and US Opens.

Even though Nastase was a constant thorn in the side for too many harassed, underpaid officials around the globe, there is no doubt that he was gifted and thoroughly deserves to be among the all-time top 10.

In a controversial career that started in the late '60s he won 2,076,761 US dollars in prizemoney, reached No 1 in the world on 23 August, 1973, and won 57 career titles, including those two precious Grand Slam titles.

But how will Nastase be remembered? The suspicion is that it will be for his temper, his showmanship and his teasing of opponents, rather than his shots that were often spun in pure gold.

Fines and suspensions made no difference to Nastase. And the location didn't matter, either. When he chose to throw a tantrum he threw it and more often than not he walked away as a winner with only a mild tap on the wrist from officialdom.

He blew up in '87 during a Davis Cup tie in Bucharest. He was banned. He performed at Wimbledon on 13 occasions and on several of them he caused both delight and despair. The worst was in '77 when he raged as he slipped to defeat against Bjorn Borg. Umpire Jeremy Shales described his performance as 'absolutely atrocious.'

In the 70's at the British Hard Court championships in Bournemouth he was thrown out after yet another disgraceful misdeed. And at the South of England championships he played Andres Gimeno and walked off court with match point against him.

Nastaste's problem was an abundance of talent. It was all so easy, so natural for him that acute boredom slowly overtook him. He also became restless, agitated. Then it was time for Mr Nasty to emerge.

Opponents were teased, made to look small. He talked to the crowd, amused them with a constant roll of wisecracks. Officials sweated and issued a stream of cautions. Sometimes they kicked him out of the tournament.

Apart from McEnroe, no one came close to having so much natural ability. The only thing he lacked was a good volley. If he had possessed that weapon he would probably have won Wimbledon three or four times.

But Nastase preferred to use cat and mouse tactics instead of going for a quick kill. Then, as he got older, a lack of nerve was his biggest and most constant enemy. Another problem was that he started to think about the game. For him, self analysis proved fatal.

Many tennis fans, though, regretted Nastase's retirement and the showmanship that was woven into his game. In retrospect, the wild man of Wimbledon somehow didn't seem that bad. In any case, he soon became a good guy, didn't he?

Nastase married twice and he later adopted one of Romania's 28,000 orphans. 'As long as I have breath and some money I can take care of another kid,' he said in May, 1990.

At that stage Nastase also announced: 'Since that wonderful event my life has completely changed and far from being a hell raiser I am a stay-at-home family man. It would be great if my son could follow in my footsteps.'

Three years earlier Nastase was playfully stating: 'Players today are not in love with the game. They are not dedicated to it. They are more devoted to making money to put them in good shape when they retire.'

That was more like the old Nasty.

Jubilation for a Jubilee – 1

That Friday in July, 1977, will be remembered forever by Virginia Wade and every tennis fan in Britain. It was the day she won Wimbledon in front of the Queen; and it was the day the ecstatic Centre Court crowd sang Land of Hope and Glory.

The clergyman's daughter played her part gloriously, reading from a script that seemed to be written in some long ago Hollywood word factory. And it still ranks as one of the most emotional moments in British sport.

That Wimbledon Final was made more dramatic than most because Wade and her Dutch opponent, Betty Stove, performed before Queen Elizabeth II at her Silver Jubilee – and it was also Wimbledon's Centenary.

The Queen, in the front row of the Royal Box, wore a pink check coat, while Stove just looked awesome. The girl from Rotterdam stood almost six feet tall and she bristled with power. Would Wade be blasted off court?

Wade, who grew up in South Africa and moved to England when she was 15, had turned professional eight years before that showdown with Stove and by then she was regarded as a British institution.

The headline writers fondly called her Ginny, while her politeness and elegance were a byword on the tennis circuit. So, too, was her talent that earned her more than one and a half million dollars in prizemoney.

On that momentous Friday an excited Wade woke up feeling stiff after a gruelling semi-final against Chris Evert. But those muscular pains were nothing compared with the unrelenting burden she carried on her shoulders.

Not only did every sports fan in the kingdom want her to win, they actually expected her to succeed. How could she lose a tennis match in front of the Queen and on her Silver Jubilee. It just wasn't part of the script.

Wade has often recalled the build up to that apparently joyous walk onto the Centre Court on Finals Day, starting with the drive to Wimbledon, then parking the car and walking to the restaurant in the All England Club grounds.

'I made myself eat,' remembered Virginia, 'because I knew I would be hungry while I played. In the end, though, I had to struggle my way through a small plate of salad.'

Outside, the crowds were gathering and an hour before the start the atmosphere was electric. 'I was nervous at the start,' she recalled. 'I forced myself to concentrate. It was close to meditation.'

Stove began as if she was sitting astride a rocket launcher. Though she was tall and well built, she seemed to glide fast and effortlessly around the Centre Court and soon she was 5-4 ahead and serving for the set.

She double faulted. Uproar. But after 37 minutes Stove took the first set 6-4. Virginia gritted her teeth in that familiar way, brushed back her hair and won the seventh, eighth and ninth games of the second set to level at 6-3.

Virginia was on a roll. This is how she described the decisive third set which she won 6-1 to become the Wimbledon champion in a pulsating 98 minutes. 'I was rolling nicely in the very first game of the third set. The adrenalin was flowing like mad.'

She added, 'I went into a trance. I don't know how, but the ball seemed to get bigger and bigger. I felt I could not miss it. Things moved so fast. I was soon 4-0 ahead and then I had won. I was the champion.'

Wade jumped excitedly into the air. She gave a two handed victory salute to the crowd; smiled towards the Royal Box. The crowd started to sing. There were tears, too, on that magical day on the Centre Court.

Wimbledon had seldom experienced anything like it. Because of the Royal flavour and the fact that it was a Centenary occasion, the clubhouse and Centre Court were repainted and special decorations were erected around the ground. On the opening day of the tournament 41 surviving singles champions paraded on the famous court.

In a funny kind of way Virginia was nervous again as she waited for the presentation ceremony. The jitters passed once the red carpet was rolled out and the Queen had made her way to the court. The pair talked, the crowd waited to unleash a thunderous cheer.

Ginny? She was engulfed in a massive emotional tide that threatened to overwhelm her. The nation expected her to win – and she had delivered magnificently. And what did the Queen say to her?

'The noise was so great that I honestly didn't know what she said to me.' said the breathless, excited champion.

Jubilation for a Jubilee – 2

It was 8.19pm on 4 November, 1978, when Pam Shriver served to Sue Baker at the Royal Albert Hall. Barker leaned back and unleashed a forehand bullet – and it went straight into the Wightman Cup history books.

Barker and her partner, Virginia Wade, beat Shriver and Chris Evert 6-0, 5-7, 6-4 in 53 minutes to give Britain a sensational 4-3 victory over the United States.

Within seconds the entire British team, decked out in red, white and blue and waving large and small Unions Jacks, leapt from their seats to cheer a victory that seemed impossible three days earlier.

But it was true. Britain, by winning that decisive doubles, had brought the Wightman Cup back to this country for only the 10th time in 50 matches. No wonder some members of the US team were left shattered – and crying!

What made the success more satisfying for the British team was that it was the golden jubilee of Mrs Hazel Hotchkiss Wighman's elegant cup; and it was Sue Mappin's last major international match before retiring to become the LTA's first professional women's team manager.

The Americans included in their line up the 15-year-old Tracy Austin (second singles) and the 16-year-old Shriver (third singles) with both of them playing in the doubles. Virginia Wade was the British captain, while Roger Taylor was the coach.

Evert, with an unblemished Wightman Cup record, started with a 6-2, 6-1 win over Barker. Then Michele Tyler chased everything to gain a superb 5-7, 6-2, 6-3 win over Shriver. Then Wade gave the crowd a roller coaster ride.

Three weeks earlier in Phoenix Wade had lost to Austin, but she was expected to win the Cup match. Austin, though, won the first set, then recovered from 1-4 to 4-5 down in the second. Then Wade answered the threat to play magnificently, winning 3-6, 7-5, 6-3.

Britain were 2-1 ahead, but the US drew level with Billie Jean King and Austin defeating Mappin and Anne Hobbs 6-2, 4-6, 6-2. The Americans swept ahead when Evert crunched Wade 6-0, 6-1 with the British girl winning the ninth game.

The first set lasted 20 minutes as Evert mesmerised Wade and the crowd with tennis of the highest quality. Then it was Barker's turn and she knew that defeat would hand the trophy to the Americans.

Fortunately for Britain, the fair haired Barker is a fighter. With her serve in perfect shape and that famous forehand at full throttle she beat Austin over three marvellous sets. Barker won 6-3, 3-6, 6-0. All square. The doubles would decide it.

When it was over and with the British camp celebrating with numerous glasses of champagne the battling Barker tried to describe how she felt. 'It is the greatest moment of my life,' she said.

'In the deciding doubles Virginia and I kept looking at each other and saying 'We've got to win.' We had total communication and we knew that Pam and Chris didn't get on all that well. They were not working as a team as we were.'

BBC TV's screens went blank at a critical moment in the match with a Scottish opera suddenly replacing the tennis. 'We had to keep to the programme schedule – anyway, you can't keep 'em happy for ever,' explained a TV official.

Wade, like Barker, was overjoyed at the success. 'I gave so much,' she said. 'I am exhausted. But I have not felt so elated since I won Wimbledon.' Tyler admitted, 'I went to a champagne reception and I got a little bit drunk.'

The Americans left for a sobering journey back across the Atlantic. It was an unexpected British success and maybe it was due, in part, to a confusing sequence of selection decisions by the US selectors.

For instance, many people believed that JoAnne Russell should have played, but would she have made that much difference or matched the spirit of the entire British team?

But 24 hours after the victory no one worried about those issues. The Americans were beaten fair and square during three days in November when London enjoyed some late, late summer warmth – outside and inside the Royal Albert Hall.

Wimbledon's Marathon Match

Though Richard 'Pancho' Gonzales was undoubtedly the best player in the world for most of the 1950s, he might be remembered most for a dramatic match at Wimbledon that lasted an epic five hours and 12 minutes.

The often angry Gonzales seemed to have saved one last great match for the Wimbledon crowd in 1969 – and it was a testimony to his fitness and determination that he was able to last so long at 41 years of age.

His opponent in the first round match was the stylish Charlie Pasarell, who was 16 years younger than the true blooded Mexican who was born on 9 May, 1928, in California.

Gonzales was a greying grandfather. He was tall, swarthy and handsome and he had a foul temper which often exploded on court. But he was a great player who was very close to the end of his career.

One of seven children, he was the son of a Mexican house painter and interior decorator and he swiftly appreciated that his aptitude for sport, his physique and good looks might provide the entry into a better life.

He was right. In his late teens and in his first serious tournament he was wearing scuffed tennis shoes that cost 4s 6d and an old sweat shirt. He was already close to six foot tall and he was the possessor of a mighty serve.

From the start Gonzales was a dramatic and spectacular competitor. He turned professional in '49 after winning the US singles the previous year and also taking the US Clay court title, the US indoor and also winning the doubles in Paris and at Wimbledon.

From then on he played his wonderful tennis away from the top stadiums of the game until, at last, open competition was allowed. By then he was 40 – and the masses had, by and large, missed a great talent.

During his glamorous pro days Gonzales, who was now 6ft 3 in tall and regularly firing his serve at 112mph, was the leader of the pack in Jack Kramer's circus of 16 players that travelled the world in search of work.

They played in big cities and hick towns. Slowly the tempermental Gonzales grew tired of the constant travel. When he was 33 he retired. 'I am tired of all the moving around and living out of a suitcase,' he said.

The good looking, cocky Gonzales made numerous comebacks and when he returned to the tennis court he licked the opposition out of sight. As the domination persisted, the great Aussie Ken Rosewall sighed, 'He is hell on two feet to play.'

No-one argued with that judgement and even in those wild days Gonzales was perfecting the mannerisms that were to dominate the TV screens in that sensational match with Pasarell that became the longest singles seen at Wimbledon.

The mannerisms ranged from a John McEnroe pick at the right shoulder of his sweat-stained shirt, the wipe of sweat from his forehead with his left or right index finger and the sweep of a hand through his mass of hair.

Throughout that performance Gonzales would smile when he was winning and growl when he was fighting for his tennis life. When he scowled opponents sensed danger, while the crowd anticipated excitement.

And so to the match that took Gonzales and Pasarell into the record books and the crowd in a maze of sporting intrigue. It began on Tuesday evening with the opening set equalling the longest played singles at the All England Club.

Pancho went into the match with a new, newspaper-inspired nickname. They called him The Old Fox and he was certainly full of stealth – a quality that suited a man who was the oldest tournament pro in the business.

The match was stopped in uproar after two sets when Gonzales suddenly announced that he could not see in the dark. He was jeered off court after the bad light row. 'Off, off,' yelled the crowd, while Gonzales asked for the floodlights to be turned on.

'It is ridiculous,' he stormed. 'I don't think I should have been made to play in the dark.' The referee, Captain Mike Gibson, said, 'The players can't really appeal against the light. It is up to me to decide when it is too dark to play.'

On Wednesday play resumed in front of 14,000 fans. In the end Gonzales and Pasarell played 112 games, used 13 sets of balls and smashed the longest singles match record previously held by Jaroslav Drobny and Budge Patty in '53.

'Towards the end I was getting cramp on the inside of my thigh,' said Gonzales. 'Suddenly Pasarell seemed nervous and tense, while I felt all right. It was my greatest comeback ever.'

Because of the tie break system it will not happen again. For the record Pancho, or should it be The Old Fox, won 22-24, 1-6, 16-14, 6-3, 11-9. It was 312 minutes of pure magic.

The Borg Enigma

On a warm, early summer afternoon in '91 at the Monte Carlo Country Club a pale, tense Bjorn Borg was sent tumbling to defeat in a highly publicised comeback match.

It does not matter who beat him, but what is significant is that Borg totally misunderstood how fast and how totally the game had changed since his retirement in '83 at the ridiculously young age of 27.

The days of wooden rackets and slow balls had gone. Borg chose to come back when the robots were in command: super fit players wielding wide bodied, high-tech rackets that boomed serves at well over 135mph.

That day in Monte Carlo was most unfortunate. A huge crowd turned up to watch a player who will always rank alongside the all-time greats and they went away shaking their heads in disbelief at what they had witnessed.

Borg stepped from a time warp. Once again he wore a head band that kept back his fair hair and once again he wore that famous white shirt with thin vertical lines that were spaced one inch apart. A dark belt, two sweat bands plus white socks and shoes completed his outfit.

The Swede also had two days' beard on his chin and though he looked immaculate he could not find the magical tennis touch that was so suddenly withdrawn from public gaze all those years ago.

Because Borg had not maintained his punishing training and practice schedules he looked slow. And because a long absence from the game had left him riddled with rust, he played everything from the baseline.

Within 20 minutes the crowd in Monte Carlo had the feeling that the occasion might, in fact, turn out to be a colossal embarrassment to him, his backers and friends, tournament officials and his fans.

When the dust had settled after that comeback flop Borg reappeared briefly at the Italian Open in Rome. Not to play, but to explain that he would be back and, the next time, he would probably be using up to date equipment.

And, when he was pressed about speculation that his tennis-made fortune had gone and that was the reason behind his comeback, he replied, 'It is all rubbish. I have no financial problems at all.'

Even now, after all those years, it seems that Borg made a mistake when he walked away from the sport. His supporters, though, insisted that he had done enough, that he had set standards between '74 and '81 that may never be bettered.

When he did go he said, 'Yes, I will miss the people, the atmosphere and the cheering. But I am glad that when I wake up in the morning I won't have to go out and practice for five to eight hours.'

But Borg had earned 3,609,896 US dollars in prize money and an awful lot more from endorsements that ranged from rackets, shoes, balls, cars, cereals, clothes, drinks, posters, puzzles to calendars, dolls headbands and teaching guides.

It has been estimated that Borg earned more than 10m dollars off the tennis court since winning the junior Wimbledon title in '72. He owned a sports boutique and he once lived on his own island retreat.

At the height of his powers Borg was hero worshipped wherever he went, setting fashion styles and creating an image that set him apart. And he was also a fantastic win machine.

Borg won 62 titles in his career. He won the Wimbledon title five times in a row and the French Open crown on six occasions. He was also the runner-up four times at the US Open. That is truly an amazing record.

He appeared in dozens of matches that have since gone down in tennis folklore. In '78 he became the first man since Fred Perry to win three straight Wimbledon singles titles, and the first man since Rod Laver in '62 to win the Italian, French and Wimbledon all in the same year.

Borg was one of the coolest match players the game has ever known. Opponents were left bewildered by his two handed backhand, his fierce topspin, powerful serve and mobility. And, of course, his inner strength.

The Swede won a record 41 matches in a row before John McEnroe beat him in the '81 Final at Wimbledon. The great American leftie robbed him of a record six titles in a classic match that is still being talked about.

From that moment Borg seemed to lose interest. He was clearly burnt out and he could no longer make a total commitment to the game. He turned to other interests, remarried and became reclusive.

Bjorn Borg started the tennis revolution in Sweden which later produced Mats Wilander and Stefan Edberg. But he will be remembered most as a truly great champion.

Chris and Jimmy – two decades at the top.

In '74, when they were both young at heart, Jimmy Connors and Chris Evert won their first Wimbledon titles to launch them to worldwide fame and considerable fortunes.

Their careers, until Evert retired to have her first baby, have more or less been in tandem, satisfying a huge American public who like their idols to be much larger than life.

Connors beat the veteran Ken Rosewall to win his first Wimbledon title and 18 years later he is still blasting away and threatening to continue until he wins just one more title.

Evert, who was once Connors' girlfriend, demolished the Russian Olga Morozova to land her Wimbledon crown and when she walked into the sporting sunset in the autumn of '89 with her husband, Olympic downhill skier Andy Mill, her fans were devastated.

Connors thought his 20 year career was over when he had a wrist operation two years ago, but he recovered to captivate a nation when he reached the semi finals of the US Open.

The 39-year-old left hander has had a magnificent career and it would not have spanned two decades if he had not taken care of himself. Only in the past few years have opponents found him tiring after a three or four hour match.

Connors was the street fighter – a snarling, win-at-all-costs battler who had countless brushes with officialdom, but it was his epic battles with Ilie Nastase, Bjorn Borg and John McEnroe that will be remembered.

'I have seen them come and I have seen them go,' recalled the man they call Jimbo. 'I am just so grateful that I was around and playing my best tennis when they were on the other side of the net.'

'I cannot honestly say I enjoyed the moment when they beat me, but I sure did enjoy beating them. They were great players and I guess we brought the best out of each other. For me, they were unforgettable times.'

Connors was ranked longer in consecutive weeks at No 1 than anyone in the history of the ATP computer – 159 weeks. He also won every major championship except the French Open, although he was a semi-finalist on four occasions.

He may hold countless records, but the fact is that his blood and guts approach was the key to his lasting popularity. The crowds worldwide loved his style. They could relate to his backs-to-the-wall situations.

Connors, who lives with his wife and family in California, has earned almost 9m dollars in prizemoney and much more from endorsements, while his future seems assured as a tennis analyst for American TV.

Evert is a tennis legend, too. Her double-fisted backhand not only launched a million girls into tennis it also flattened hundreds of opponents who ranged from champions to also-rans. It was like clockwork: a precision stroke that hardly ever faltered. Her approach never changed. She had a superb figure (some say her shapely legs were the best), she was always beautifully dressed and her conduct and manners on court were perfect.

Way back Evert was called The Ice Maiden. Off court she enjoyed a joke and mixed easily with the other players and her vast army of fans. But on court she became decidely chilly. The only thing on her mind was winning.

The late Ted Tinling, the legendary tennis dressmaker and expert on women's tennis, sat courtside at most of Evert's matches and when she retired he spoke for everyone when he said, 'She gave America what America wanted. She is totally American, the apple pie girl, if you like. She was the pathfinder, the one who set the standards and then watched everyone follow.'

Evert, like Connors, won almost 9m dollars in prizemoney and she also added to that fortune with a long list of top quality endorsements. But once her future husband, Andy Mill, came into view the tennis appetite faded.

She won at least one Grand Slam title in 13 consecutive years and a record 157 titles which was recently passed by her long term friend, nine-times Wimbledon champion, Martina Navratilova.

Chris Evert called it a day at the '89 US Open when the former No 1 was ranked fourth in the world. 'This is it,' she said. 'No more maybes, no more depends upons and no more probables.'

She kept her word.

The Nearly Man

It seemed so unfair. After a long and brilliant career Ken Rosewall was finally packing away his tennis rackets and calling it a day. And, regrettably, it mean that he would never win the Wimbledon singles title.

Over a quarter of a century the slighly-built Aussie, who was nicknamed 'Muscles' by all his other play-mates, had performed with a graceful, economical style that delighted the connoisseurs.

Rosewall was the champion at the Australian, French and US Opens, but he walked away empty handed from four Wimbledon Finals – against Jaroslav Drobny, Lew Hoad, John Newcombe and lastly Jimmy Connors in '74.

The final throw of the dice at Wimbledon ended in disaster when a young, brash Connors overwhelmed him 6-1, 6-1, 6-4 in an embarrassing 93 minutes.

But for so many years, in wind, rain or sunshine, the British public rooted for Rosewall. They felt he should be rewarded for a wonderful career. And the only reward worth mentioning was the Wimbledon singles title.

Rosewall, who was winning local tournaments in Sydney when he was eight years old, began serious work as a Hopman prodigy and it was not until '79 that he retired from Grand Prix tennis.

He turned professional in '57 and he took over the leadership of the professional circuit from Richard 'Pancho' Gonzales until Rod Laver's arrival in '63. Five years later he won his first open tournament at Bournemouth.

When fellow Aussie Newcombe beat him over five memorable sets in the '70s Final he, too, felt some pity. He put it this way, 'It was quite lonely for me out there on the Centre Court. Just about everyone wanted Ken to win that singles crown.

'I would have supported that if only I wasn't his opponent. Ken had always been one of my heroes and here I was having to do my best to stop him getting the one major title that had always eluded him.

'We were the perfect contrast – Ken all deftness and artistry, while I was concentrating on power and mobility. I reckon I played the best fifth set of my life to finish the winner. I thought it would be his last appearance in a Wimbledon final.'

The crowd thought that way, too. They gave him a tremendous ovation at the end of the match against Newcombe – and yet, four years later he was again savouring that walk to the Centre Court to face the rising Connors.

'Muscles' really did have a distinguished career and years after the Connors Final he explained his feelings regarding Wimbledon. There was no regret, no permanent blues.

'People often stop me to say that I deserved to win Wimbledon because of the way I had played over the years. Well, in sport things don't quite work out like that. I had my chances, you know.

'I lost to Drobny because of my inexperience, while Newcombe had the strength. Jimmy Connors made the most of the 19 year gap between us. He was much too strong, though I surprised myself and others by reaching the Final.'

That Connors match will be remembered for the way in which the American punished Rosewell's medium paced serve. Long before he passed the net Connors was in position – and swiping massive winners.

Rosewall was 5ft 7in and he weighed around 10st. David Gray, writing in The Guardian newspaper, described him thus, 'He was a ghost with a rapier in his backhand.'

There is no doubt that Rosewall was the best of the old style pros . . . a player with easy, fluent shots, grace and speed of movement. In a way Rosewall agreed with those sentiments.

But 'Muscles' summed himself up this way, 'Nature gave me a great deal and I am grateful.' He never did say, though, whether he would have preferred, say, Lew Hoad's thunder and lightning.

146

The Young Turks

When the stony-faced Ivan Lendl and the ultra-serious Martina Navratilova ruled hardly anyone else got a look in at the very summit of the world rankings.

Then along came Stefan Edberg and Steffi Graf, only to be replaced by Jim Courier and Monica Seles. Somewhere down among the young pretenders is someone who will seriously menace their status.

That is the beauty of professional tennis. The men's game, in particular, is brimful of talented young players eager to dedicate their lives to becoming the best. And it does take dedication.

Tony Pickard, the long time coach of former world No 1 and twice Wimbledon champion Edberg, is very precise about what it takes to become the leader of the pack. 'To get there means a player must make some serious sacrifices,' he said.

'Assuming the player has all the normal attributes like talent, even a gift, physical and mental strength and belief in himself, he must also be totally single minded. It is demanding a lot of a young man.'

Edberg may have been upset at losing ground, but he was highly respectful of Courier's achievement. 'He is a very hard worker,' he said. 'He is a tough competitor and at the moment everything is running for him.

'He is also having all the luck and to beat him you have to play some really good tennis and the reason is that he has improved a lot. He plays the big points much better than he used to.'

Then Edberg got to the guts of the matter in a quick run-down of his main rivals. 'Pete Sampras is playing very well and you can never forget about him,' he said. 'Then you have a guy like Wimbledon champion Michael Stich, but he is not really up there at the moment.

'Guy Forget? You have to watch out for him at any tournament. Boris Becker needs to get back to work again, but he is always going to be a danger. It is not just Courier to worry about. There are a lot of guys out there.'

Everyone who follows the pro tour agrees, particularly when you glance down the rankings. What about the tall, willowy Goran Ivanisevic, who is building a reputation as the master of the ace serve?

Close behind him are the totally dedicated Petr Korda, David Wheaton, Andre Agassi, Michael Chang, and Richard Krajicek – and that is nowhere near the end of the young pretenders.

The women's game is rich in eager young talent and at the moment it is dominated by the incredible 18-year-old Seles who, by January '92, had won 21 titles and almost five million dollars. But '91 was a bumper year.

The grunting left-hander from Novi Sad, Yugoslavia, won three Grand Slams, excluding Wimbledon, and she reached the final of all 16 tournaments where she competed. To say that she was invincible is an understatement.

But to get to the pinnacle of her profession Seles has been one-tracked, even to the point where at one tournament she suddenly admitted that she does not have the time to smell the roses anymore.

Edberg was told about that and he replied, 'If you want to stay up there there is only one way of doing it and that's playing as many matches as you can and concentrating on each tournament – and working as hard as you have ever done before.'

He then warned, 'The moment you don't work as hard you will sooner or later start to fail. It would be only a matter of time. I know what it takes to stay up there. It is all hard work.'

Seles is not afraid of hard graft and neither is the pack behind her. That includes Graf, who hit a rough patch and, of course, Navratilova who is in the twilight of her distinguished career.

Gabriela Sabatini, Mary Joe Fernandez and Arantxa Sanchez Vicario will remain threats, but poised ready to pounce are two youngsters who have not yet hit the peaks – Jennifer Capriati and Anke Huber.

Capriati has only been a pro since March, '90, but in that time she has made a fortune, becoming a media favourite and already she has won a string of important matches against well established opponents.

Just how seriously the Florida-based kid and her family take the mission to be a champion is proved by the appointment in '91 of coach Pavil Slozil who shared so much success with Graf.

Huber, the 5ft 8in German, has rocketed up the rankings and though at first she did not mind being branded the new Graf she is now fashioning a career of her own. Most experts believe she will soon be a major force.

There are enough young pretenders around to guarantee that the top dogs will sleep uneasily at night.

The Bad Boy

The wonder is that John McEnroe, who has consistently failed to ditch his Superbrat image, has had enough time over the past 16 years to actually play such magnificent tennis.

So many times at so many different locations the left-handed American has infuriated himself, officialdom and his fans with his dire on-court conduct that was more suited to a mad house.

Mad, that is, in the sense that too often there seemed no logic behind the outbursts which, over the years have cost McEnroe countless fines and suspensions.

But after accepting the punishment and then publicly promising to stay on the straight and narrow he has predictably tumbled swiftly back into trouble, leaving him to mutter black oaths at the game in general.

Though Ilie Nastase might well have started the bad times McEnroe stands supreme as the game's bad boy. Almost two generations of young tennis fans have grown up with McEnroe's zany blast ringing in their ears.

McEnroe's angry bleatings have embraced every level of competition from the Davis Cup, the Grand Slams, regular tournaments and even exhibition events. And he has exploded with or without the TV cameras in attendance.

The worst three instances, in my opinion, were in the Davis Cup Final against Sweden in Gothenburg, the Masters at Madison Square Garden and at the Australian Open in Melbourne.

The fact is that there have been so many tiffs over the years that most are difficult to recall; and who, one might ask, makes a point of remembering a highly disagreeable situation on purpose?

In the US v Sweden tie McEnroe screamed abuse at officials and his language was so bad that he should have been permanently banned from the competition. But he survived to argue on another day.

Down Under two years ago at the magnificent Flinders Park, McEnroe was thrown out of the Grand Slam event midway through his match with Mikael Pernfors – and that was the right decision.

McEnroe ranted and raved in front of the British umpire Gerry Armstrong and finally the supervisor, Ken Farrar, had no option but to send McEnroe on that long, embarrassing walk to the locker room.

It was one of the few occasions when officials actually acted in perfect unison. They gave McEnroe every chance, but they could not stop his ravings. They tried to reason, they failed. So he had to go and the crowd didn't seem to mind at all.

Superbrat was full of remorse and it has to be said that since then his outbursts have been fewer as he has made a conscious effort to tone down the darker side of his act. 'I can do no more than try,' he said.

What bugs McEnroe most, though, is that even though he is the proud father of three young children he still allows himself to be dragged into situations that clearly embarrass the entire family unit.

He knows he would be on cloud nine if, when he finally calls it a day, he knew for absolute certainty that all his wife, kids and fans would remember about him at sport was his superlative tennis gifts.

The hard, galling fact about McEnroe is that he is acknowledged by all his fellow professionals as being a rock solid certainty for any all-time greats list. And the man would be damn close to the top three.

In the early '80s he was the world No 1, winning tournaments galore and getting himself involved in classic matches with his friends, Bjorn Borg and Jimmy Connors, during that truly golden time for the game.

Though McEnroe is now in his 30s he is still winning consistently, although he moans constantly about the hi-tech rackets, faster balls and the new breed of he-man he has to face on a daily basis.

McEnroe has earned almost 12m dollars in prizemoney, won almost 80 titles and seven Grand Slams, the last of them was in '84 when he was beating the hell out of everyone – and arguing, of course.

But these days he is more concerned with beating the big hitters rather than whether or not he should retire. The veteran trouble-shooter said, 'I'll know when to go and it will probably be when I don't want to work at it on the practice court any more.'

But the subject is Superbrat and on that well worn issue he commented, 'I've made mistakes over the years and I have learned from them, whatever anyone else thinks. Sometimes officials are right, sometimes they were wrong.

'But at the end of the day I am proud at what I have achieved. And when people actually get around to talking about my tennis and my titles they might state that I could play a bit.'

Agreed.

Player Power

By far the most bizarre and significant meeting held in professional tennis occurred in a dusty car park in '88 during the US Open at Flushing Meadow.

It was the afternoon in which the players, through one or two specially selected administrators, made it plain they they were going to run the men's multi million dollar game.

The Association of Tennis Professionals stated once again that they were unhappy at the way the game was being administered by the Men's Tennis Council and they later produced a document to support their argument. Though time had tended to soften the edges, there is no doubt that the word Revolt would not have seemed too hysterical in those dark, noisy days when the sport seemed in danger of collapse.

The document was sub-titled 'A Critique of the Opportunities and Problems Facing Men's Professional Tennis' and it initially caused a huge stink and then outright alarm. The ATP were head-hunting. They wished to remove the three members from the International Tennis Federation, the sport's ruling body, on the Council's nine-man voting panel and to reduce the Federation to non-voting observer status.

In their place would be two 'independent businessmen' with the third ITF voting place going to ATP and boosting its total to four. When this was rejected that famous car park meeting took place.

It was headed by ATP's chief executive Hamilton Jordan. The players later claimed the meeting was held in the car park because officials at the US Open had refused them a room in the stadium.

Jordan said that, 'Our guys are burned out and frustrated. Something is wrong with the sport,' while other ATP officials insisted that they had no wish to take over the four Grand Slams. 'They are the pillars of the sport,' they chorused.

Words like 'solidarity' and 'united' were constantly in the locker room air, while the MTC administrator Marshall Happer held a last ditch meeting in New York, while several leading players openly wore T-shirts with the new ATP logo on them.

Happer was desperately trying to salvage an organisation that he called the 'Institution of our sport' – adding, 'Up to now our tennis family has worked.' He then revealed a new MTC format for 1990 suggesting a restructuring of the MTC to give the players 50 per cent representation. Offering also a programme of some 79 tournaments to include 13 one week World Series events and another 13 Super Series he said:

'The top players ought to like this format. It is the best they have ever seen.' He also put forward a long list of other proposals. Twenty four hours later Jordan held a meeting and said the existing system was 'badly flawed.'

He added, 'The MTC would not have offered any of these changes if they had not been under pressure. They have come a long way to try and accommodate us, but our preference is to have our own tour. We are not just chasing dollars. We are going to pay attention to tournaments that have a tradition in the history of tennis.'

The follow up was that tournaments were invited to apply for specific weeks on the calendar – leaving a circuit built around the existing Grand Slam events and the Davis Cup weeks.

The dust has, of course, almost settled on that momentous phase in professional tennis, but one last big shot was fired by the men who run the Grand Slams in Australia, Paris, Wimbledon and New York.

Some people insist that the Slammers wanted some sort of revenge for the mayhem that the ATP and their players had caused. So they plonked a 6m dollar tournament called the Grand Slam Cup at the end of the season.

It has already secured top player interest, worldwide TV and media coverage and there is every chance that the women's tour will be represented in the future – a decision that will cause world No 1 Monica Seles to bleat again about equal pay.

Meanwhile, the ATP tour seems watertight. There are 81 events in 29 countries on six continents. The players scrap for more 40m dollars and three players are on the board. ATP states 'The tour is run by those directly concerned with the presentation of the sport, the players and the tournament directors.'

And the launch pad was that meeting in a New York car park.

OTHER SPORTS

Mick Dennis

The Sultan of Swat

Today, when the politically correct make us all aware of our use of language, we would have to call him 'differently sized', but in America between the two World Wars they did not hesitate to call him a giant.

Babe Ruth was a mountainous man, or rather, he seemed to be. He was six feet tall, shorter than many contemporary players, but had a gargantuan presence, emphasised by a barrel chest and a huge head. Although his weight varied, even at the peak of his powers he seldom weighed in at less than 15 stones. Sometimes he was considerably heavier. It is said that he once nearly died from over-eating and it is certainly true that he was a glutton, perhaps because as a young child he frequently went hungry.

His jungle of dark brown, almost black hair was never quite under control, so that unruly curls peeked out of the back of his Yankees' baseball cap or the cloth, working man's cap that he favoured when off duty. His heavy features were ill-defined and weather-beaten. His nose was flat. He had piggy eyes. His big face was weighed down by jowls. He was, in truth, plug ugly.

In the 1992 film about his life, Babe was played by John Goodman, who is famously fat and best known for playing Roseanne Barr's large, blue-collar, television husband. Even Goodman's friends do not accuse him of being handsome.

And as well as looking rough-hewn, Babe Ruth spoke roughly as well. He used profanities which seem mild now and which were commonplace on the streets of his early boyhood but which often shocked the polite society which which he mixed in later years.

But if Babe did not have the frame, face or manners of a classic sporting hero, there can be no doubt that he was a giant metaphorically as well as physically.

The British cannot really begin to appreciate his sporting stature, because he carved his career in baseball, a sport we do not play, watch or understand. But we do know that three baseball players stand head and shoulders above the rest in folklore and fact: Joe Di Maggio, Mickey Mantle and Babe Ruth. And many of those who love baseball insist that the Babe was the biggest of them all; that he was a sporting colossus to rank alongside Muhammad Ali, W. G. Grace, Pele, Jack Nicklaus or Jesse Owens.

And, as with many such giants, it is difficult to separate truth from myth or legend.

Take, for instance, the story of Johnny Sylvester. The legend, perpetuated in most of the many films about Babe Ruth, was that when Johnny was about 11 year old he was kicked on the head by a horse and became critically ill. As he lay in hospital expecting to die, he whispered, 'Gee, I wish I could see Babe Ruth hit one more home run before I go.'

Newspapers reported the 'dying wish' story and Babe visited the hospital, taking with him a signed baseball bat and promising to hit a homer for Johnny in the Worlds Series.

The newspapers reported that promise as well, and so the nation listened on radio as Babe strode to the plate for the New York Yankees against the St Louis Cardinals. Sure enough, Babe hit one ball into the stand and then two more over the fence 'for the little sick kid'.

And Johnny got better.

That, at any rate, is the legend. Unfortunately, the facts are a little more prosaic. Johnny Sylvester is not thought to have been very ill at all, and Babe may not have been motivated by anything more altruistic than the desire to guide the Yankees to victory. In fact the Yankees lost the series.

But perhaps it doesn't matter whether the Johnny Sylvester story is entirely true. What matters is that people thought it extremely likely that an ailing youngster would dream of seeing a Babe Ruth homer. People also thought it completely probable that Babe would be able to respond by delivering homers to order and that the child would recover. People thought, in short, that Babe Ruth could perform miracles.

What is certain is that when Johnny Sylvester died, aged 74 in 1990, the New York Daily News carried his obituary under the headline: 'Now He's With Babe.'

There are other elements of the legend which may or may not be true. For instance, Did Babe really greet a startled George VI by saying: "Hiya King"?

What we do know is that Babe Ruth was born George Herman Gerhardt, that his early years were spent in poverty in Baltimore, that later he would never talk about his parents and that at the age of six he found himself in a Roman Catholic institution which was a cross between an orphanage and a correction school. It was there that his baseball potential was first spotted. He had prodigious strength which he allied to remarkable timing. The priests at the orphanage recommended him to the local side. The journey which was to take Babe to Boston, on to the Yankees, fame and a massive fortune had started.

He was paid a total of £150 for his first season in the big time in 1914 when he was 19, but the big money was not long coming. His transfer from Boston Red Sox to the New York Yankees cost a remarkable £25000 and by 1931 he was on between £16000 and £20000 a year. And, that, remember was at a time when British football stars were on £8-a-week.

In his 20 years at the top, Babe earned a million dollars in wages alone, and there was money as well from a ghosted, syndicated newspaper column and from Babe Ruth baseball bats, balls and gloves. There was even a Babe Ruth candy bar, which he enjoyed eating as well as advertising.

Babe was a slugger. He could hit the ball huge distances, and he become known as The Sultan of Swat. When he tried his hand at cricket on a visit to London, he smashed the bowlers out of the ground and broke at least one bat. His baseball achievements do not mean a lot to people not steeped in the game's lore, but he hit 50 home runs in two consecutive seasons, and, at the time of writing, nobody has managed that feat since.

But it was his capacity for producing miracles to order which filled his fans with awe.

He did it one last time in the final world series in which he appeared. It was 1932, and the Yankees were facing the Chicago Cubs in a hostile Chicago stadium. When Babe came out to bat, the Chicago fans whistled and booed, and when he swung and missed at the first pitch, they jeered and cheered. Babe raised one finger, as if to say, 'I've only missed the first one.' The crowd hated that and, when Babe swung and missed a second time, the home crowd exploded into hoots of derision. Babe extended his forefinger and pointed to the flagpole at the far side of the stadium, indicating that was where he intended to hit the next delivery. It was an imperious gesture, and the crowd booed and booed at his arrogance.

But, astonishingly, Babe did indeed smash the third ball out of the ground over the flagpole.

When Babe Ruth died of cancer at the age of 53, America mourned. More than 100000 filed past his coffin as it lay in state at the Yankee stadium and a Requiem Mass at St Patrick's Cathedral brought New York almost to a standstill. A giant had died.

The Golden Reign of Kaiser Franz

Franz Klammer reached the top by going downhill . . . extremely quickly. It made him a millionaire by his late-20s, showering him with such riches that the facade of Olympic amateurism was irretrievably damaged.

One of his less endearing traits was that he wanted to be much richer. Other skiers with smaller talents were also making fortunes and it rankled with Klammer that the Austrian skiing federation adhered to amateurism rules more closely than some other European nations. He had to turn away many of the sponsors, advertisers and skiing equipment manufacturers who queued up to make him even wealthier.

But Klammer did not do too badly for a farmer's boy and few would argue that he did not deserve his riches. Hurtling down mountainsides at 90 mph takes a certain type of bravery, and Klammer did it better than anybody, driving himself on to the limit to find a quicker line, a faster route to the finish. He called it 'skiing on the edge of my courage.'

That courage earned him a secure place in the history of sport and made him a truly great champion. Other skiers, notably Jean-Claude Killy, might claim to have had better all-round ability and perhaps more grace, but Klammer was fast; extremely fast. And in one gloriously memorable 12 months, he was faster than anyone. In 1975 he won eight out of nine World Cup downhill events, six of them in succession. Then, in 1976, he took the Olympic Gold Medal in Innsbruck with a breathtaking, scintillating performance in which he teetered close to crashing half-a-dozen times.

As he clutched the medal, Klammer told reporters, 'I've got everything now. I don't want anything else.' But he did want more, and, despite 'retiring' several times, he skied on for more than nine years. In the end he was losing more often than winning, but he usually lost with a smile and won as many friends and admirers in defeat as he had done when he was an exhilarating winner.

But it was 1975 and 76 which made the man they called the Kaiser a sporting sensation. It made the open-faced, tousle-haired Klammer a national hero, and turned the remote Austrian Alpine village of Mooswald into a shrine.

It was in Mooswald that Klammer was born in December 1953, and people, particularly Austrians, wanted to see the farm where he lived, where he first put on skis and where he built his strength helping his parents. Eventually his parents turned the farm into a tourist centre.

Like other Austrian youngsters, Klammer skied to school, but, unlike many other Austrians, he did not start regarding skiing as a serious sport until he was 14. Even then, his progress to the top was not particularly quick, but he learned from watching others and he learned from his mistakes. Finally he learned to relax. Years later he explained, 'You have to relax. You must realise that you will make mistakes but that they need not matter.'

It was a philosophy which he demonstrated in that remarkable run of World Cup victories in 1975. Only Jean-Claude Killy had previously recorded five in a row, and when Klammer matched that record, the whole of Austria willed him to go at least one better.

The sixth World Cup race was on his 'home track'; the Innsbruck course which would be used for the Olympics the following year, so a win for Klammer there would be a psychological blow to his rivals. But Klammer made a hash of the start, messed up one of the early corners and was only third fastest as he went past the intermediary timer. Klammer was relaxed, however. Or as relaxed as anyone can be at 85 mph. Using his technical skill to find the quickest line on the lower, more demanding part of the course and his exceptional strength to keep to it, Klammer went faster and faster. He finished the 3145 metre run in one minute, 55.78 seconds to win by less than half a second from Switzerland's Bernhard Russi, the world champion.

That confirmed Klammer as a superstar, and he was unable to walk anywhere in Austria without being mobbed. Klammer revelled in the adulation and felt charged by the passionate support which welled up and engulfed him before races. That passion was never more apparent than when Klammer returned to Mount Paterscherkofel in Innsbruck for the 1976 Olympics. Austria did not only want a Klammer victory, the whole country demanded it. The downhill is the blue ribband event of the Winter Olympics, and Austria just had to win the downhill at its own Games.

A massive back-up team was assembled to give Klammer any possible advantage. Austrian servicemen danced attendance on his every whim and his physical and psychological wellbeing was nursed and cherished. The latest technical innovations were placed at his disposal and a helicopter whisked him up the mountain. But nobody could help him get down it. That was up to Klammer. The descent would take less than two minutes, but Klammer's reputation depended on how much less.

The whole of Austria held its breath as Klammer's great rival, Russi, prepared for his run. He was third out of the gate and pelted down the ice-hard course at a pace which defied all the laws of physics and anatomy. At the finish, the clock showed one minute 46.06 seconds. That was nine seconds inside Klammer's course record, and the Austrians in the crowd let out a groan which drowned the Swiss cheers. An expectant nation began to doubt whether Klammer would be able to take the gold.

We will never know whether Klammer harboured the same misgivings but he certainly had long enough to foster doubts. He had to wait for 40 minutes at the top because he had been drawn to go 15th, the last of the first group and the worst possible draw of any of the seeded competitors. Every skier who went before him churned up the course, leaving ruts and ridges which would make Klammer's own task that much harder. But Klammer could only wait while skier after skier tried and failed to match Russi's incredible time. Three competitors managed to finish inside one minute 47 seconds, but only Italy's Herbert Plank got close to Russi, clocking one minute 46.59.

When Klammer's turn came, he started brilliantly, clocking 33.2 seconds to the first timer. That was a fifth of a second faster than Russi, and the Austrians began roaring themselves hoarse. But Klammer made some obvious blunders on the next section. It should have been the fastest portion of the course, but Klammer bounced off too many ruts and spent too long in the air. When the second intermediate time was announced it was bad news . . . one minute 13.24 seconds, slower even than Plank and a whole fifth of a second behind Russi. Still the Austrians, and thousands of others, roared their deafening encouragement and Klammer responded. Recklessly, brilliantly, he stole every available millimetre; his yellow suit was a blur.

The daunting 'bear's neck' was negotiated at such breathtaking pace that even now watching a recording of Klammer's perilous progress is enough to make you gasp. Then, with the crowd screaming and screaming, Klammer hurled himself into the very last section. All pretence at style had gone. All that mattered was speed, and Klammer thundered over the finishing line to a storm of cheers.

There was a pause of perhaps a second before Klammer and his adoring audience realised that the clock had stopped at one minute 45.73 seconds. He punched the air with both fists and accepted the ecstatic acclaim of the crowd, who began chanting: 'Franzi, Franzi.'

There had never been a race like it. Klammer had won with a stirring combination of derring-do and expertise and in the most demanding circumstances.

Life was never the same for him. The fame, glory and wealth were very acceptable to him, but in some ways everything after Innsbruck had to be an anti-climax. In pursuit of similar emotional highs, Klammer kept skiing, even when his powers were waning and even after his 16 year old brother, Klaus, was paralysed from the waist down in a ski-racing accident. Then, in eventual but reluctant retirement, Klammer took up saloon car racing but demolished too many expensive Mercedes. And, anyway, it was not the same.

Klammer cannot explain what made him a great downhill skier. Perhaps it was courage. He said, 'All those times I crouched over the start line peering down at the slope I never felt a twinge of real fear. If I had, I would have had to walk away and pack it in. You must have complete belief in your ability to complete the course without a serious crash. Without that belief, you are finished. There is no room for fear in downhill racing.'

The Night Britain Didn't Sleep

It is estimated that 18.5 million Britons stayed up late into the night to watch the television coverage of the final of the Embassy World Snooker Championships in 1985. It was the biggest British television audience for any sporting event and the biggest audience for any programme after midnight.

All those armchair fans had switched on to see what promised to be an engrossing contest between the reigning champion, Steve Davis, and an unlikely challenger, Dennis Taylor at the Crucible Theatre, Sheffield. In fact, the drama which unfolded on those millions of small screens and kept the goggle-eyed viewers out of their beds had more twists than the most outrageous thriller, more emotion than the most soppy soap operas and an unbelievably tense climax.

The final of the World Snooker Championship is always the best of 35 frames. In other words, the first to 18 wins and, although four sessions are set aside for it over two days, it is possible for the final to be over fairly quickly.

In 1985, it lasted the full four sessions. Indeed, it lasted to the very last ball of the 35th frame. Nobody who saw it will ever forget it.

The two participants were opposites, perfectly cast for a television duel. Tall and dapper Davis, from working-class Plumstead in London, is not at all as dull as the public imagine (in fact he has a laconic, self-deprecatory sense of humour) but he is serious about his snooker and looks it. When he is on the top of his form, moving ruthlessly around the table to pot ball after ball, he has a robotic quality. It is not a quality which endears him to the public, and in 1985 there was a further antipathy towards him becaue he was so good. The British, who love an underdog, do not love someone who keeps winning and Davis had won the title in 1981, '83 and '84.

Taylor, born in Coalisland in Northern Ireland, chats to the audience and to himself and does not have the Davis trick of keeping a tight rein on his feelings. Emotions twitch across Taylor's face, lending a certain pathos to an appearance which is otherwise comic. Taylor is a dumpy, rounded man. His 'upside down' spectacles, especially designed to help his snooker, make him look owlish, or like a clown. And the British love clowns. There was no doubt who people wanted to win.

There had been an inevitability about the way Davis progressed methodically to the final, and although Taylor had claimed some impressive scalps on his way to the showdown, Davis was expected to win fairly comfortably, and began as if he would do so.

The first session was easy for him. He won all seven frames without any particularly high breaks. Taylor spent most of the session sitting in his corner, his head sinking lower and lower; a hand darting nervously to his mouth from time to time. In the first frame of the second session, Davis moved up a gear, building breaks of 64 and 57 to win by 121 to nil. It was eight frames to Davis, none to Taylor.

To his evident relief, however, Taylor won the next frame (the ninth) on the pink. At least now it could not be an 18-0 whitewash. Taylor relaxed visibly, and began to play with real aplomb. Davies was rattled by the trans-formation, lost some of his own confidence, began to opt for easier shots and missed some of them. Although Taylor lost the tenth he won the close, untidy 11th frame 63-48. The crowd clapped long and loud, and Taylor beamed back at them. Davis, as ever, masked whatever emotions he was feeling behind a deadpan countenance.

Taylor won the next three frames, playing like a dervish and dragging the frame score back to 9-5. Then, in the 15th frame, Taylor compiled an amazing break. He followed seven reds with seven blacks and scented the possibility of a maximum 147 break, worth £60,000. The break finished on 100, but Taylor still smiled and accepted the applause. The fact that he had shown sufficient nerve to go for a 147 in a world final, attempting some risky shots along the way, demonstrated how his mood had changed. He won the next two frames and finished the day just 7-9 down.

And so the second day began with newspaper headlines about 'The Great Comeback'. Taylor, advised by his son during a telephone call to his Blackburn home to change into his lucky navy blue suit, continued where he had left off by extending his winning run to seven consecutive frames by winning the first of the afternoon session. But the tension was apparent to everyone and both men were playing mistake-strewn snooker, riddled with errors. Taylor make a series of particularly bad blunders and lost two frames to trail 11-8, but then pulled himself together. He won the 20th frame, with the help of some careful safety play and then restricted Davis to just three scoring shots in the next two frames. For the first time in the final, Taylor was level at 11-11.

If Taylor had pulled away then we would still have called it a great final but what lifted it into the realms of sporting sensation was the refusal of Davis to buckle. He won the next two frames, each of them on the black. He ended the afternoon 13-11 ahead and made millions of people change their plan for the evening. It was going to be some last session.

Taylor won four of the first six frames of the evening, to level again at 15-15, but then Davis restricted Taylor to six points in two frames to edge two ahead with three remaining. One more frame would give Davis the world title again.

Davis had three good opportunities to win the next frame, but missed them all. A relatively easy brown came back off the jaws of the pocket, the last red stopped a fraction short of the lip of the pocket and when Davis potted the green he left himself snookered. Taylor made fewer errors, won 71-47 and was back in the match at 16-17.

The penultimate frame was more one-sided. It was Taylor's as soon as he put together a 51 break, and finished 71-24 in his favour. The frame score was 17-17, the world final was going to the wire and 18,500000 people could not leave their armchairs.

The last, epic frame lasted 68 minutes and was a cat and mouse affair. Davis and Taylor took turns to pot a few balls and then play a gentle, safety shot.

Davis had an opportunity to pull clear but missed a blue from short range. Then he sunk a lucky green, missed a long-range brown and led by 18 points with 22 points left on the table. Taylor, knowing he could not afford a slip now, played three of the best and boldest shots of the final to sink the brown, blue and pink, and then bravely (or foolishly) tried to 'double' the black by hitting it against the side cushion so that it rebounded across the table into the opposite, middle pocket. Taylor said later, 'I thought it was in,' but in fact it rebounded from the jaws and the crowd and Taylor groaned in unison.

Davis and Taylor then each played a nerveless safety shot on the black, but when Davis attempted to do it once more, he hit the black too strongly and watched in thinly disguised horror as the balls ricocheted around the table. The white 'kissed' the black a second time and they ended in line with the pocket.

Taylor, who had not been in front at any stage of the final, crouched down and looked through his peculiar glasses down his cue at the long, diagonal shot which could make him the champion. The black missed the pocket by two inches, and Taylor turned away in disgust and disappointment, not bothering to see where the balls would end.

In fact, however, the cue ball ended near the side cushion, leaving the obviously anxious Davis with the task of attempting a difficult cut. But again the black missed the pocket. This time is bounced off two cushions and slowly came to rest dead in line with the same pocket.

Taylor stepped up for the simplest of shots and . . . down went the black.

Gripping his cue with both hands and holding it horizontally across his chest like Friar Tuck holding a jousting staff, Taylor's face broke into unbridled exultation. He repeated one word over and over again. 'Yes! Yes! Yes!'

Over in Coalisland, despite the late hour, a brass band marched up and down the street as the villagers celebrated the remarkable, heartstopping victory, and back at the Crucible Theatre, equally improbable celebrations began. Taylor, the rank outsider who had seemed destined for humiliation during the first session of the final, kissed the cup. Davis stood nonplussed with the worst ever Monday morning feeling. He was probably still in shock when the BBC's David Vine thrust a microphone in front of him for an interview immediately after the match. Davis made a few stunned comments which did not sound particularly gracious and gave the false impression that he was a bad loser.

Davis suffered another crushing disappointment the following year when he lost again in the final (to Joe Johnson), but then he won three consecutive world championships (in 1987, '88 and '89). So he appeared in eight out of nine successive finals and won six of them.

Dennis Taylor only reached one world final. But it was the best of them all.

The Poisoned Chalice

In some sports, you can make a fortune. In America's Cup sailing, you need a fortune to start and will almost certainly lose it.

The Cup's history is strewn with cautionary tales of men who have spent profligately; rich men who have become very much less rich trying to win sport's oldest international trophy.

In fact, you don't even need to compete to lose a fortune. In 1992, when the event had grown so gross that it was in danger of collapsing under the weight of overspending, the president of the organising committee had to make a personal loan of £1.4 million which he later wrote off. Another member poured in £390000.

But it is the yachtsmen (or weathly men who want to be yachtsmen) who get through the real money. Sir Thomas Lipton, the tea baron, squandered a fortune mounting five unsuccessful challenges at the start of the century. Peter de Savary, who led two British challenges in the 1980s, spent another £18 million before deciding that he could not afford to build the boat he wanted for another challenge. And, in 1992, came Italy's Raul Gardini, who was ousted from the board of his family firm (the agricultural chemical giants Ferruzzi) for spending too much time and money on his bid. How much had he spent backing the Italian boat? About £39 million.

That is an awful lot of money to spend on one yacht for a boat race, but of course it is not any old boat race.

The Cup gained its name when the schooner America beat 15 British yachts in a single race around the Isle of Wight in 1851. In 1870 an English yacht, Cambria, challenged the Americans to defend the trophy, which they did, again in a one-off, single race. Thereafter, the competition developed into a more complex event. Nations began competing for the right to challenge the Americans and the challenge round itself changed from a single race to a series. But although the format altered, the result remained the same. The Americans kept winning. In all, there were 25 consecutive successful defences by American yachts, and people began to believe that the Cup was called 'America's' because it belonged to America. The New York Yacht Club bolted it to a display plinth, confident they would never have to give it to anyone else.

By the 1980s the America's Cup had become the third biggest sporting spectacle after only the Olympics and football's World Cup, and such was the stubborn brilliance with which Americans had defended it for 132 years that the trophy became a symbol of that nation's power and importance. The world's best designers, the world's best boat-builders and the world's best helmsmen made winning the Cup their holy grail. So did some world's wealthiest men, and Alan Bond, at that time, was one of them.

Bond was seriously rich, the wealthiest man in Australia. He had been born in Ealing, West London, and was the class dunce when he started school. But, in the best self-made millionaire tradition, he emigrated at the age of 13 to join his parents and made his fortune. By the time he was 30 he was travelling everywhere by private jet or private yacht and able to buy anything he wanted. Among the things he wanted and bought were aircraft, boats, two adjoining houses in London (paying £7 million for the pair), several breweries, half a dozen restaurants, more sheep than it was possible to count, the complete Chilean telephone system, a handful of oil rigs, some gold mines, a couple of hotel chains, a string of ten-pin bowling alleys, one village in Oxfordshire and one island.

But despite that purchasing power, he could not, apparently, buy success in the America's Cup.

In 1970 he had been in New York with his yacht Apollo when he spotted the newly-launched Valiant, the 12-metre yacht which had been built for the defence of the America's Cup that summer. Bond was invited aboard and was fascinated by the high-tech equipment and by the attention which had been paid to detail. He turned to Ben Lexcen, who had designed Apollo and said, 'I want you to build me a boat like this.'

Lexcen tried, but Bond made three unsuccessful bids to wrest the America's Cup away from the Americans. He later estimated that the whole adventure cost him nearer £20 million than the £10 million he had budgeted for, but still the trophy, a rather ugly thing, remained fixed to its plinth in the New York Yacht Club.

Then, in 1983, when Bond was 42, he began dropping broad hints that Lexcen had produced an innovatory design, but did not drop any clues at all about just what innovations had been made. When Bond arrived off Newport, Rhode Island, he was determined to keep everyone guessing. In fact he was determined to keep everyone away from his yacht, Australia II. Bond mounted such a tight security operation that one journalist recalls, 'It was like a secret nuclear base, only more efficient.' Bond's secrecy only spawned more interest, and that provoked an even greater degree of secrecy. Armed security guards patrolled Australia II's berth day and night. Reporters and other visitors were frisked and kept at a distance. Submarine nets were used to make sure there was no underwater espionage and every time Australia II was lifted out of the water for adjustmements, a huge canvas shroud hid everthing below the water-line.

Reporters and rivals were intrigued. There was obviously something odd about the keel. But what? In fact, although nobody had realised it, the mystery could have been solved fairly easily, because Bond's team had been compelled by law to lodge details of the keel's design with the Patent Office whose documents were available for public scrutiny. In the event, however, the secret was only revealed when racing began.

Australia II, we learned, had a revolutionary, winged keel. Lexcen's design looked as if he had tacked a Vulcan bomber on the bottom of an orthodox keel. It gave the boat such great stability that Lexcen was able to make the rest of the yacht lighter and more responsive. The keel also enabled Australia II to head into the wind at a more direct angle than is normal, and with Lexcen also making use of the latest synthetic materials in the sails, the whole design was summed up by British designer Ian Howlett in one curt sentence. 'She will be,' he said 'very fast.'

And she was. Seven foreign yachts competed for the right to meet the Americans but it quickly became apparent that Australia II would emerge to face the Yanks. Australia II's 11-men crew were not the best, but their boat was peerless. It manoeuvred like a living creature.

That much also became clear at 37 West 44th Street, Manhattan. Behind the stained glass windows of the New York Yacht Club the members began to mutter that the Australian chap might actually beat their man. Their man was San Diego draper Dennis Conner, and his boat, Liberty, was very conventional.

So, amid the marble, old leather and antiques of the NYYC, the venerable members decided that Australia II's 'winged appendages' must be illegal. It did not matter that the design had already been passed without a qualm some months earlier. The lawyers of the NYYC studied the extremely complicated rules governing the construction and racing of 12-metre yachts and tried to find something with which Autralia II did not comply. They could not find anything. So they fastened on to the fact that Lexcen had spent some time in Holland, using facilities there to perfect his design. If it could be shown that the keel design was part Dutch, Australia II would be disqualified on the principle that America's Cup yachts must be designed and made in the challenging country.

The NYYC sent emissaries to the Dutch National Aerospace laboratories and the Netherlands Ship Model Basin, where Lexcen had worked. But the scientists in Holland insisted the design had been all Lexcen's own work and that they had only helped him test it. Astonishingly, the NYCC representatives then met Dutch politicians and other prominent figures and asked them to put pressure on the scientists to change their mind. Again, the NYYC failed.

Undeterred, the nine-member NYYC America's Cup committee met in secret session on the eve of the first challenge between Australia II and Liberty and discussed whether the Australians should be disqualified for cheating and the America's Cup races cancelled. In the end, fear of the outcry there would be if racing were cancelled at such a late stage outweighed the desire to stop Australia II from taking part. But only just. The committee voted 5-4 to let the America's Cup continue.

Then it was Bond's turn to cry 'foul' as the desperate Americans continually tinkered with Liberty, so that she handled completely differently. Not surprisingly, his protests were over-ruled.

By now the world was hooked on the contest which was dubbed 'The Race of the Century,' and millions tuned in to watch the elegant duels between two beautiful yachts. The tension built up by all the on-shore arguments continued as Conner built a 3-1 lead with Liberty only for Australia II, superbly skippered by John Bertrand, to stage an unprecedented comeback to 3-3. The best-of-seven challenge was to be determined by the very last race.

The scene was set. One airship, a US frigate, a liner and almost 3,000 other, smaller craft waited as the wind shifted wildly for two hours, but then . . . the wind died completely and the organising committee declared that the decisive race would have to be postponed 24 hours.

Then Conner claimed the following day as a rest day so that yet more alterations could be made to Liberty, and the race was postponed again.

When the showdown finally came, Conner made the better start, snatching an eight-second lead and stealing the best line. The Australian yacht chose an entirely different course and for 20 minutes it was impossible to tell which was in front, but when they came together again there were gasps. Australia II was four boat-lengths in the lead.

Off they went on different lines again, and when they converged 10 mintes later it was Liberty which was in front. The Ivy League gentlemen in all the watching American yachts applauded the 29 second advantage with obvious relief.

The Australian yacht made some impression on the lead but then fell away again and Liberty approached the finish with a seemingly impregnable 57 seconds lead.

Then, on the fifth downwind leg, Australia II's greater manoeuvrability changed the history of the America's cup. Bertrand sailed past Liberty and on to the front pages of the newspapers of the world. Australia II won the four hour race by 41 seconds.

Conner cried at the post-mortem press conference, aware, that as far as America was concerned, the title of his autobiography was particularly appropriate. He had written it some years previously. It was called 'No Excuse To Lose.'

In Perth the partying began. Untold quantities of lager were consumed and there were at least a billion tuneless renditions of Waltzing Matilda. The parties were still going on when Bond arrived back with the Cup. The Australians were not modest in their hour of triumph.

But the America's Cup is a poisoned chalice and so the story could not end happily. Conner snatched the Cup back in 1987 but then defended it in San Diego with a catamaran. Although he beat New Zealand's huge yacht 4-0, many doubted the legality of the Conner cat and there followed a series of lengthy court (and, of course, expensive) squabbles. Conner was eventually declared the winner, but the fact that his victory came in the New York Supreme Court and not in the water debased the sport and led to a growing public apathy toward the Cup from which it did not fully recover.

And there was no happy ending for Bond either. The 1983 triumph made the buoyant entrepreneur a national hero and encouraged him to live even higher on the hog. Yet within nine years he was bankrupt; his personal company went into liquidation owing £675 million.

SPORTING SENSATION AND THE MEDIA

Michael Herd

Mother Teresa once said that facing the Press was more difficult than bathing a leper, Graham Greene said that media is a word which had come to mean bad journalism and Adlai Stevenson said a journalist separates the wheat from the chaff and prints the chaff. They were all saying roughly the same thing: no-one loves the Media though few can do without us. In the case of sport, there is no doubt it has a symbiotic relationship with newspapers, television and radio. They are two difficult organisms, each on occasions accusing the other of being a bloodsucker but always being attached one to the other and each needing the other.

Without the Media there would be no sporting sensations because without the Media there would be no communication. At the same time, there is no doubt that the relationship between the Media and sport is constantly changing. Let me explain. There have been, if you like, five floors to the relationship. If you were in a lift, it would be like ascending from the ground floor to the Fourth, though many have a feeling that for some years the lift has actually been descending to the basement. Once upon a time, a journalist simply reported the events of the day. It might have been another century by Denis Compton, another League championship for Arsenal or a Wimbleton title for Rod Laver. It might have been a British gold medal at the Olympic Games.

With the arrival of the popular tabloids, reporters not only commented upon the events of the day but the events of the night. Some editors decided that a sportsman caught 'playing away' from home, indulging in 'rumpy-pumpy' instead of batting practice, or having a couple of drinks too many instead of an hour on the training track, was fair game. Indeed, his night life was of more interest to readers than his sporting prowess. That is still the case though newspapers soon learned that the more they paid sportsmen and women the more lurid the stories became.

Newspapers reached the third floor when they discovered they could not only print the news, they could not only pay for scandal, but they could create it, too. And then the full circle. The media learned they could ferment sporting sensation by ignoring the players and writing or talking about each other, newspapers about television, television about newspapers and radio about the other two. Let me take you in the elevator.

Ground Floor

Within the space of a few days the Evening Standard and the Daily Mail, sisters papers belonging to Associated Newspapers, led their front pages with stories about Ian Botham. 'Beefy' always has been and always will be one of those men and women who move sport from the back of the newspapers to the front, make the Nine O'Clock News and regular radio bulletins. In these instances, the first story in the Standard was about his performance on the field, the second in the Mail about his behaviour off it. Both were judged to be of huge interest to readers, a belief borne out by increased circulation on each occasion.

In the first instance, in March, 1992, I wrote, 'Ian Botham, once rejected by England team-mates as a 'fat has-been,' smashed Australia in cricket's World Cup in Sydney today. Botham, who arrived from England three weeks later than the rest of the squad because he was starring in a pantomine, Jack and the Beanstalk, took four wickets for no runs in seven balls. And, as he smelled the blood of Australians, he finished with four for 31.

'Afterwards a smiling team-mate said, 'Ian may be overweight and overpaid but thank God he's over here. Just don't tell him I told you.' With 36-year-old Botham back at his menacing best, roaring defiance at the Australians, the world champions slumped to 171 all out in 49 overs and were in danger of crashing out of the one-day competition. Sydney Cricket Ground was a sea of red, white and blue as England's record-breaking cricketer relived the incredible Test Matches of a decade ago when he single-handedly destroyed Australia.

'While England prepared for the World Cup with matches in New Zealand, Botham had been on stage at the Pavilion Theatre, Bournemouth. Critics said he just about out-acted the beanstalk, but he didn't care. Today he out-acted the rest of England's cast with a sensational maiden over in which he took three wickets that left England, still to bat, poised for victory and virtually certain of a place in the World Cup finals.

'When the England hero, also known as Guy the Gorilla, returned to the action today after his first spell in which he had conceded 18 runs from four overs, Australia were moving along nicely at 145 for four. By the time Botham had finished, they were 155 for eight. Beefy was back!'

First Floor

A couple of weeks later Botham made the headlines in just about every newspaper in the land. The Daily Mail's headlines read 'DON'T INSULT OUR QUEEN' with a story from Melbourne.

'England cricket stars Graham Gooch and Ian Botham stormed out of the official eve of the World Cup Final dinner in protest at a tasteless send-up of the Queen. They would have been followed by the rest of the squad if manager Micky Stewart had not intervened to placate the others.

'Botham said: 'It was a bloody insult. I love my country and I'm not going to sit around listening to someone insult the Queen.' The target of his fury was Australian drag artist Gerry Connolly, who marched into Melbourne's Exhibition Building in a white sequinned dress, blue sash and tiara giving regal waves and cracking anti-royal jokes.

'With cricket mania rampant back home, the incident marred the last hours of the build-up to England's showdown with Pakistan in Melbourne this morning. Connolly, known as the king of satire in Australia, delivered a series of jokes about the Queen, including one about the break-up of the marriage of the Duke and Duchess of York. Connolly said, 'You think you've got troubles . . . what about mine with Andrew and Fergie?'

'The routine had hardly started when Botham glanced across at team captain Graham Gooch and said, 'Come on, let's get out of here.' Another member of the team added, 'Gooch and Botham got it dead right. A lot of players wanted to go as well.'

It didn't seem to occur to anyone at the time that Elizabeth II is also the Queen of Australia or that she and her family are lampooned on Spitting Images, a hugely popular British television programme, far more savagely than anything Gerry Connolly could come up with. That was neither here nor there, though some of Botham's critics suggested he had stormed out because he was fet up with the dinner and looking for an excuse to be away.

Months later, the affair still seemed to rankle with Botham. He rushed out a book, 'Botham hits back,' in which he declared, 'I found it quite amazing that we had to go to a dinner on the eve of the World Cup final – one of the biggest moments in our careers – and be paraded in front of seven or eight hundred people. It just seemed crazy that we had to sit through his boring dinner.

'That was bad enough but to have to put up with what was meant to be wit with a drag artist appearing as the Queen was just too much. I'd had enough when he took the mickey out of the Royal Family, who have no comeback and cannot defend themselves. I thought it was completely out of order and unnecessary to belittle them. It was all in bad taste.

'I didn't see why I had to sit there, so I walked out and was pleased to see that the captain had done the same thing. Graham was very upset. He was very emotional and almost in tears. I was just angry and wanted to punch the drag artist's lights out. I am very proud of our heritage. Unlike the Australians, at least we have one.'

Second Floor
This is the floor on which papers like The Sun, The Star and The Mirror

have their offices. The Sun front page on Monday, April 6, 1992, was devoted to the news that Graeme Souness, manager of soccer club Liverpool was to enter hospital the following morning for a life-saving heart operation at the age of 38. As the fitness-mad manager watched his team scrape a 1-1 draw against Portsmouth in their FA Cup semi-final, the 42000 crowd and even his own players were unaware that he was to undergo a five-hour triple heart bypass operation the following day that would save his life. Souness's full story was on pages, 2, 3, 4, 5, and 36!

The manager had sold his story to the newspaper, which was somewhat unusual. The rest of us would have been too damned concerned about the operation than thinking of flogging the news but there you are. The headline screamed 'MY LIFE IS ON THE LINE.' Souness explained that he had had a heart attack without knowing it. 'They told me one artery was 70 per cent blocked and the other 90 per cent. Apparently if the arteries were any more blocked I could have died at any time. It could have been six days, six weeks or six months, who knows.' He explained how he had broken the news to his family at a tearful and emotional conference at his home in Cheshire three days earlier. His estranged wife Danielle, son Jordan and daughter Chantelle, his father James and his brother Bill were stunned. So was Souness's girlfriend Karen.

It was not long before Souness and The Sun were under attack from other papers. Should he have sold a story about his operation? Well, so what if he copped a bob or two? The lions' share of the money was going to a local children's hospital, wasn't it? Soon the muck was being raked over. The Souness children were mortified about his girlfriend and never wanted to see him again. His wife was fuming at the way in which Souness, wearing pyjamas, appeared on the front page of The Sun in a passionate embrace with his girlfriend. The headline was 'LOVERPOOL'. With extraordinarily bad timing, the kiss photograph appeared on the third anniversary of the Hillsborough tragedy in which 95 fans died, many of them from Liverpool.

Merseyside and the rest of the country was angry. Souness's association, disliked on Merseyside after its coverage of Hillsborough, provoked an uproar and several relatives of those who had died demanded that Liverpool dismiss their manager.

Souness apologised. 'That picture was just a Cup win reaction. But long hours in hospital have given me time to analyse the events. I now feel I must explain them. I apologise unreservedly for any hurt I may have done concerning the people of Liverpool and the club's loyal supporters. It was never my intention to offend any of them. The picture of me kissing Karen was taken after our lads had won the semi-final and reached Wembley.

'I do not apologise for kissing my girlfriend. It was a spontaneous reaction to the result and not a posed picture. Those who know me will understand my strong emotional feeling for football and Liverpool and, in my case, it was a natural response at a time of celebration.'

Souness was quick to explain that, yes, he was surprised when the photograph was used on the anniversary of the Hillsborough disaster, yes he may have been wrong in agreeing to the photograph and, yes, he received payment from the newspaper after given them the exclusive story. Of course, he thought by handling it that way he would have better control of what was going on.

There was more trouble for the manager. Before Liverpool had beaten Sunderland 2-0 in the FA Cup Final at Wembley, Souness appeared from the tunnel, walked slowly round the ground and took his place to watch the match. Less than a week later, Liverpool Football Club issued a statement in which the club made clear Souness had been admonished for the way in which he made public his health problems.

A statement issued by the club said that Souness had expressed his sincere regret for entering into an exclusive agreement with The Sun and had given an assurance there would be no repetition.

Peter Robinson, the club's chief executive, said: 'The board expressed their disapproval at what has happened but accepted that, at the time of entering into the agreement, Mr Souness was under considerable medical and emotional pressure. Mr Souness has already expressed his sincere regret for what has happened, has repeated this and has now given clear assurances that there will be no reoccurrence of any such incident. He has accepted the board's recommendation that it is inappropriate for the manager of Liverpool Football Club to enter into exclusive arrangement with any section of the media.'

Third Floor

In some ways the most curious floor to be on. This is the level on which newspapers do their damnedest to outmanoeuvre each other not by commenting on sensations but by actively, deliberately, creating them. The classic case took place in the mid-Eighties and concerned Zola Budd, a 17-year-old South African who was granted a British passport after the Daily Mail exerted pressure on the British Government. The child, a world record-holding runner was then smuggled into this country by the Mail much to the consternation of other papers, television and radio. It was a story that ran and ran. The most complete account appeared in a book written by Neil Macfarlane and me. Macfarlane, later knighted, was Minster for Sport at the time.

I make no apologies for repeating much of that account. On 6 January, 1984, Reuters, the London-based international news agency, reported that Zola Budd of South Africa had clipped more than six seconds off the women's 5000 metres world record of the American Mary Decker during a race in

169

Stellenbosch near Cape Town. According to one writer, the teenager had lapped the track with the precision of a metronome and the grace of a gazelle as the crowd chanted 'Zo-la. Zo-la,' making it sound like a tribal chant.

Three months later, two weeks after she and her parents had been flown to Britain from their home in Bloemfontein by the Daily Mail, she was told she had been granted British citizenship on the personal instructions of the then Home Secretary, Leon Brittain. The application had been made ten days earlier. At the time the average delay between submission and decision in applications made in the United Kingdom for British citizenship was, in the case of naturalisation, just about 21 months and in registration cases generally about 14 months.

A few days later David Waddington, Minister for State at the Home Office, explained to the House of Commons what criteria had been used in the case of Miss Budd's application. 'Applications are generally considered in the order they are made, but are sometimes taken out of turn if there is a request for priority and the merits of the case and the circumstances surrounding it justify such treatment. Miss Budd has come here with her parents to live in this country to try to qualify to run for it, if possible in this year's Olympic Games. The timetable this imposed for considering her application was necessarily short.'

Waddington later explained that Zola Budd's father was a British citizen by descent who had decided to come to live with his wife and daughter in this country, as they were entitled to do. Miss Budd did not automatically acquire her father's British citizenship but while she was a minor she could apply to be registered under section 3(1) of the British Nationality Act 1981.

It transpired that Leon Brittain had taken into account Miss Budd's connections with the United Kingdom and her own exceptional talent. Other papers and other political parties did not fail to point out that the Home Office had also taken into account that the request for urgency had been made by the Daily Mail, one of the Government's greatest supporters. After all, hadn't Brittain been approached by the Mail editor, Sir David English? The editor's motives, naturally, were to enable Zola to compete throughout the world and, hopefully, to win a gold medal for Britain at the Los Angeles Olympics. It must be said, however, that there were those who said that any contribution to the prestige of the nation was influenced by the effect it would have had on the Daily Mail's circulation.

One could never pretend that Miss Budd had thought longingly of England during her athletics isolation in South Africa. She was brought up in the Afrikaans-speaking heartland of the Republic, her cat was called Stompie, her terrier Fraaier and the old vehicle she used was a Bakkie. Since the day she was born, Zola's parents had called her their Laatlammethie (Afrikaaans for late lamb) and, until she arrived in Britain, she was at Orange

Free State University studying political science and the native language of South Sotho.

David English and the Mail sports editor, Tom Clarke, met Macfarlane at the Department of the Environment and was convincing in their earnestness to assist Miss Budd. The Minister had a feeling that his Government was allowing itself to be swept along. Nevertheless, swept along it was.

The Daily Mail had set up a trust fund for Zola Budd worth more than £200000 and the departure of the Budd family from South Africa was as well planned by David English and his cohorts as any wartime operation to lift an agent from enemy-occupied territory. Accompanied by English's envoys, the Budds flew from Jan Smuts Airport, Johannesburg, to Schipol Airport, Amsterdam, where a private Piper Chieftain aircraft chartered by the Mail was waiting, parked close to the main runway.

An hour and a half later the Budd party landed in a heavy rainstorm at Southampton Airport and were swept in a two-car convoy to a quiet manor house on the edge of the New Forest. In Johannesburg the Budds had been shown into the Royal Lounge until a Mercedes saloon had driven them to the foot of the waiting KLM jumbo jet. In Amsterdam, a 40ft bus had been laid on to get the party out of the charter aircraft and in Southampton the flight had been organised with such secrecy that the control tower could not help casual enquirers.

At the end of March, when the Budds were finally British to the core, the Daily Mail announced that it had brought the wonder girl to Britain. It was a great coup for the Mail and there was much gnashing of teeth elsewhere in Fleet Street. As the Daily Express and other papers were left scrambling for stories, the Mail was hitting them between the eyes.

The rest is history. There were huge pressures from without on the waif-like distance runner. Her parents' marriage broke up, she was a target for anti-apartheid protesters, and she became the most famous athlete in the world. She also demonstrated her talent by winning a record-breaking 3000 metres in the Europa Cup, two world cross-country titles and a five-mile road race over the freezing cobbles of Zurich.

Alas, she failed in her biggest race, the final of the Olympic 3000 metres in the Los Angeles Coliseum. The South African teenager who had become a Britain versus the mature American, Mary Decker, whose fiancé was Richard Slaney, a field event member of the British team. On the day – 10 August, 1984 – only four months after Zola had first flown to Britain, neither woman won because halfway through the race Decker clipped the left leg of Zola and the young Briton, just in front, moved into the inside lane. Decker tore the plastic number from Zola's back as she tried to save herself from falling. The American pitched toward, twisting as she fell, lunging over the trackside kerb, screaming in her anguish and frustration. Zola Budd ran on, the boos of thousands of Americans ringing in her ears but the will to win had gone. She finished down the field.

Today Zola Budd is back in South Africa, married to an Afrikaaner and probably speaking Afrikaans. But her arrival in Britain was a sporting sensation and a great coup for the Daily Mail.

Fourth Floor

This is the floor where one branch of the media reports gleefully on the warring antics of two sections of another branch. The sport is almost irrelevant. It is the ultimate in sporting sensations. Take the case of soccer's new Premier League, and its decision to award a contract to a partnership of BSkyB and the BBC instead of to ITV. It was another show that ran for days much to the merriment of newspapers, not least my own.

There was amazement in May of this year when the Premier League announced that live soccer matches were to be shown only on satellite television in an astounding £304 million deal with BSkyB and the BBC. The deal between unlikely bedfellows – Rupert Murdoch of BSkyB and Marmaduke Hussey of the BBC – was by far the most expensive in British sporting history. Football or, at least, the Premier League clubs were being handed undreamt of riches. It was for five years, during which only viewers with cable TV or satellite dishes would be able to watch live Premier League football. The BBC would show only recorded highlights, reinstating its Saturday night Match of the Day Highlights and lunchtime Football Focus. BSkyB would screen live League matches on Sunday afternoons and Monday evenings, with the Sunday match part of a five-hour programme.

The BSkyB offer (to which the BBC were said to be contributing only £5 million a year) was much larger than ITV's. But within hours there were accusations by the independent channel of unfair dealing, the leaking of confidential information and so on. ITV even went to court in an effort to force the Premier League to reopen bidding for the soccer coverage.

The ITV companies sought a 14-day suspension of the Premier League's deal with BSkyB to allow them to put in an increased offer. They claimed the deal was secured unfairly by the leaking of confidential information on ITV's bid. Mr Justice Ferris refused, saying it could not be right to make an order forcing the League to consider a new ITV offer which the League had already indicated it was not prepared to consider.

During the hearing the Premier League chief executive, Rick Parry, admitted he was responsible for the late tip which led to a last-minute and dramatic bid by BSkyB. But he told the High Court he did not tell BSkyB the precise details of the ITV's rival bid. He said he telephoned Sky chief Sam Chisholm, a tough talking Australian said to be the best televison executive in the world, simply to increase the money soccer would gain from selling off its TV rights.

172

'I knew of Sam Chisholm's determination to secure the rights and felt this would be an opportunity to obtain even more money for the Premier League.' Speaking to the High Court through a statement read by a barrister, Parry said he did not reveal the amount of the ITV offer but told him it was still below BSkyB's bid 'although it was very close.'

He said that as the deadline drew nearer, he advised Chisholm to increase his offer and be sure of a recommendation to clubs which would approve the deal. Mr Parry said that, following his call, the satellite station made an increased offer which was ultimately approved by the clubs.

Before the case and shortly after the original League decision, there had been much arguing between the Premier League clubs themselves. David Dein, vice-chairman of Arsenal, had suggested to the meeting that Alan Sugar of Tottenham should not be allowed to vote because he also ran a company which manufactured satellite dishes. Sugar was said to have been overheard ringing someone and advising them urgently to up their offer. He denied he had done anything unethical. Before the meeting of the club representatives in a London hotel, ITV executives had stood outside the room, handing out papers containing details of their latest offer. It was a good murky tale and Fleet Street's finest had a field day.

Within a week of the court cvase, there was more trouble at mill. BSkyB and the BBC revealed they had succeeded with a £75 million bid to clinch coverage of the FA Cup and England international matches for the following five years. In other words, within the space of a few weeks, they had broken the back of ITV's sports coverage.

ITV executive accused the Football Association of 'another stitch up' as they awaited confirmation of the bid acceptance, pointing out that they had offered substantially more than the BBC's share of the bid.

It reminded me of a comment I had made in the Evening Standard two years earlier. I pointed out that, in my opinion, the Government was correct when they said that it would be wrong to deny sports the opportunities to sell themselves to the highest bidder. Hadn't the BBC and ITV screwed football when they worked not as rivals but as team, I asked. Hadn't they paid millions less each season than they should have done? One day, I said, one of them, or both, would get their comeuppance. But I'm a newspaperman, aren't I?

INDEX

174

175